THE EVALUATION OF Information Services and Products

DONALD W. KING
EDWARD C. BRYANT
Westat Research, Inc.

Information Resources Press
WASHINGTON, D.C. 1971

Published September 1971. Second Impression December 1979.
Printed in the United States of America.

Available from
Information Resources Press
1700 North Moore Street
Arlington, Virginia 22209

Library of Congress Catalog Card Number 76-141595

ISBN 0-87815-003-X

Foreword

Although it is only in the last decade that serious attention has been devoted to the problem, the importance of evaluation of bibliographic services is now widely recognized. The study of MEDLARS, conducted by the National Library of Medicine, has shown that evaluation of an operating retrieval system is essentially an analytical and diagnostic procedure applied to measure performance level, disclose major system weaknesses, and suggest ways in which the performance may be improved. An evaluation program, if properly applied, should lead to system modifications designed to improve the effectiveness or cost/effectiveness of the system.

The literature of evaluation is now voluminous. However, although many have written on the subject from various viewpoints, few evaluations of information retrieval systems, operational or experimental, have actually been conducted. This is at least partly because very few individuals or groups have developed expertise or experience in this type of evaluation. Consequently, many system managers have received little guidance in methods applicable to the design and conduct of an evaluation program, and the analysis and interpretation of results from such a program.

Westat Research is one of the few organizations that has developed expertise in evaluation procedures applicable to bibliographic products and services. This book presents a distillation of Westat experience and serves as a very useful methodological guide for anyone contemplating or planning an evaluation program. The authors are statisticians of considerable ability and reputation. The most useful aspect of the work, to my mind, lies in the explanation of applicable statistical procedures. For the nonstatistician, the chapters on basic statistical concepts, experimental design, and sampling are refreshingly clear and to the point. The authors also discuss various subjects that previously were sadly neglected in the literature, including the important topic of marketing as applied to bibliographic products. While I do not agree fully with everything presented (I feel, for example, that the application of some of the mathematical models is appropriate to the understanding of retrieval problems, but may have limited use for real-life evaluation), I find this volume to be extremely useful and would urge that it be studied by all contemplating the evaluation of any type of bibliographic system for current awareness or retrospective search.

F. W. LANCASTER
University of Illinois
Urbana, Illinois
June, 1970

Preface

The continuing need to put scientists in contact with the research of others, coupled with the rapidly expanding volume of published material during the past several decades, has placed new emphasis on the old arts of assembling, coding, and disseminating recorded knowledge. In some instances, the emphasis has manifested itself in research on improvement of traditional library systems. In other instances, it has resulted in the assembly of specialized collections and their intensive indexing for access in a variety of ways. Still other systems have progressed from the passive role of responding to requests to the active role of supplying documents, or references to them, to researchers as the documents become available. For lack of a more descriptive terminology, all of these activities are referred to in this book as "document transfer systems," implying that the product being retrieved (or disseminated) is a document rather than the information (if any) in it. That is, intelligence systems or fact retrieval systems (if facts are indeed retrieved) are excluded from our concern. The document, of course, may be a book, a journal article, a drawing, an abstract, a piece of film, or a piece of magnetic tape.

Examination of the documentation literature of the late forties and early fifties shows that a great deal of experimentation was performed with indexing systems which, it was then hoped, would provide improved identification of the subject matter of the document. During this period a variety of searching devices also came under scrutiny, including the then developing digital computer. Most of the experiments were of the let's-try-it-and-see-if-it-works type, and evaluation, if conducted at all, was highly subjective. This period might be characterized as the "innovative period" in documentation.

The innovative period was followed in the sixties by a period of increasing attention to matters of experimental design and statistical evaluation of results. A number of systems were also implemented, but there was, and continues to be, an obvious reluctance to commit extensive amounts of funds to widespread implementation of new systems. Part of this reluctance appears to stem from the lack of definitive evaluative results. One might, then, characterize the current period as the "period of evaluation."

The 1970 *Annual Review of Information Science and Technology*, published by the American Society for Information Science, listed well over 100 papers on the design and evaluation of information systems. These papers reveal wide divergence of opinion concerning what to measure, how to measure, and how to interpret the results. This book is designed to give some guidance in these matters.

Some disclaimers are in order. We do not presume that the methodology presented here is the only methodology, nor that it is even the best. We anticipate that experienced evaluators will find many ways of improving the illustrative techniques. However, it is hoped that this text will give the inexperienced student and evaluator a better idea as to how to proceed. These two groups are our principal concern.

The first draft of this book was a two-volume report to the Office of Science Information Service, National Science Foundation, prepared under contract NSF-C491. These two reports, "Evaluation of Document Retrieval Systems: Literature Perspective, Measurement, Technical Papers" and "Procedural Guide for the Evaluation of Document Retrieval Systems," were prepared by staff members from Westat Research, Inc. Among the contributors to the reports were Edward C. Bryant, Project Director; Donald W. King, Principal Investigator; Robert R. V. Wiederkehr; Robert H. Shumway; Stephen K. Dietz; David G. Weinman; and Mrs. Cynthia Siehler White. In addition to these contributors, the authors would like to thank Miss Nancy W. Caldwell, Mrs. Peggy W. Neel, and Miss Anita M. Brown, who helped with calculations of the new examples; Mrs. Irma N. Klein, who typed the initial reports; and Mrs. Judith M. McPhie, who typed most of the revisions that resulted in this book.

DONALD W. KING
EDWARD C. BRYANT

Bethesda, Maryland
June, 1970

Contents

Chapter One
Systems, Evaluation and Measures: Some General Considerations

1.1 Document transfer systems

This book is concerned with the evaluation of systems that record and transmit scientific and technical knowledge by means of documents. Such systems include those commonly referred to as information retrieval systems or document retrieval systems. We will call all such systems *document transfer systems* because they really deal with *all* functions and processes necessary to complete the transfer of documents from authors to users, whereas *document retrieval* and *information retrieval* tend to imply only one step in the transfer process, the recovery of documents from some store. However, we are not restricting ourselves to one specific kind of system. The word "document" may be interpreted very broadly to include published material, research notes, magnetic tapes, microfilms, or any other vehicle for the storage of knowledge (information) that may be transmitted from one individual to another or from an individual in one time frame to the same individual in another.

A document transfer system is comprised of (1) functions, (2) processes, (3) organizational structure, and (4) components (documents, buildings, personnel, computers, files, and so on). Since all four facets are important to evaluation, each is discussed below to set forth a framework within which evaluation takes place.

Document transfer systems involve the flow of information via a message unit from a source (author) to a destination (user). The message unit may be a collection of words or symbols such as a book, the full text of a report, a research finding, or a journal article that is transmitted from an author to users. Document representations such as abstracts may also be considered message units if their purpose is to inform or to provide access to the full texts. Furthermore, it is conceivable that some day scientific and technical research reports or articles may be formatted so that only portions of full texts will serve as message units. However, full texts are considered the primary message units and, for convenience, they are called "documents" although a broader meaning, as stated above, is intended. The transfer process is not considered complete until the document is transmitted from author to user.

Presumably, the transfer of documents from author to user will result in productive use of the information such as gained knowledge, research, or proposals. The use may, in turn, result in composition of new documents. However, before a user obtains a document, the document may go through a complex system of functions and processes. Document transfer from author to user usually consists of a series of six basic system *functions* as given in Figure 1.1.

The arrows in the schema represent flow only to the extent that the document transfer functions often occur in the sequence shown. These basic functions are defined below, with examples of the *processes* by which they are accomplished:

(1) Composition – recording, preparation, and editing of a document.

(2) Reproduction – duplication of the original document (e.g., by typing, printing, keyboarding, tape recording, or filming) to allow wider dissemination.

(3) Acquisition and storage – procurement, maintenance, and preservation of copies of documents at identified locations (e.g., on library shelves, in vertical files, or on magnetic tape or disk).

(4) Identification and location – determination of the identity

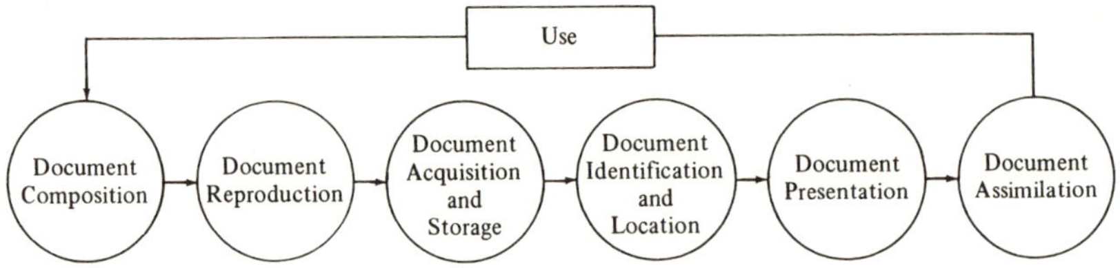

Figure 1.1 Basic document transfer functions.

and location of documents to be transmitted (e.g., in response to retrospective searches or by selective dissemination).

(5) Presentation – physical transmittal of a copy of a document to a user (e.g., by mailed copy, audio-tapes, or microfilm viewer).

(6) Assimilation – perception by a user of the information, if any, in a document (e.g., by reading or listening).

Clearly, most document transfer processes involving the flow of documents from authors to users incorporate all of the six basic functions to some degree.

Document transfer systems are managed by *organizational entities* that provide services to reproduce, acquire and store, identify and locate, and present documents by one of several processes. The functions may be accomplished at any one of several levels of organizational complexity, including:

(1) An individual.

(2) A "local" library such as that of a university, government department, or industrial organization.

(3) A central reservoir service such as the Library of Congress, the National Technical Information Service (NTIS) [formerly the Clearinghouse for Federal Scientific and Technical Information (CFSTI)], or the National Library of Medicine.

We define a "proprietary system" as that part of the document transfer system which is under the management control of a given organizational entity. Evaluation almost always takes place within a proprietary system. A system may perform transfer functions within the proprietary entity, outside the proprietary entity, or both, depending on the particular system. For example, evaluation of a university library should include assessment not only of the in-house services but also of the use of external services such as an inter-library loan service and the facilities of regional and national information centers.

A transfer of a single copy of a document may be accomplished at any one of the three levels of organizational structure above. For example, all six functions could be performed by an individual if he were both the author and the user of a document, or by a central agency if the agency were both author and user. In most cases, however, documents are transmitted from an author to users by a myriad of information transfer channels comprised of numerous organizational entities and processes.

System *components* refer to specific items such as hardware, books, staff, and buildings. Each component may itself be the object of evaluation, or at least an important element in evaluation decisions. Evaluation processes may be used to compare two methods of implementing a particular component (e.g., two photocomposition devices). We cannot evaluate system processes without also evaluating system components, since the processes are dependent upon the individual components.

The functions, processes, organizational structure, and components of information transfer systems dictate, to a large degree, evaluation objectives, methodology, and measures. For example, evaluating reproduction and identification processes may well stem from different objectives. The document identification process, retrospective searching, requires different evaluation methodology from that used to evaluate selective dissemination. Further discussion of the relationship of the four system dimensions to evaluation is given in this chapter following the next two sections on evaluation and measures.

1.2 Evaluation

Evaluation must have a purpose – it is not an end in itself. Its purpose arises out of a need to "set a value on" a system (or component or difference). The term evaluation implies quantification. The need derives from the decision-making process which is a prelude to action. Without the possibility of alternative courses of action, one cannot conceive of a need to evaluate. A system performs *functions*, and these functions are designed to accomplish *objectives. Measurement* of the extent to which these objectives are met is a major part of system evaluation.

System objectives can be stated very generally, such as "to increase accessibility of research references to researchers in the field of biochemistry." Presumably, then, any increase in accessibility would be counted a success. Upon probing, one may find that certain goals have also been set, such as "to produce 80 percent of the documents requested within 24 hours." Or it may be that a fixed budget has been provided and the goal is to maximize service within this fixed budget.

Note that a simple verbalization of the system objectives and goals may be inadequate as a basis for evaluation. For example, it may be impossible to maximize service and minimize cost simultaneously, although this may be the verbalized goal. The point is that one must discuss objectives and goals with system managers and operators to set a realistic framework for evaluation. The accurate verbalization of objectives and goals is the first step in a successful evaluation.

One must distinguish between the objectives of the system and the objectives of the evaluation. The latter are motivated by the need to make decisions, and these decisions can be classified broadly as follows:

(1) Decisions to design or implement a new system.
(2) Decisions to modify an existing system.
(3) Decisions to discontinue a system.
(4) Decisions arising from the continuous monitoring of system effectiveness.

The last category is not independent of the first three, but is so important that it merits a special class.

Presumably, evaluation is done at the request of, or at least for the information of, some person or group. Although the evaluation may be used by various groups, it is important to identify the primary target, that is, the person or group whose decisions are expected to be influenced by the evaluation. These targets may be identified broadly as (*1*):[1]

(1) The funding entity of the system.
(2) The system management.
(3) The system technical staff.
(4) The user population.

The focus of the evaluation will be affected not only by the target, but also by whether the evaluation is done by system personnel or by an outside agency. The choice is governed by monetary resources, availability of qualified personnel, and desire to guard against bias.

Another consideration affecting the objectives of the evaluation is the status of the system being evaluated, that is, whether the system is being designed, developed, implemented, or operated. In any case, one must identify the *decisions* which depend upon the evaluation, the *decision-makers,* the *status* of the system, and the *evaluators,* as a prelude to evaluation.

[1]Italicized numbers in parentheses throughout this book refer to items cited in *References* at the end of chapters.

Evaluation costs money (frequently, more than one anticipates), so the decision to evaluate should not be taken lightly. There are few guidelines on how much an evaluation *should* cost. Even in the field of manufacturing, determination of the "reliability" of an item may range from many times its other costs in the case of an aerospace item to a very small fraction of its other costs in the case of a mop handle. In developing a system, there is always great pressure to use all available funds for "productive" components such as documents, hardware, and indexing rather than for "unproductive" evaluation. The point of view is sound, unless evaluation is made a part of the dynamism that converts an idea into a successfully operating system. While it may be fashionable to evaluate a system with no other objective than to see how well it works, such an application of funds must be secondary to the application of funds for productive items.

As has been noted earlier, evaluation implies quantification of the performance characteristics of a system. Since such quantification after modification or control of specified influences is *experimentation*, it seems to be convenient, if not imperative, to include experimentation as a part of evaluation. One cannot experiment without evaluating. Therefore, in discussing the methodology of evaluation, the application of such methodology may include experimentation with systems rather than only the narrower determination of performance characteristics under natural environmental constraints.

In addition to the potential for taking action, the resources to do the evaluation must be available and there must exist a possibility that the resources applied to evaluation will return at least their cost in terms of cost saving, increased service, or both.

Decisions in this area must be made largely upon intuitive grounds, backed up by knowledge of the state-of-the-art, predictable evaluation costs, system objectives, and system constraints. At no other place in evaluation does expert judgment play such an important role. If there were quantified facts upon which to base the judgment to evaluate, one would not need to perform the evaluation.

However, the *need* to evaluate may be evident prior to the evaluation. No system can operate without leaving some tracks on the landscape. Such tracks tend to be in the form of trend statistics of use, user complaints, cost statistics, resistance on the part of the funder, excessive turnover of operating personnel, and so on.

It is difficult to formalize the decision-making process through which the decision to evaluate is reached. The following questions might be asked:

(1) Is there substantial evidence that the system needs improvement?

(2) Is there expert opinion that "better" procedures exist?

(3) Is there reason for believing that resources are available for implementing recommendations, or that management will be willing to modify or drop a system if evaluation suggests this?

If the answer to these three questions is "yes," evaluation is clearly in order. Note that all three questions require subjective judgment.

Document transfer systems require funding, planning, and management, and these activities require decisions. If evaluation has anything to offer in the field of document transfer, it must make its contribution to the decision-making process. Such evaluation can range from the purely subjective to the highly objective. It is obvious that measurement is at the heart of objective evaluation; this subject constitutes the principal focus of attention in the remainder of this chapter.

1.3 Measurement

There are two aspects to evaluation: the first is description and the second is comparison. We *describe* systems in order to acquire knowledge of their operating characteristics under specific environmental conditions, and we *compare* alternative systems with regard to particular characteristics. Both description and comparison require specification of system characteristics, or measurement. Measurement implies quantification, although in the field of documentation there has been a singular lack of consensus as to what to quantify or how to quantify it.

Certain questions are assumed that must be answered in a discussion of measures of evaluation. Among them are:

(1) Why measure at all?
(2) What should one measure?
(3) What measures are appropriate to specific requirements?
(4) How does one use measures?

These four questions are discussed below.

Why measure at all?

"Measure" is a highly flexible word, which, in a typical English dictionary, has well over a dozen meanings when used as a noun and perhaps half that many when used as a verb. For our purposes it seems desirable to take a simple meaning of the verb, i.e., "to take or mark the limits or the dimensions of," and for the noun, "the extent or dimensions of anything." The connotation of a standard scale is avoided, since this is a luxury not permitted by the systems being measured. In other words, measurement is simply quantification.

One measures (quantifies) as an aid to evaluation, but it must be realized that not all evaluation requires quantification. A wine taster can evaluate a wine without knowing its exact chemical composition. However, in the universe of document transfer systems, it seems reasonable to presume that quantification leads to more consistent, and hence more meaningful, evaluation.

What should one measure?

Every document transfer system has virtually an endless list of characteristics that describe the system, the environment within which it operates, and the ways in which it responds to stimuli from that environment. Some of these characteristics are worth measuring and some are not. Which of the characteristics one decides to measure depends upon the objectives of the evaluation, that is, upon the kinds of decisions that might be affected by the evaluation results. These decisions may be broadly categorized as *funding decisions* and *management decisions.*

Funding decisions include the allocation of resources to the system, as well as decisions to establish or discontinue systems. Management decisions are those that govern the use of funds to acquire documents, to index documents, to provide search and reference services, and so on. These decisions are highly dependent upon funds available, of course, and decisions to provide funds are dependent upon management's use of funds previously provided. The distinction between funding decisions and management decisions is useful in determining whether to focus upon economic measures or performance measures.

What measures are appropriate to specific requirements?

At the risk of oversimplification, we can say that one would like to be able to measure *cost, effectiveness,* and *benefits* (*20*).There is little question about the unit of measurement for cost – the dollar provides a convenient unit. There is some uncertainty about whether one should use discounting techniques, but this is a minor problem. However, there is a great deal of doubt over what constitutes cost.

More attention has been paid in the literature to measures of effectiveness of system performance than to measures of cost and benefits. Most of the difficulties arise because performance is not a uniquely defined property – it is many things to many people. No single measure can be expected to satisfy all groups of persons who wish to quantify performance effectiveness, although some attempts to do so appear in the literature. Even within the management of a system, one person will be interested in acquisition, another in indexing, another in hardware, and so on. Thus, it seems wise to establish as a first principle that one must provide multiple measures of performance effectiveness.

All of the problems associated with measurement of cost and effectiveness are magnified when one tries to measure benefits. Even though some benefits can only be expressed artificially in monetary units and some not at all, one must consider the consequences of the system; otherwise evaluation is only partially complete and may be seriously misleading.

Some of the practical considerations involving measurement are discussed below.

How does one use measures?

A framework for use of measures is presented in Table 1.1, which lists five principal functions – composition, reproduction, acquisition and storage, identification and location, and presentation – along with some of their major components that require evaluation. The table also shows some aspects of the system which one might consider measuring in order to form evaluative judgments about those functions and components. The listing is not intended to be comprehensive, but for illustrative purposes it covers some of the principal items of interest to the typical evaluator.

One of the problems in evaluating document transfer systems is that frequently the thing we would like to quantify cannot be measured directly. For example, it would be convenient to have a single measure of performance so that, in comparing two systems, one could select the one with better performance. Most often, however, performance is a composite of many things, some easily quantifiable and

Table 1.1 Partial List of Measurement Candidates for the Evaluation of Document Transfer Systems

Functions and objects to be evaluated	Examples of candidates for use of measures
1. Composition	a. Degree of editorial review b. Extent of information
2. Reproduction	a. Form of reproduction b. Reproduction process
3. Acquisition and	a. Responsiveness to requests from users b. Selection of high-demand documents c. Ordering mechanics
Storage	a. Composition b. Location c. Organization d. Storage form e. File purging
4. Identification and location	
Indexes	a. Indexing procedures b. Index structure – Specificity & exhaustivity Hierarchical structure Correlation of terms c. Index languages
Retrospective searching	a. Entry vocabularies b. Assistance c. Procedures d. Equipment e. Screening (use of document representations) f. Interaction with system
Selective dissemination	a. Screening b. Current awareness c. Use of document representations
Referral	a. Extent b. Accuracy
5. Presentation	a. Form b. Timeliness

others almost impossible to quantify. Also, while it may be desirable to measure one thing, frequently one must measure a substitute (proxy). For example, user satisfaction is a concept that is desirable to quantify. It is not measurable directly, however, so one measures such indicators of satisfaction as continued use of the system, the number of relevant citations obtained through the system, the amount of search output examined by the user, or his qualitative assessment of satisfaction with particular services.

1.4 A system model for evaluation

Evaluation measures should, on intuitive grounds, contribute something to one's knowledge of a system and its performance. What is needed is a framework for tying together evaluation measures so that one can see their implications with respect to the overall system viewed as a unit. Such a framework is called a "model." The literature contains many attempts to construct document transfer models – some quite primitive and some utilizing sophisticated mathematical concepts. A great deal more must be learned before global document transfer models can be constructed that faithfully picture a generalized document transfer system operating in a real-world environment. This is not to discourage model-building – far from it – but rather to point out that any models presented here must be considered as stages in an evolutionary process in which perfection is still far in the future.

Clearly, an understanding of how a system works, what its environmental constraints are, and what will happen to it as a result of certain operational patterns is a necessary prerequisite to the use of measures in the formation of evaluative judgments. With this in mind, some macro-models are discussed below that rely heavily on the concepts of cost/effectiveness and benefits.

Cost describes the *input of resources* to a system in terms of monetary units. Measures of system effectiveness are used to describe *attributes* that can be controlled by system management, such as speed, accuracy, and quality – all subject, of course, to budgetary constraints. Benefits describe *consequences* of system performance in terms of value, return on investment, effect on behavior of the user, effect on other systems, and nonquantifiable consequences that may be a direct result of the system or a result of interactions with other systems.

When possible, system decisions should be based on a comparison between the *cost* necessary to attain a particular degree of performance effectiveness and the *benefits* that are derived from this performance. System effectiveness measures should be chosen with two purposes in mind. The first purpose is to relate performance effectiveness to costs and to benefits so that they may be compared. The second purpose is to enhance diagnosis of the system when performance is found to be unsatisfactory.

The schema in Figure 1.2 gives a general relationship among cost-effectiveness-benefits measures and the six basic functions of document transfer. As shown in the schema, effectiveness measures serve to relate system performance to cost and to benefits. For example, in retrospective searching (one process of document identification), *system cost* is partially determined by average number of documents identified (since it costs something to screen or look at each identified document), by the number of searches completed (since each search has an identifiable cost), and by average time per search. *System benefits* are partially derived from such effectiveness measures as search accuracy and response time.

The schema is purposely oversimplified. System cost, for example, must be subdivided into fixed costs and two kinds of variable costs. Fixed costs include component, development, and operational costs that do not vary by number of searches or by alternative system processes. The first kind of variable cost is related to the number of uses of the system, and the second kind of variable cost is that attributable to the alternative system processes under investigation.

An example may help explain the general philosophy of choosing measures of effectiveness to determine costs. Suppose a government agency's information center is considering indexing at one of two distinct levels of exhaustivity (that is, number of terms per document) for input to a retrospective search system. The variable costs attributable to the two alternative index processes are fairly well defined. Greater exhaustivity represents higher indexing costs (per document). However, the variable costs attributable to the number of retrospective searches not only affect the cost of identification but also are reflected in the cost of other transfer functions. Greater exhaustivity (1) yields a larger number of documents identified by the system (for a given query), (2) affects search time because of the increased number of terms to be matched, (3) requires more documents to be screened and located, and (4) potentially yields more documents re-

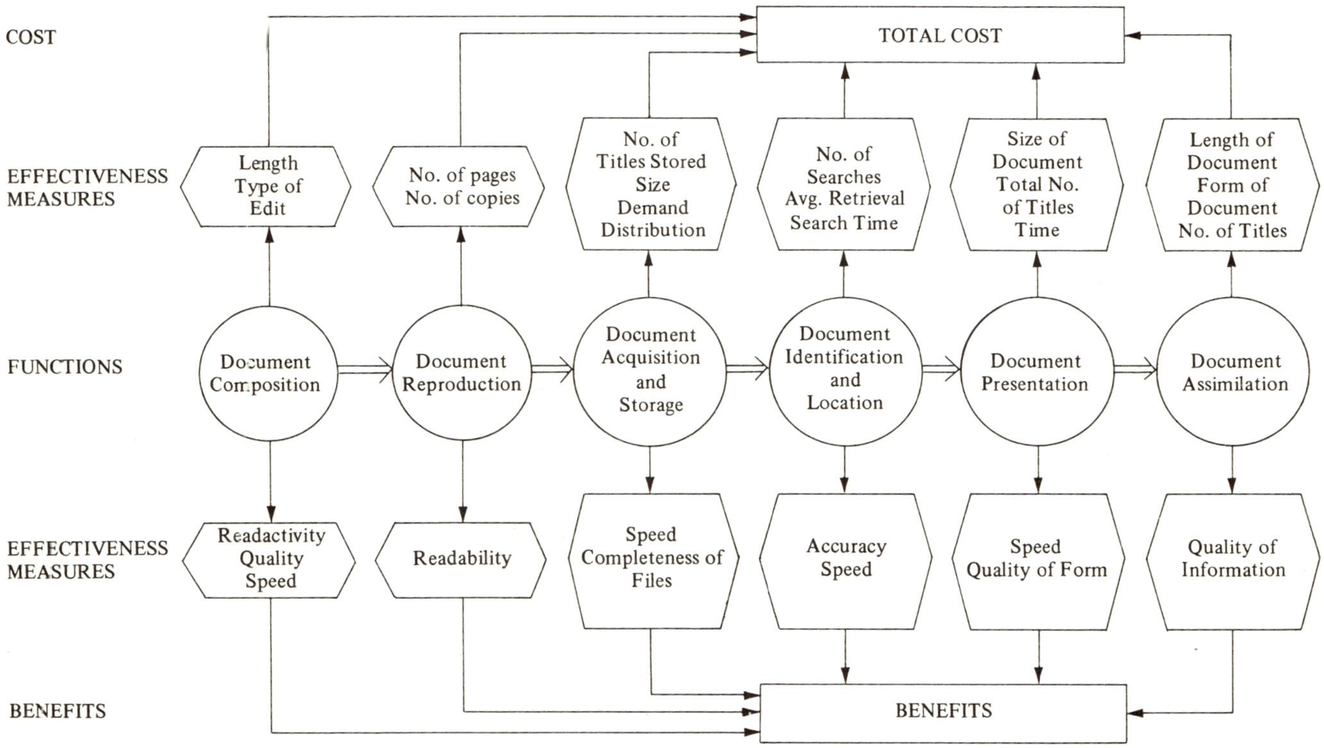

Figure 1.2 Schema for cost, performance, and benefits measures for composition, reproduction, storage, identification, presentation, and assimilation in document transfer systems.

trieved and used. All of these variables directly yield measurable increased costs. Of course, the question of indexing exhaustivity is not entirely resolved by estimating its effect on system costs. Greater exhaustivity will tend to allow retrieval of a greater proportion of the documents relevant to a particular request (i.e., improve *recall*) which, in turn, should yield greater benefit from the system.

One of the most important considerations in determining performance variables and benefits measures is whether or not a user is a part of the system being evaluated. If he is a part of that system, performance effectiveness directly affects the overall goals and objectives of the organization. Therefore, the management of the proprietary entity, as system funders, will want to know whether or not system expenditures yield sufficient benefits to make them worthwhile. Furthermore, if a user is part of the system under evaluation, his use of the system can be more easily investigated.

If the user *is not part* of the proprietary entity, system management has no administrative control over what the user does with the information or over the ultimate consequences of the information use. However, management should know the consequence of the service and whether or not the user will continue to employ the system. Thus, when users are not a part of the proprietary system, the system resides in a market-like environment, and all the economic, marketing, and competitive ramifications of the environment must be considered in evaluation.

The schema in Figure 1.3 shows relationships between performance effectiveness and benefits when users *are not part* of the proprietary system being evaluated. The user assimilation function is no longer assumed to be directly involved. However, processes necessary to accomplish composition, reproduction, acquisition and storage, identification and location, and presentation all have effectiveness measures such as accuracy, speed, and quality. These effectiveness attributes determine the user's degree of satisfaction with service. User satisfaction and price of the service, along with promotion and advertising, provide motivation to begin or to continue using the system. As shown in the schema, price is determined by cost and anticipated income. The price per use times demand determines income produced by the system.

When users are not a part of the proprietary system under evaluative consideration, the system is usually one of two kinds: either (1) a local facility, such as a public library, in which system functions are performed in-house or by request from another service facility, or (2)

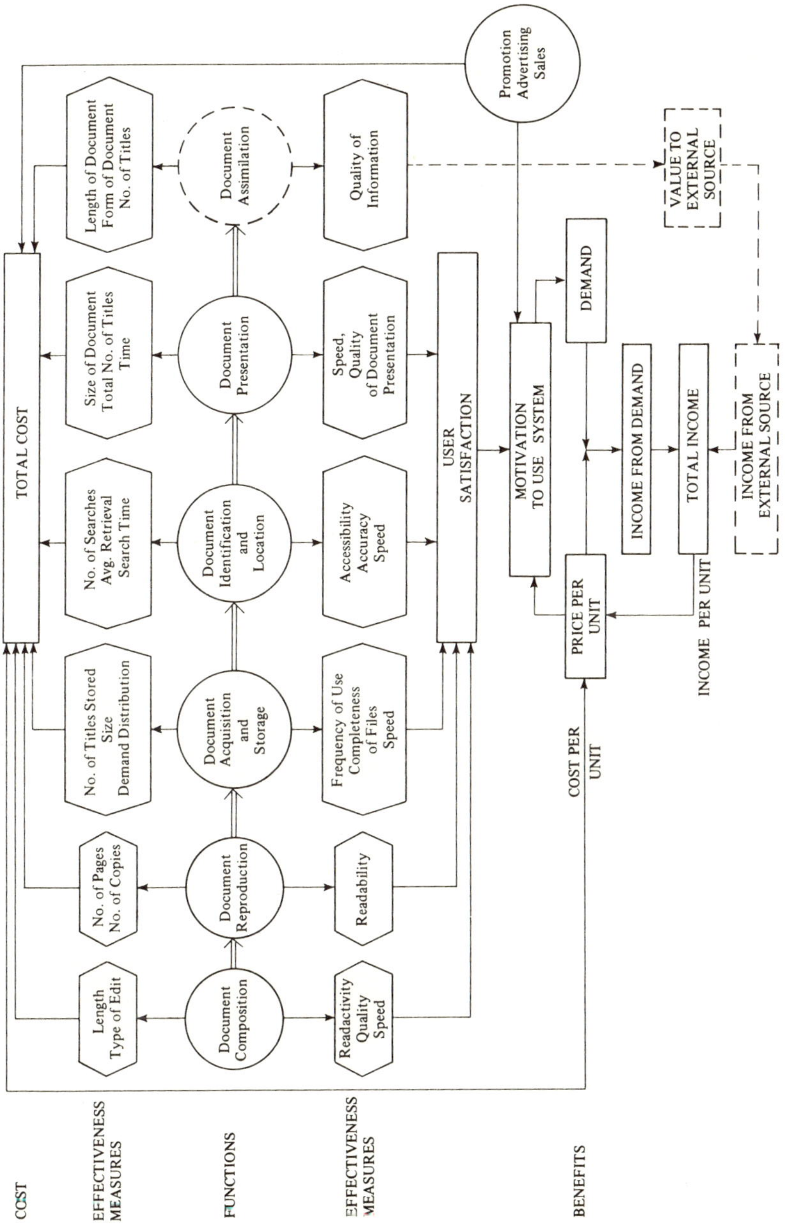

Figure 1.3 Schema for performance and benefits measures when users are not a part of the proprietary system.

a central reservoir, such as the National Technical Information Service, that provides one or more system functions.

A local library may identify a document in-house but may send away to obtain it. The performance variables cited in Figure 1.3 still apply, as do their relationships to user satisfaction, motivation to use the system, and income. Cost of document delivery in this case is the price paid plus internal handling costs.

In some instances, the Federal Government or some other external source partially supports development or operation of a system in order to ensure that the system will be available to the professional communities. Thus, as shown in Figure 1.3, income may also be derived from an external source. In these instances, the sponsoring agencies should have an interest in the use of the system and the value derived from the system in order to determine if their own resources are properly allocated.

Figure 1.4 depicts the system schema when users *are part* of the proprietary system. Document assimilation by the user becomes an integral part of the system, and this function has effectiveness attributes that contribute to user satisfaction, which creates greater demand. Document assimilation also determines the use made of the information, which in turn affects user behavior and, hopefully, increases the value of the system to his organization.

In summary, we have attempted to establish a meaningful framework within which evaluation can take place. This framework includes four broad dimensions including six basic system functions, processes for accomplishing these functions, organizational structure, and system components. Evaluation must have a purpose, which usually is the need to make decisions concerning the system. A system performs functions and the degree to which these functions accomplish objectives is the focus of evaluation. The heart of system evaluation is measurement of the extent to which system objectives are met. The measure may be broadly classified by cost, effectiveness, and benefits, where cost describes the input of resources to a system, effectiveness describes performance attributes, and benefits describe the consequences of a system.

The remainder of this book is devoted to evaluation of specific system functions and their processes, as well as to evaluation methodology. Particular emphasis is placed on evaluation of identification systems and their processes. In fact, Chapters 2 through 7 are all devoted to the identification function because of its relative importance and the problems of its evaluation. Chapters 8 and 9 discuss

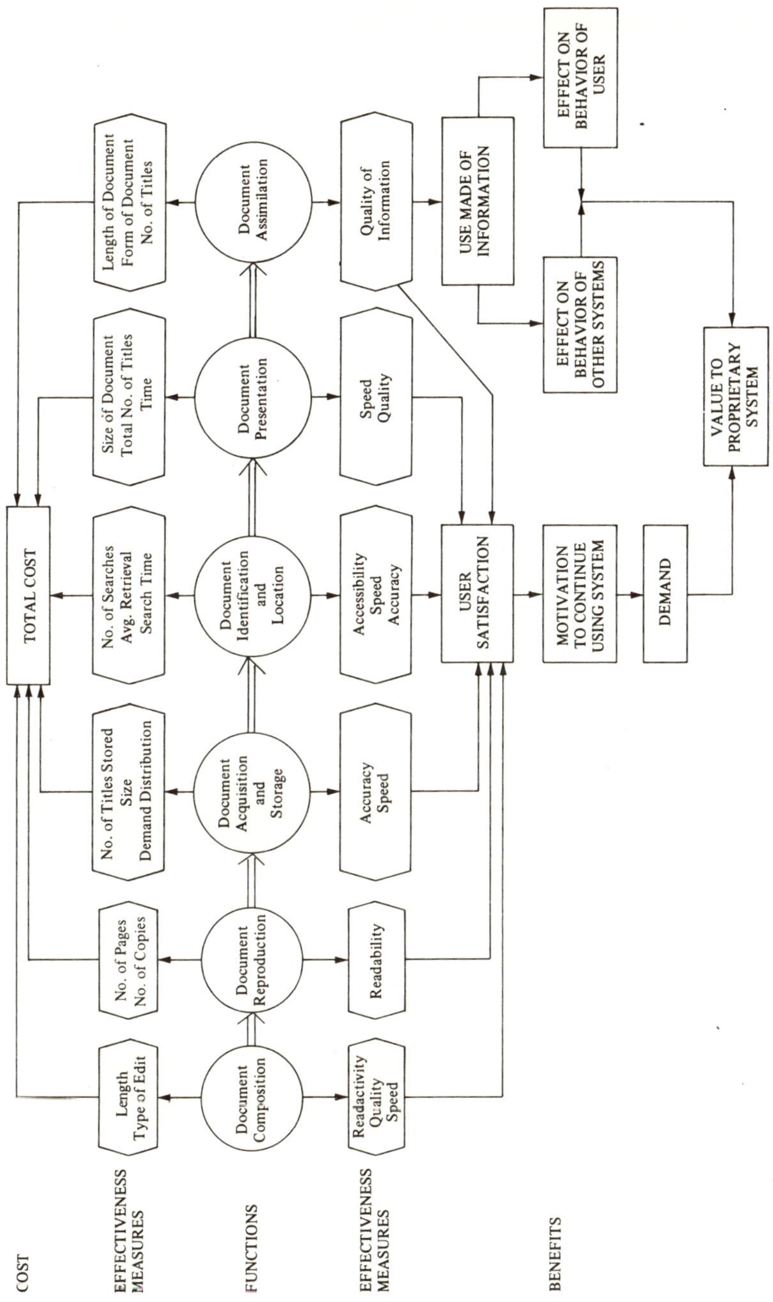

Figure 1.4 Schema for performance and benefits measures when users are part of the proprietary system.

evaluation of the other system functions and their processes. Chapter 10 deals with user surveys and marketing research related to information products and services, and Chapters 11 and 13 provide elementary discussion of statistical methodology as it applies to evaluation of document transfer systems.

References

1. Baker, N. R., *A Descriptive Model of Library/User Funder Behavior in a University Environment.* Presented at Conference on "The Library-College: A Method of Learning," Graduate School of Library Science, Drexel Institute of Technology, Philadelphia, December 18-21, 1966. (Research sponsored by the National Science Foundation, Office of Science Information Service.)
2. Baker, N. R., Nance, R. E., *The Use of Simulation in Studying Information Storage and Retrieval Systems.* Presented at the 32nd National Meeting of the Operations Research Society of America, Chicago, November 1-3, 1967.
3. Bednarek, A. R., Belzer, J., "A System Performance Function." *In*: Kent, A., Taulbee, O. E., Belzer, J., Goldstein, G. D., eds. *Electronic Handling of Information: Testing and Evaluation.* Washington, D. C., John I. Thompson & Co.; London, Academic Press, 1967, pp. 237-244.
4. Borko, H., "Design of Information Systems and Services." *In*: Cuadra, C. A., ed. *Annual Review of Information Science and Technology.* New York, Interscience, Vol. 2, 1967, pp. 35-61.
5. Bourne, C. P., "Evaluation of Indexing Systems." *In*: Cuadra, C. A., ed. *Annual Review of Information Science and Technology.* New York, Interscience, Vol. 1, 1966, pp. 171-190.
6. Churchman, D. W., *The Systems Approach.* New York, Delacorte Press, 1968.
7. Davis, R. M., "Experimentation and Evaluation: The Challenge." *In*: Kent, A., Taulbee, O. E., Belzer, J., Goldstein, G. D., eds. *Electronic Handling of Information: Testing and Evaluation*. Washington, D. C., John I. Thompson & Co.; London, Academic Press, 1967, pp. 3-12.
8. Fairthorne, R. A., "Morphology of 'Information Flow'." *Journal of the Association for Computing Machinery,* Vol. 14 (October 1967), pp. 710-719.
9. Henderson, M. M., *Evaluation of Information Systems: A Selected Bibliography with Information Abstracts.* Washington, D.C., National Bureau of Standards, December 1967. (NBS Technical Note 297.)
10. Herner, S., "System Design, Evaluation, and Costing." *Special Libraries*, Vol. 58 (October 1967), pp. 576-581.
11. Herner, S., Leyman, E., Herner, M., *A Study to Determine the Feasibility and Design for a New England Technical Information Referral Service.* Washington, D.C., Herner and Company, November 1969.
12. Hyslop, M. R., "The Economics of Information Systems: Observations, Development Costs and Nature of the Market." *In: Proceedings of the American Society for Information Science Annual Meeting, Columbus, Ohio, 20-24 October 1968.* New York, Greenwood Publishing Corp., Vol. 5, 1968, p. 301.

13. Information Dynamics Corporation, *A Method for Systems Design and Analysis.* Wakefield, Mass., (n.d.). PB 176 191.
14. Katter, R. V., "Design and Evaluation of Information Systems." *In*: Cuadra, C. A., ed. *Annual Review of Information Science and Technology.* Chicago, Encyclopaedia Britannica, Vol. 4, 1969, p. 31-70.
15. King, D. W., "Design and Evaluation of Information Systems." *In*: Cuadra, C. A., ed. *Annual Review of Information Science and Technology.* Chicago, Encyclopaedia Britannica, Vol. 3, 1968, pp. 61-103.
16. Koch, H. W., Herschman, A., *A Network for Physics Information.* New York, American Institute of Physics, October 1968.
17. Lancaster, F. W., "Design and Evaluation of Information Systems." *In*: Cuadra, C. A., ed. *Annual Review of Information Science and Technology.* Chicago, Encyclopaedia Britannica, Vol. 5, 1970, p. 33-70.
18. Lancaster, F. W., *Information Retrieval Systems: Characteristics, Testing, and Evaluation.* New York, Wiley & Sons, 1968.
19. Morse, P. M., *Library Effectiveness: A Systems Approach.* Cambridge, Mass., M.I.T. Press, 1968.
20. Murdock, J. W., Liston, D. M., Jr., "A General Model of Information Transfer." *American Documentation,* Vol. 18, No. 4 (October 1967), pp. 197-208.
21. Orr, R. H., Pings, V. M., Pizer, I. H., Olson, E. E., "Development of Methodologic Tools for Planning and Managing Library Services. I: Project Goals and Approach; II: Measuring a Library's Capability for Providing Documents." *Bulletin of the Medical Library Association*, Vol. 56, No. 3 (July 1968), pp. 235-267.
22. Orr, R. H., Pings, V. M., Pizer, I. H., Olson, E. E., "Development of Methodologic Tools for Planning and Managing Library Services. III: Standardized Inventories of Library Services." *Bulletin of the Medical Library Association,* Vol. 56, No. 4 (October 1968), pp. 380-403.
23. Rees, A. M., "Evaluation of Information Systems and Services." *In*: Cuadra, C. A., ed. *Annual Review of Information Science and Technology.* New York, Interscience, Vol. 2, 1967, pp. 63-68.
24. Whittenburg, J. A., Schumacher, A. W., *An Information System Planning Guide: Preliminary Development and Checkout.* Alexandria, Va., Whittenburg, Vaughan Associates, Inc., February 1968. PB 177 601.

Chapter Two
Measures for Evaluating Identification Systems

2.1 Introduction

The identification function in document transfer systems was described briefly in Chapter 1 as the determination of the identity and location of documents. Clearly, this is one of the most important functions in the transfer of documents from author to user and we place a great deal of emphasis on it in evaluation. In most document transfer systems this function is accomplished by one of the two following modes:

(1) A *passive mode*, in which the document identification process is initiated by the user; e.g., retrospective search.

(2) An *active mode*, in which the document identification process is initiated by the system; e.g., selective dissemination of information and current awareness services.

In the *passive mode*, retrospective searching may be performed (1) by the user having prior knowledge of a document's identity (by title, author, or subject matter), (2) by the user requesting desired references by subject matter without prior knowledge of specific documents, and (3) by the user "browsing" to generate new ideas or to investigate new fields without prior knowledge as to what documents are actually sought. In the first instance, document identification is not difficult (or at least should not be), since the user already knows the identity of the document and he merely attempts to locate and to retrieve the full text. In the second case, however, document identification involves retrospective searching processes. Browsing requires more complex document identification processes since a user must peruse the full text, or at least informative document representations, from a large but ill-defined file.

In the *active mode,* document identification results from action taken by the system. The identification process often occurs by prior agreement between the user and system, in which case the system disseminates identification information (title, author, keywords, or abstracts) to a user or group of users. This process presumes that the user will need and subsequently retrieve a document for his use. Document identification in both the active and passive modes involves a number of subprocesses such as indexing, abstracting, dissemination, and user matching techniques.

A general discussion is given in the remainder of this chapter on evaluation measures for identification processes. Measures for evaluation of subprocesses such as indexing, searching, and screening are given in subsequent chapters.

2.2 Effectiveness measures

We indicated in Chapter 1 that the performance effectiveness of document identification can be characterized by such measures as speed, timeliness, accessibility, and accuracy. These measures can then be related to system benefits. Cost, on the other hand, may be found from such measures as number of searches, number of references identified, and search time. The question of which measures one applies depends on which identification mode and processes are being used.

Identification by searching requires different measures of effectiveness, depending largely on the degree of knowledge the user has about the desired documents. When a search is performed by a user who has prior knowledge of desired documents, the citation may be subject to error, but search accuracy may not be as important as duration of time between making the request and receiving the item requested. On the other hand, when a search is performed by a user who does not have prior knowledge of desired documents, the accuracy of identifying documents becomes highly important. When a user is browsing, accessibility to the full texts of documents may be the most important measure.

Particularly important, from the standpoint of evaluation, is the search situation where users need references in a subject without prior knowledge of specific documents. This situation is important because in identifying correct documents it is subject to error. The ability of the system to identify correct documents without error may be called *system accuracy*. However, in reviewing evaluation literature, it has not been abundantly clear exactly what accuracy is. We will develop the notion of accuracy by first discussing the concept of document relevance.

We assume that a user can verbally characterize his need for information found in documents. Researchers engaged in two major research projects to investigate relevance agree, in principle at least, that relevance should be defined as the relationship between a user's information question (or information requirement statement) and a document (*5,15*). There is such a relevance relationship between the user's question and every document in the file. This relationship is called user relevance judgment.[1] A user relevance judgment can be a dichotomy (i.e., a document does or does not answer the user's information question); a multi-valued scale, such as a "degree" of relevance given by scale values (e.g., 0 to 10); or continuous values, in which case relevance can take on values from low to high degrees of relevance.

User questions are processed through the system, resulting in a response for every document in the file. The system response may also be a dichotomy with a value of one or zero (i.e., a document is identified or not identified), or it may be multi-valued such as is the case with weighted responses from associative retrieval systems. The system response value also exists for every document in the file and this value is called *system relevance response*. The *system relevance response* is the system's assessment of the relationship between the user's question and a document. Hopefully, it accurately predicts (or resembles) the user relevance judgment.

Continuous valued measures of user relevance judgment and system relevance response can be plotted against one another, as shown in Figure 2.1. Each point represents one document from the file. Each document has a user relevance judgment value and a value found by processing the user's question through the system. For a given user question, most documents in a file are likely to have low values on the scales of user relevance judgment and system relevance response,

[1] It is noted that, even though we refer to "user" relevance judgment, the judgment of relevance can (and sometimes should) be made by a proxy on behalf of the user.

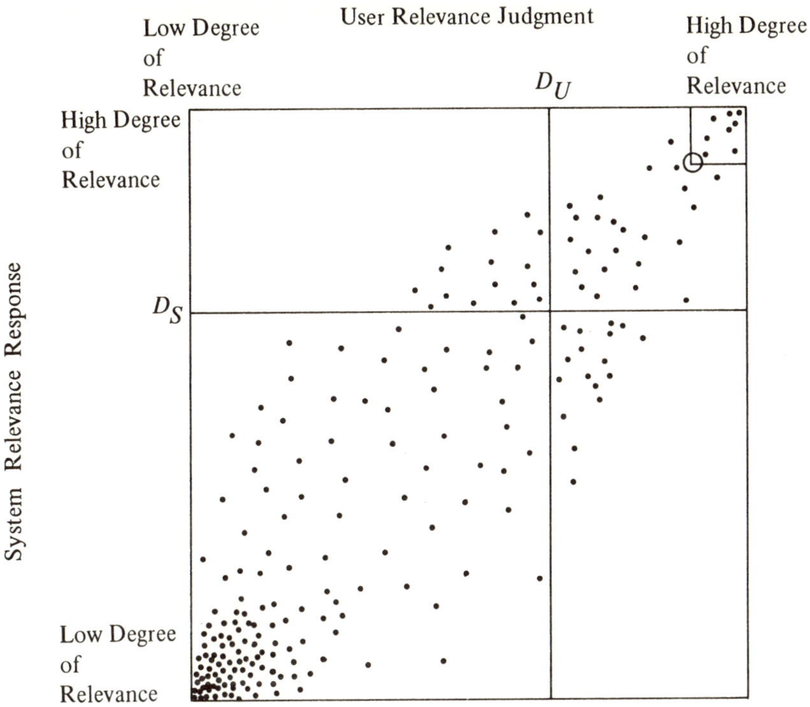

Figure 2.1 User relevance judgment plotted against system relevance response for individual documents and a given search question.

which accounts for the large cluster of documents in the lower left corner. It is highly unlikely that values of system relevance response will be the same as user relevance judgment. The degree to which system relevance response predicts the user relevance judgment is called *accuracy*. If the system processes a user question perfectly and no errors occur, all documents in the file would have values that fall on a 45° line drawn from the lower left corner to the upper right corner, which would imply perfect accuracy for the system.

System relevance responses are independent of user relevance judgments in the sense that the relevance numbers are assigned by different entities. For example, if a system is improved to raise or lower the system relevance response value to the 45° line, the value found by user relevance judgment remains the same. On the other hand, if a user changes his relevance judgment left or right, the system relevance response remains the same. Therefore, accuracy must *not* be considered the user relevance judgment or system relevance response alone, but rather the degree to which the system relevance responses resemble the user relevance judgments.

User relevance judgment[2] can be estimated from system relevance response mathematically, by measures of correlation or by conditional expectation. (See Chapter 11.)

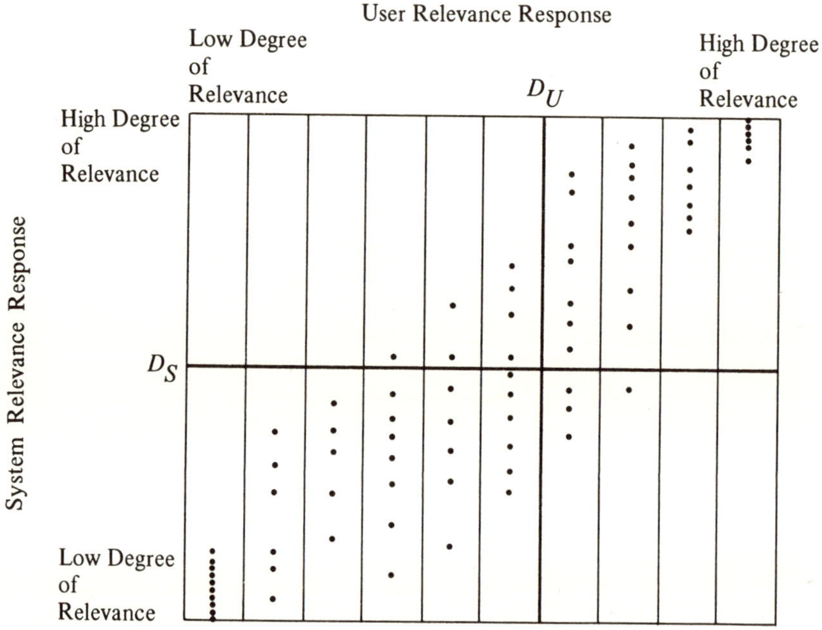

Figure 2.2 Multi-values of user relevance judgment plotted against system relevance response.

[2]Someone must judge the relevance relationship between a question and a document to establish the value of user relevance judgment for the document. Also, an information system intermediary may judge relevance between a question and a document to produce the system relevance response. Two studies (*5, 15*) on human judgments of relevance indicate that these judgments are subject to considerable variation due to differences in documents, judgment conditions, questions, judges, and even different judgments made by the same judge over time. Another study (*12*) indicates that, even though judges are not fully consistent concerning relevance, these variations in judgment do not affect the ranking of alternative retrieval procedures in terms of their effectiveness. Even though these factors are not directly related to cost or to benefits, they should be isolated, if possible, to permit better estimates of user relevance judgments (hence, benefits) and also to enable a researcher to diagnose system processes more effectively.

We can depart from continuous values on both axes, as given in Figure 2.1, by having scaled user relevance judgments plotted against continuous values (as depicted in Figure 2.2) or vice versa (as depicted in Figure 2.3). Discussion of these relationships is given later in this chapter. Despite some advantages inherent in the relationships indicated above, we feel that dichotomous assessments of relevance are more meaningful for evaluative purposes, since the decision processes of both the system relevance responses and the user relevance judgments are typically dichotomous in nature. Even though user relevance judgments may be multi-valued, the user may feel that a relevance decision depends on whether or not his relevance judgment exceeds a critical value, designated by D_U in Figure 2.1. Similarly, a decision may be made to send or not to send documents to a user, depending on a critical system relevance response value, labeled D_S in Figure 2.1. Thus, dichotomous values may be necessary either because of decision requirements or because the relevance assessments are dichotomous in nature. In either case, the values in Figure 2.1 can be transformed into the retrieval categories of Figure 2.4, where the cell

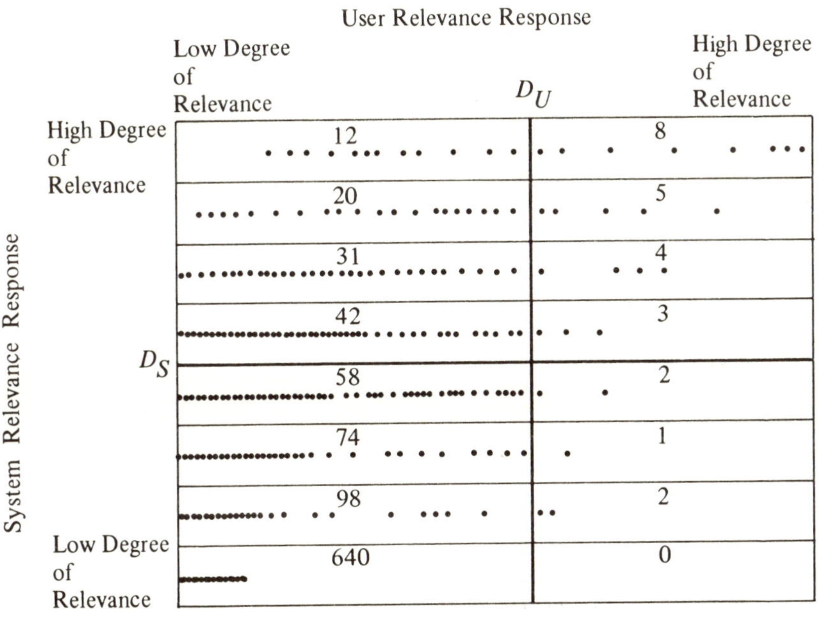

Figure 2.3 User relevance judgment plotted against multi-values of system relevance response.

		User Relevance Judgment (V)		
		Not Relevant ($V_{\bar{r}}$)	D_U Relevant (V_r)	Total
System Relevance Response (R)	Relevant (R_r) D_S	a	b	$a + b$
	Not Relevant ($R_{\bar{r}}$)	c	d	$c + d$
	Total	$a + c$	$b + d$	$a + b + c + d$

Figure 2.4 Retrieval categorization with dichotomous values of user relevance judgments and system relevance response.

values a, b, c, and d correspond to the number of documents observed in the four quadrants in Figure 2.1.

Performance measures for estimating value from system output can also be determined from the entries in the table in Figure 2.4. For example, the probability that a user will judge a document relevant, given that the system assesses it as relevant, is $P[a|(a+b)]$ or $P(V_r|R_r)$, which corresponds to the well-known *precision ratio*.

Given a user relevance judgment, the expected system relevance response is estimated by $P[b|(b+d)]$ or $P(R_r|V_r)$ which corresponds to the well-known *recall ratio*. Another measure of system performance effectiveness is the *fallout ratio* which is estimated by $P[a|(a+c)]$ or $P(R_r|V_{\bar{r}})$. Finally, two other measures that characterize the 2×2 table in Figure 2.4 are the *proportion of documents retrieved*, $P[(a+b)|(a+b+c+d)]$, and the *generality ratio* estimated by $P[(a)|(a+b+c+d)]$.

It is common practice to compare two retrieval measures such as precision and recall to establish the trade-off found by broadening system searches. Referring to Figure 2.3, searches can be broadened by beginning the search output (D_S) at the scale of high degree of relevance and successively broadening the search (depicted by lowering the system decision point D_S). In the highest degree of system relevance, the system retrieves eight documents judged relevant by the user and twelve documents judged nonrelevant. If we broaden the search one scale, the system retrieves a total of 13 relevant and 32 nonrelevant documents.

The process can be continued through eight scales of search broadness yielding eight new search results. The values for the eight search results are given in Table 2.1 for recall ratio, precision ratio, total retrieved, fallout, proportion retrieved, and generality.

There are several ways in which two of the measures may be compared graphically. For example, Cleverdon (*2*), Salton (*12*), and Lancaster (*11*) have all incorporated a comparison between the precision ratio and recall ratio in their studies. Usually when a search is broadened, the recall and precision ratios will be inversely related as shown in Figure 2.5. The relationship more or less describes the tradeoff between the search accuracy defined by recall and search effectiveness defined by the precision. However, it is difficult to assign actual costs and to relate these measures to system benefits.

Another relationship commonly given is recall versus fallout; this relationship is shown in Figure 2.6. Robertson (*16*) presents an excellent argument for using these two measures for comparative purposes.

Swets (*19*) has considered continuous values of system relevance responses and dichotomous values of user relevance judgments. He suggests that the frequency distribution of documents found to the

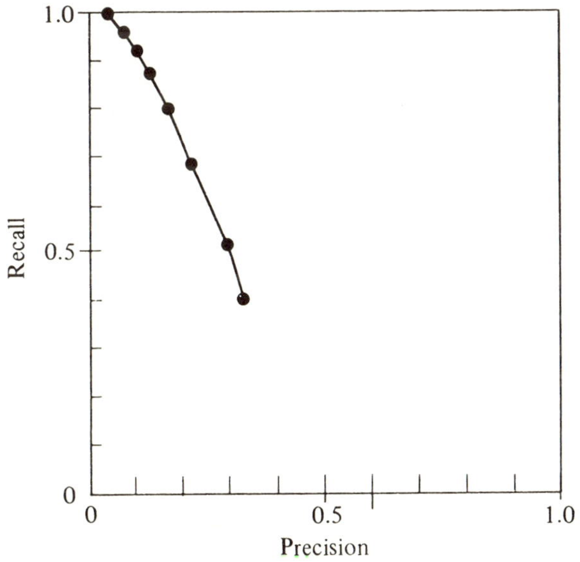

Figure 2.5 Recall vs. precision.

Table 2.1 Estimates of Recall, Precision, Total Retrieved, Fallout, Proportion Retrieved, and Generality from Figure 2.3

Search level	Cell values[a] *a*	*b*	*c*	*d*	Recall $[b/(b+d)]$	Precision $[b/(a+b)]$	Total retrieved $(a+b)$	Fallout $[a/(a+c)]$	Proportion retrieved $[(a+b)/(a+b+c+d)]$	Generality $[(b)/(a+b+c+d)]$
1	12	8	963	17	0.32	0.40	20	0.012	0.020	0.008
2	32	13	943	12	0.52	0.29	45	0.033	0.045	0.013
3	63	17	912	8	0.68	0.21	80	0.065	0.080	0.017
4	105	20	870	5	0.80	0.16	125	0.108	0.125	0.020
5	163	22	812	3	0.88	0.12	185	0.167	0.185	0.022
6	237	23	738	2	0.92	0.09	260	0.243	0.260	0.023
7	335	25	640	0	1.00	0.07	360	0.344	0.360	0.025
8	975	25	975	0	1.00	0.025	1.000	1.000	1.000	0.025

[a]Cell values correspond to the number of documents observed in the quadrants of Figure 2.1.

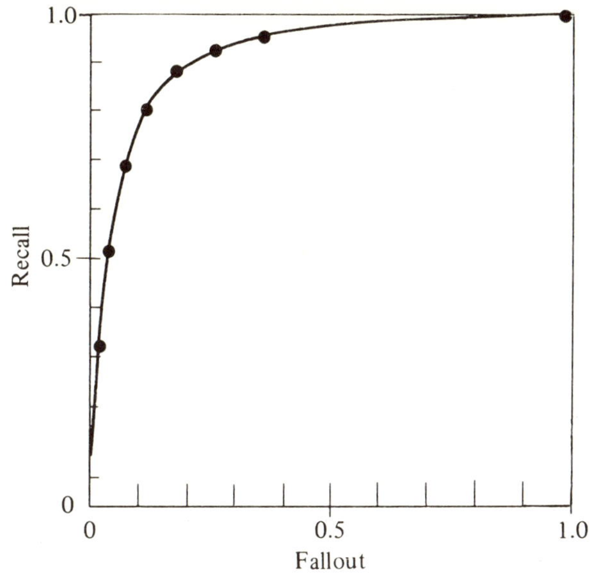

Figure 2.6 Recall vs. fallout.

right of the user decision point D_U in Figure 2.3 (i.e., those judged relevant) and the frequency distribution of documents found to the left of D_U (i.e., those judged not relevant) are plotted against values on the system relevance response scale as shown in Figure 2.7.

Swets also defines D_S as a critical point above which the system selects items for examination. The area under the high relevant curve to the right of D_S in Figure 2.7 can be characterized as the probability of retrieving a document, given that it is relevant. The area under the low relevant curve to the right of D_S may be defined as the probability of retrieving a document, given that it is not relevant. Swets plots the probabilities against one another for all values of D_S and refers to this relationship as the operating characteristic curve, which he recommends as a measure of performance. This relationship is given in Figure 2.8.

Another common way of characterizing retrieval performance is to plot the recall ratio against the proportion of documents retrieved. This relationship is given in Figure 2.9. The diagonal in that graph represents the relationship if one were to randomly search, that is, if searches were conducted by randomly selecting documents from the file. Thus, one would expect to achieve a search curve above that line

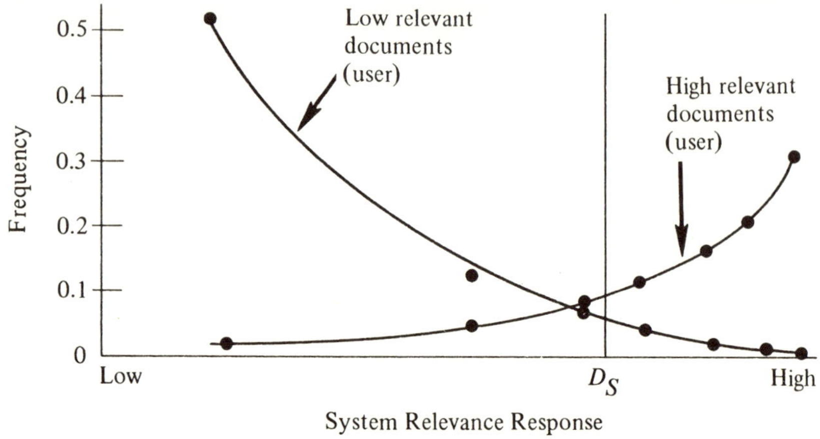

Figure 2.7 Frequency of system relevance response for documents judged of high and low relevance by users.

if the system were superior to a random search. The line to the left of the curve drawn from the origin to *G* (the Generality Ratio at 100 percent Recall) represents the best the system could be expected to perform. That is, if, when we broaden each search, only relevant documents are retrieved, the search performance characterized by recall versus proportion of documents retrieved would follow the line drawn from the origin to *G*. Thus, perfect performance of the system is described by that line. The normal search performance, then, will lie somewhere between these two lines.

Finally, another relationship that is used is the recall plotted against the total number of documents retrieved. This relationship has been used by King (*10*) and is closely related to the expected search length suggested by Cooper (*3*). The advantage of this relationship is that recall can be transformed to system benefits and total retrieval can be transformed to cost since the number of documents retrieved and investigated is directly related to the cost of screening. This relationship is shown in Figure 2.10, with total retrieval given in a log form and recall given on a probability scale. This relationship has been shown to be close to linear in several evaluation projects by King.

Several attempts have been made to arrive at a single figure of merit for measuring system performance. For example, Swets (*19*) plots the fallout ratio against the recall ratio on a single probability curve (similar to the operating characteristics curves used in statistics). This relationship is given in Figure 2.8. He then describes system performance by the slope of this curve. Orr (*13*) has discussed the

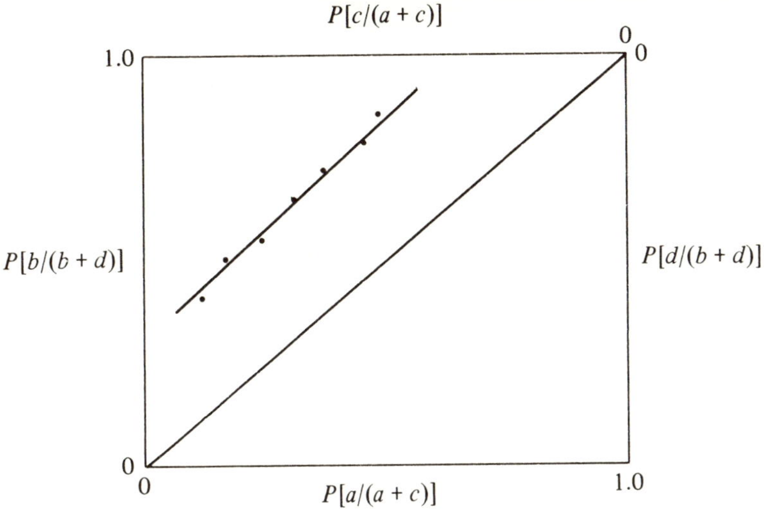

Figure 2.8 Frequency plots of system relevance scores for documents judged relevant or nonrelevant by the user.

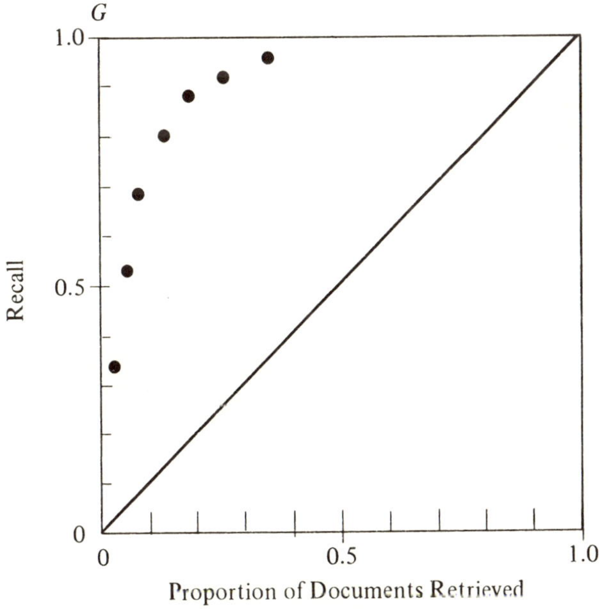

Figure 2.9 Recall vs. proportion of documents retrieved.

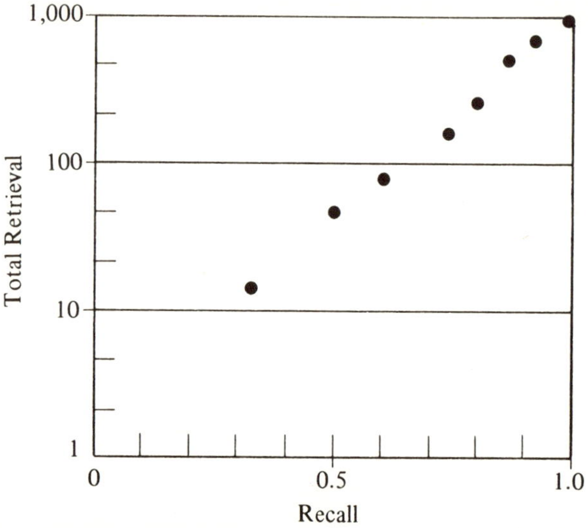

Figure 2.10 Recall vs. total retrieval.

interpretation of data contained in plots of recall versus proportion retrieved as used by several researchers. Salton (*12*) measures performance by summing the area under the curve of the recall ratio plotted against the proportion of documents retrieved, divided by the entire area to the right of the line drawn to *G.* Thus, this relationship ranges from zero to one and increases as the performance curve of the system approaches the generality line. Rocchio (*17*), on the other hand, recognizes that the area below the diagonal line really does not contribute to system performance. Since this area is described in both the numerator and denominator, the ratio is not truly repesentative of the actual performance divided by the ideal performance. Thus, Rocchio applies the same ratio with one-half subtracted from both the numerator and denominator. Wiederkehr (*24*) has developed a single measure of merit based on the net benefit of a system. That is, he translates the measures of accuracy into cost and into the relative value of the system. He then subtracts one from the other to arrive at a net benefit value for the system. This procedure is discussed thoroughly in Chapter 9.

When a user is not part of the proprietary system, it is not as essential to determine the value of the output as it is to determine how well the system satisfies the user. As was shown in Figure 1.3, the best gross measure to observe for determining the effectiveness of the system is the demand placed on the system by users. However, this measure is neither timely nor discriminating enough for sensitive management control. Therefore, it may be a better procedure to estimate user satisfaction from accuracy, speed, quality, accessibility, and similar measures. User satisfaction can be estimated by regression modeling (see Chapter 11) where satisfaction scores are assigned by the user and estimated from the performance measures. It is also important to obtain a statement from the user that he intends to continue using the system and then to observe whether or not he actually does use it. The group of users in the test can be compared with users not in the test to determine their relative use of the system. Then, at least in theory, system demand (hence, income) can be estimated (utilizing the regression model mentioned above) from system accuracy as measured by the precision ratio and by total retrieval.

References

1. Bourne, C. P., Peterson, G. D., Lefkowitz, B., Ford, D., *Requirements, Criteria, and Measures of Performance of Information Storage and Retrieval Systems.* Menlo Park, Calif., Stanford Research Institute, 1961, 132 p. AD 270 942.
2. Cleverdon, C., Mills, J., Keen, M., *Factors Determining the Performance of Indexing Systems.* Vol. 1: Design, Part 1: Text; Part 2: Appendices; Vol. 2: Test Results. Cranfield, England, ASLIB Cranfield Research Project, 1966.
3. Cooper, W. S., "Expected Search Length: A Single Measure of Retrieval Effectiveness Based on the Weak Ordering Action of Retrieval Systems." *American Documentation,* Vol. 19, No. 1 (January 1968), pp. 30-41.
4. Cornell University, Department of Computer Science, *Information Storage and Retrieval.* Scientific Report No. ISR-14 to the National Science Foundation. Ithaca, N. Y., October 1968.
5. Cuadra, C. A., Katter, R. V., "The Relevance of Relevance Assessment." *Proceedings of the 30th Annual Meeting of the American Documentation Institute, New York, October 1967.* Washington, D. C., John I. Thompson & Co., 1967, pp. 95-99.
6. Good, I. J., "The Decision-Theory Approach to the Evaluation of Information-Retrieval Systems." *Information Storage and Retrieval,* Vol. 3 (April 1967), pp. 31-34.
7. Gotterer, M. H., "Identification of Performance Criteria of an Electronic Information System." *In*: Kent, A., Taulbee, O. E., Belzer, J., Goldstein, G. D., eds. *Electronic Handling of Information: Testing and Evaluation.* Washington, D. C., John I. Thompson & Co.; London, Academic Press, 1967, pp. 51-62.

8. Hertz, D. B., Wynne, B. E., Jr., Corrigan, J. J., Schaffir, K. H., Moody, L. A., Littauer, S. V., *Research Study of Criteria and Procedures for Evaluating Scientific Information Retrieval Systems.* Final Report. New York, Arthur Andersen & Co., March 1962. AD 273 115.
9. Katter, R. V., *Measuring Fidelity in Components of Document Retrieval Systems.* Presented at 33rd Conference of FID and International Congress on Documentation, Tokyo, September 12-22, 1967.
10. King, D. W., *Evaluation During File Development of the Glass Technology Coordinate Index File.* Bethesda, Md., Westat Research, Inc., November 1967.
11. Lancaster, F. W., *Evaluation of the MEDLARS Demand Search Service.* Bethesda, Md., National Library of Medicine, January 1968.
12. Lesk, M., Salton, G., "Relevance Assessments and Retrieval System Evaluation." *Information Storage and Retrieval,* Vol. 4, No. 4 (December 1968), pp. 343-359.
13. Orr, R. H., Private communication.
14. Pollock, S., *Evaluation and Comparison of Information Retrieval Systems.* Presented at the 31st National Meeting of the Operations Research Society of America, New York, June 1, 1967. (*See also* abstract of his "Measures for the Comparison of Information Retrieval Systems, and the Normalized Sliding Ratio," *Bulletin of the Operations Research Society of America*, Vol. 15, Supplement 1 (Spring 1967), p. B57.)
15. Rees, A. M., Schultz, D. G., *A Field Experimental Approach to the Study of Relevance Assessments in Relation to Document Searching.* Final Report (July 1, 1965-June 30, 1967). Cleveland, Center for Documentation and Communication Research, Case Western Reserve University, 1967.
16. Robertson, S. E., "The Parametric Description of Retrieval Tests." *Journal of Documentation*, Vol. 25, No. 1 (March 1969), pp. 1-27.
17. Rocchio, J. J., "Performance Indices for Document Retrieval Systems." *In: Information Storage and Retrieval.* Report No. ISR-8, Harvard University, Computation Laboratory, Cambridge, Mass., December 1964.
18. Saracevic, T., "Comparative Effects of Titles, Abstracts and Full Texts on Relevance Judgments." *Proceedings of the American Society for Information Science Annual Meeting, San Francisco, 1-4 October 1969.* Vol. 6: *Cooperating Information Societies,* pp. 431-435.
19. Swets, J. A., "Effectiveness of Information Retrieval Methods." *American Documentation,* Vol. 20, No. 1 (January 1969), pp. 72-89.
20. Welch, J. T., Jr., "Measures and Criteria for Evaluation." *In*: Kent, A., Taulbee, O. E., Belzer, J., Goldstein, G. D., eds. *Electronic Handling of Information: Testing and Evaluation.* Washington, D. C., John I. Thompson & Co.; London, Academic Press, 1967, pp. 231-236.
21. Wessel, C. J., "Criteria for Evaluating Technical Library Effectiveness." *ASLIB Proceedings,* Vol. 20, No. 11 (November 1968), pp. 455-480.
22. Wessel, C. J., Cohrssen, B. A., *Criteria for Evaluating the Effectiveness of Library Operations and Services. Phase I: Literature Search and State of the Art.* Washington, D. C., John I. Thompson & Co., February 1967, p. 399. AD 649 468.

23. Wessel, C. J., Moore, K. L., *Criteria for Evaluating the Effectiveness of Library Operations and Services. Phase III. Recommended Criteria and Methods for Their Utilization.* Washington, D. C., John I. Thompson & Co., January 1969. AD 682 758.
24. Wiederkehr, R. R. V., "A Net Benefit Model for Evaluating Elementary Document Retrieval Systems." *In: Evaluation of Document Retrieval Systems: Literature Perspective, Measurement, Technical Papers,* Chapter 3.5. Bethesda, Md., Westat Research, Inc., December 31, 1968.

Chapter Three
Macroevaluation of Identification Systems

3.1 Introduction

In the previous chapter we discussed measures for evaluating identification systems. This and the succeeding five chapters are devoted to identification systems and processes whose performance is under evaluation. While economic evaluation is discussed with respect to specific document transfer functions, our principal purpose is to present a methodology for measuring performance effectiveness. Since the measurement of effectiveness implies the ability to compare features of systems within the same environment, we will not attempt to distinguish this type of evaluation from evaluation against specified objectives. Also, no attempt is made to present methodology for answering a question such as "Is System A in chemistry better than System B in geology?" since differing environments make such questions meaningless.

As has been stated earlier, the objectives of an evaluation determine its scope and format. While an in-depth evaluation provides more information than a more superficial one, it costs more and takes a much longer time. Frequently, decisions affecting funding and administration of document transfer systems must be made quickly and at minimum cost. Under these circumstances, gross measures of input, output, and effectiveness may suffice; we refer to this kind of evaluation as "macroevaluation."

Evaluation can serve many objectives, but two distinguishable classes of objectives can be characterized by the following two questions:

(1) How *well* does the system work?
(2) *How* does the system work?

The first question can be answered by macroevaluation, but the second cannot. It requires "microevaluation," a kind of evaluation that will be discussed in the next chapter.

In macroevaluation it is appropriate to think of a document transfer system as a black box, thus concentrating on inputs of time delays. Thus, macroevaluation can be likened to performance testing of completed assembly – the outputs *may* reveal sources of failures, but there is no guarantee that they will. Microevaluation, on the other hand, may be likened to the testing of parts, components, and subassemblies, so that failures permit one to point directly to the source of the deficiencies.

3.2 Determination of objectives

One way to start macroevaluation is to determine what functions the system performs, and how well, in the views of administrators and potential users, they are performed. The task begins by asking the question: "What is the system supposed to do?" Answers may be found in:

(1) Enabling legislation, charters, or other documents which define the objectives of the system.
(2) Regulations, procedures, instructions, and other management records of the system.
(3) Interviews with system management.
(4) Interviews with users.

One can expect that there will be some inconsistency among these sources of information. Inconsistency may be of substantial importance if management's views of the role of the system differ from those of the potential users.

For the gross level required for macroevaluation, one feasible way of proceeding is to conduct group interviews among researchers in the population which should be served by the system. In some instances this population is homogeneous and easily definable, but in others it may be so diverse as almost to defy definition. In spite of the difficulties, one must identify persons who have the knowledge and willingness to serve in a group interview.

Generally, it is easy to obtain lists of principal users, but these should not be employed exclusively insofar as they may bias responses toward the provision of services already part of the system. One might be equally interested in persons who do not use the system at present, but who might do so under different circumstances. Thus, a selection from the present users should be augmented by a list of nonusers if they can be identified. Possible sources of nonusers include research laboratories, university departments, and governmental agencies. A brief interview with the library (or information system) administration should reveal classes of nonusers whose opinions might be valued.

For a small system with homogeneous coverage of the literature, a single group of 8 to 10 persons might suffice. For larger, more heterogeneous systems, one might want to utilize a half dozen such groups.

The group interview should be conducted away from the physical location of the system being evaluated and should be conducted by a person not connected with the staff of the system. The interviewer's role is to stimulate discussion (see Chapter 10), to guide the meeting, and to record reactions and responses. His objective is to reach a consensus of the group with respect to services (or products) that should be provided by the system. A table with the following sample format could be used for determining needed services.

	Importance characterization		
Service	Imperative	Useful but not imperative	Not needed
(1) Permuted title index		X	
(2) Interlibrary borrowing service, etc.	X		

The following checklist may be used to focus attention on services which the system might provide:

(1) The collection.

- (a) Subject categories covered
- (b) Monographs
- (c) Serials
  - Current
  - Back issues
- (d) Government documents (by subject)
- (e) Abstract publications
- (f) Acquisition of requested items

(2) Indexes.
- (a) Catalogs
- (b) Permuted title indexes
- (c) Citation indexes
- (d) Coordinate indexes
- (e) Other special type indexes

(3) Other searching services.
- (a) Bibliographies on call
- (b) Searches in response to questions
  - Assistance with queries
  - Screening
  - Processing (by machine or by hand)
- (c) General reference service
- (d) Mechanical searching aids and technology

(4) Interlibrary borrowing services.
- (a) Union catalogs
- (b) Other locator services

(5) Current awareness.
- (a) Notification
- (b) Selective dissemination

(6) Other services.
- (a) Browsing capability
- (b) On-site study facilities
- (c) Abstracting services
- (d) Translation services
- (e) Photoduplication

The above procedures should permit the evaluator to make a reasonably clear statement of objectives against which to evaluate the system. A simple comparison of the services offered and the services established as needed by the consensus represents a major step forward in evaluation at the policy-making level.

Document transfer systems can assume an active role in making the researcher aware of the literature which might be useful to him, or they can take a passive role in responding to requests put to them. Many systems do both, but it is important to recognize which role is being evaluated. As noted in Chapter 2, the passive role can be subdivided as follows:

(1) Response to requests in which the references have been identified (at least in part) by the requesters.

(2) Response to requests for subject matter with no bibliographic clues to specific references.

(3) Response to the needs of researchers to browse through literature in which the specification of subject matter of interest will be crystallized as the activity progresses.

The first case is typified by a request such as: "Get me an article on liver flukes by Anderson in *Animal Health* of a couple of years ago." The second is typified by: "Get me some references on the life cycle of liver flukes in sheep." The third cannot be verbalized in advance, but might arise through the need to prepare a paper on some aspect of a very general problem, or through the desire to acquaint one's self with the background literature for a new project being undertaken. The services and facilities required to fulfill the three roles are substantially different, so their evaluation will be discussed separately in the following sections.

3.3 Retrieval of references identified by the requester

The attribute which characterizes this class of requests is the identification, in the mind of the requester, of a reference which he wants. The citation may be subject to error, and in practice frequently is, but the requester knows of the existence of a reference which he wants. As suggested by Orr *et al.* (*16*), the variable which measures performance for this kind of retrieval is the length of elapsed time between making the request and receiving the item requested. One is not really concerned with where the item is physically located, but it is clear that items held in the collection should, on the average, have a shorter response time than items obtained from "reservoir libraries." What one tries to test is how well the system responds to such requests. The following test procedure should provide the kind of evaluation needed.

(1) Identify a group of users who, by reason of their scientific disciplines, publications, or research interests, might reasonably be expected to be users of the system. They need not be actual users.

(2) By interview, or by questionnaire, obtain from each of them a list of no more than five references which the potential user has read, or which he has seen and intends to read, or which he has used in any other way in his research work. Also, ask for five or fewer items which he would "like to see," but does not now have in his possession.

The first question provides a list of items which may be biased by easy availability; the second question may be biased in the direction of items which are difficult to obtain.

(3) For each of the recently used items, determine how it was identified and supplied to the user (whether from his personal collection, the organizational library, selective dissemination, interlibrary loan [and source], purchase, and so on), how long the retrieval process took in each case, and what the out-of-pocket costs were.

(4) For each of the items wanted, determine how the user would proceed to obtain the item.

The references given in (2) constitute a test set. For each of them, one needs to know whether the system being evaluated can retrieve the item, and, if so, how long it takes. Out-of-pocket costs can also be observed at this step, if desired. Orr *et al.* (*16*) suggest that the list be checked against the collection of the system being evaluated, then against a "reservoir" collection for items not in the proprietary system, assigning approximate times for retrieval based upon the location of the needed item and "reasonable" imputed time lags. There is substantial danger in performing the test in this way, because all it really accomplishes is to test the adequacy of the collections rather than the efficiency with which requests are processed, lost items are located, and so on. It seems much safer to actually submit the requests and to observe what happens. In doing so, however, one must be careful not to overload the system by an unusually heavy number of requests. Therefore, the requests should be fed into the system a few at a time in an approximation to a normal pattern. Also, it is important to submit the test requests in such a way that system personnel will not give them special treatment.

A summary of the test might appear as given in Table 3.1. Additional details can be obtained easily, but the format in Table 3.1 should serve most uses.

Table 3.1 Summary of Identified Reference Retrieval Test

Item	References used	References wanted	Total
(1) Number of test references			
(2) Actual source of references used:			
(a) From selective dissemination			
(b) From search of test system			
(c) From browsing test system			
(d) From using test system as intermediary			
(e) Other			
(3) Sources to be used on wanted references:			
(a) Test system			
(b) Others			
(4) Test results:			
(a) Number obtained from (or through) system			
(b) Elapsed time:			
4 hours or less			
1 day or less			
2 days or less			
1 week or less			
2 weeks or less			
2 weeks or more			
(c) Source of successes:			
1. In system and available			
2. In system, on loan			
3. In system, not available			
4. Interlibrary loan			
5. Other			
(d) Causes of failures:			
1. Not locatable			
2. Cannot be loaned			
3. Other			
(e) Number of requests with bibliographic errors:			
1. Retrieved			
2. Not retrieved			

The question of errors in the citations has been left open. Note that Section 4e of Table 3.1 provides a place for recording such errors. If we wish to test the ability of the system to compensate for such errors, we can deliberately introduce errors in dates, spelling, journal titles, and so on.

How large a sample is required? To determine the percentage of failures, or percentage in the test library, or percentage taking longer than a specified number of days, one can estimate the standard deviation by $\sqrt{p(1 - p)}$, where p is the expected proportion of references having the characteristic of interest. To determine a percentage within 5 percentage points with risk of 0.10 (certainty factor of 0.90), one needs a sample of no more than 271 references. To be within 3 percentage points with the same certainty requires almost a thousand references. This precision is probably outside the feasibility range for macroevaluation.

One other procedure may provide useful information in the evaluation of a system's ability to provide previously identified references. This is a survey of potential user behavior and attitudes toward the system. The test procedure outlined above will provide an estimate of where users actually obtain their references, but it will not show what motivates them. A few well-chosen questions at the time of interview may provide this information at very low cost (see Chapter 10 on conducting the user survey).

Analysis of the data collected as above should reveal how well the test system competes in the total market for document retrieval services. The survey of potential users shows where they obtain their references and some reasons for their behavior. It also provides some gross timing measures which can be compared with actual times observed in the retrieval test. It might occur to the evaluator that, if there is a principal competing service, the requests should be submitted to that service as well as to the system under testing so that the results can be compared. This test can be accomplished, but must be handled carefully. It is clear that if both the test system and its principal competitor use the same reservoir library for items not in their files, and if both submit a request for an item at nearly the same time, one of them will be unsuccessful because the item will be on loan to the other. Thus, such a comparative retrieval test must be spaced over time in such a manner as to minimize this kind of eventuality.

In summary, then, we see that three classes of measures are of interest in judging the effectiveness of the system to retrieve references identified in advance. They are:

(1) Measures of elapsed time.
(2) Measures of operational success.
(3) Measures of user satisfaction.

The first can be obtained by recording calendar time. The second can be obtained as the fraction of successful requests (including whatever adjustment one wishes to make for garbled requests). The third can be obtained by user survey and by actually tabulating use of the test system and competing systems.

3.4 Retrieval of references whose identity is not known in advance

In the macroevaluation of a system's capability to retrieve references which are responsive to the subject-matter interests of users, one is interested in judging the ability to find material and to screen it.

As mentioned in the previous chapter, it has become customary to measure the ability to find subject matter by the recall ratio, which is the fraction of total relevant references produced by the search. This measure of effectiveness has some weaknesses, including the problem of deciding what is relevant and the possibility that the user might not want all of the relevant references and, in truth, might be totally swamped by all of them.

Since a system can have perfect recall, that is, not miss anything, everything could conceivably end up on the desk of the user in response to every question. Clearly, then, there must be some measure of the system's ability to screen. It has become customary to measure this ability by (1) the precision ratio, that is, the fraction of references presented to the user which are relevant to his purposes, (2) total retrieval, or (3) the fallout ratio (all of which are defined in Chapter 2). Precision and fallout measures suffer from our inability to determine what is relevant.

These measures were discussed in Chapter 2, and will be discussed in more detail in the next chapter on microevaluation. However, it may be observed here that no simple and inexpensive way has been found to estimate the recall ratio because the total number of relevant references is unknown and can only be estimated unbiasedly by large samples. It is therefore not an appropriate measure to use in macroevaluation.

Some evaluators (*8,12*) have employed a substitute measure for the recall ratio, which has proven successful and which is simple enough for use in macroevalution. The basis of the plan is that the requester identifies, in advance of the search, a list of references which are relevant to his purpose. He does not inform the system of these identified items, but submits his request in the normal manner. The fraction of his previously identified references which the system returns to him is an estimate of a pseudo recall ratio. Shumway (*17*) shows the conditions under which this is a good estimate of the true recall ratio.

Estimation of the precision ratio is relatively straightforward in spite of definitional problems with the relevance concept and special problems which may arise when the output is so great that the requester is unwilling to screen it for relevance. The latter problem can be handled by computing the precision ratio from only the items screened. An output so large that none of it is screened is considered an unsuccessful try and measures of time are aggregated with subsequent trials.

Another gross measure of effectiveness is the amount of user effort that is required to search for references. The effort expended by the system presumably can be obtained by a cost analysis of the accounting records, and we are not concerned with it as a measure of *effectiveness.* It is important, of course, to consider system cost in measuring *efficiency.*

In Figure 1.2, we indicated that system benefits are found from measures of effectiveness where these measures contribute to user satisfaction, which in turn, partially determine system demand and, hence, system value. Thus, it is important to choose measures of effectiveness that can be related to user satisfaction, if possible, and to attempt to establish the degree of satisfaction from these measures.

Assuming that a literature search can be identified, one can measure the number of hours spent by the user from initiation of the search until termination, including screening of the output. It may also be important to record elapsed calendar time, since that may have an important bearing on user satisfaction. The user may terminate his search because he has found exactly what he is looking for, or because he feels that additional search effort is not likely to yield a satisfactory return on the time invested. Thus, it seems important to record some measure of the user's satisfaction with the search, regardless of the reason for the termination. Satisfaction might be recorded as simply "satisfied" or "dissatisfied," thus making it possible to consider the response as a binomial variable with a value of one for satisfied and zero for dissatisfied. Or a verbal scale of completely satisfied, moderately well satisfied, moderately dissatisfied, and completely dissatisfied might be used. For macroevaluative purposes, it is doubtful whether the more extensive scale is warranted.

Thus, we have identified the following five measures which indicate the performance effectiveness of the system in searching for references:

(1) Recall ratio (or pseudo recall).
(2) Precision ratio (or fallout ratio).
(3) Total retrieval.
(4) Hours expended by user.
(5) Elapsed calendar time.

These can be thought of as five dimensions, and any test search can yield a figure for each, although some, such as recall ratio, may be more meaningful than others when averaged over a sample of searches.

All five measures are highly related to each other, but each presents some bit of information not contained in the other. The measures of effectiveness should, in some way, reflect the user judgment expressed by user satisfaction.

It is suggested that analysis of test results proceed as follows:

(1) In consultation with system management and after reviewing the updated system objectives, determine what values for each of the five measures should be considered unsatisfactory. For example, one might determine that a recall less than 0.4 and a precision ratio below 0.1 are unsatisfactory. Also, it might be determined that the user should not spend more than 2 hours searching and screening and that elapsed calendar time should be less than 24 hours. A user satisfaction judgment carries its own criterion.

(2) Construct the following summary tabulation:

Five effectiveness measures	Number of searches		
	System criteria	User score	
		No. satisfactory	No. unsatisfactory
All five satisfactory			
Four of five satisfactory			
Three of five satisfactory			
Two of five satisfactory			
One of five satisfactory			
None satisfactory			

The first column expresses satisfaction from the viewpoint of the system and the last two columns, from that of the user. The two judgments will not be alike, but there should be some correspondence.

(3) As a means of obtaining some diagnostic capability, cross-

tabulate the user satisfaction judgment against each of the first five measures. An example follows:

Search and screening time	No. satisfactory	No. unsatisfactory
Less than 1 hr	______	______
1 hr and under 2 hrs	______	______
2 hrs and under 5 hrs	______	______
5 hrs and under 10 hrs	______	______
10 hrs and over	______	______

(4) To show the joint relationship of recall and precision (or fallout) to user satisfaction, construct the following table, where "S" identifies the number judged satisfactory and "U" identifies the number judged unsatisfactory:

		Recall ratio				
Precision ratio		Under 0.2	0.2 and under 0.4	0.4 and under 0.6	0.6 and under 0.8	0.8 and over
Under 0.2	S					
	U					
	%S					
0.2 and under 0.4	S					
	U					
	%S					
0.4 and under 0.6	S					
	U					
	%S					
0.6 and under 0.8	S					
	U					
	%S					
0.8 and over	S					
	U					
	%S					

We consider now how one might design a test to produce the data described above. The method is essentially that used successfully by Lancaster (*12*). Two principal problems arise: the first is the selection of sample searches and the second is the determination of relevance.

For test searches there is no very good substitute for real-life searches, that is, searches conducted by or at the request of researchers in the normal course of their work. If searches are submitted formally, one modifies the request form to provide for relevant literature known in advance (from which pseudo recall can be computed) and designs a follow-up form for the user to complete. This form can be given to the user with the output of the system and will identify the references which he decides are relevant, the time he spent formulating his search request and screening, and his overall satisfaction judgment. Elapsed calendar time can be obtained by the system and entered on the request form. A matching of the request form and the user response form will then provide all five of the effectiveness measures and measures of user satisfaction.

If the request is modified and resubmitted, it is important to consider all submissions as one search. The aggregation can be accomplished in the following way:

(1) Use the last request form to identify previously known references.

(2) Use the aggregate output of all responses, with each identified document counted only once, as the total output for computation of the recall and precision ratios.

(3) Aggregate separate user-time responses to obtain total user time.

(4) Aggregate separate calendar times to obtain total calendar time.

(5) Use the last user satisfaction judgment, making sure that his judgment refers to the entire search rather than to the output of the last request.

Pro forma request and user response forms are shown in Figures 3.1 and 3.2. Such forms will vary depending on the particular system being used and the kinds of other data being routinely collected. The amount of detail on the examples is minimal.

Unfortunately for the evaluator, all systems do not require the submission of a formal request and the actual searching is frequently done by the user himself. System management may actually be unaware of the use. Under these circumstances, one may not be able to draw a sample of searches (uses) but may have to draw a sample of users, relying on their cooperation to identify their searches and to record the desired data.

Since the user of the informal system normally does not write down his request, requiring him to do so may impose an unnatural constraint on him. He will feel particularly constrained if much of his

____
System Serial Number

User Request Form

Name of User______________________________ Date______________________

Is this a new request?______yes;______no.

If no, what was date of last submission?______________________

Request: (Form varies with system)

List below all references (if any) which you know in advance are relevant to the request you have made.

(For use of system staff only)

Previous request serial number______________________

Date and time this request received______________________

Date and time output submitted______________________

Attach copy of output.

Figure 3.1 Pro forma User Request Form.

literature activities are of the browsing nature. In this case he may be searching (although that is hardly the right word) for references which may be of interest to him over a wide spectrum of projects or research, much of which may not yet be formalized.

Under such circumstances, it seems advisable not to force the user's behavior into the mold of formal search. Instead, it may be desirable to ask him to keep a record of his literature activities. There is a natural tendency for him not to keep such a diary or journal, so substantial follow-up may be needed. Of course, there is always the possibility that his normal behavior will be modified by the requirement to record what he is doing.

An alternative is the personal interview in which one tries to establish, through recall, the user's literature-oriented behavior during a preceding interval of time. One week may be a maximum time over which he can be expected to have reasonably accurate recall. Even then, one should obtain detailed data on behavior during the previous day to serve as a check on longer recall.

Whether data are obtained by interview or by diary, the following should be established:

(1) How much time is spent searching?

(2) How much time is spent on the system being evaluated?

(3) How much time is spent on other (identified) systems?

(4) How many useful references per searching hour are obtained from the test system? Other systems?

(5) After identification of desired documents, how much calendar time elapses before presentation of documents?

(6) What is the overall judgment as to the effectiveness of the system?

(7) What are its principal weaknesses?

User Response Form

Name of User ______________________

Serial number of request ______________________

List below the documents which were submitted to you in response to the above request which you found to be relevant to your purposes.

How much time did you spend preparing your request?

hrs ______ min ______

How much time did you spend screening the documents submitted to you?

hrs ______ min ______

Please indicate below your opinion about the effectiveness of ______ System with respect to this search. If this is one of a series of requests, please make your judgment about the entire series to date.

Satisfactory ______ Unsatisfactory ______

If unsatisfactory, explain:

Please list below any references, not supplied by this system, which you found relevant:

Figure 3.2 **Pro forma User Response Form.**

3.5 Use of browsing services

In fulfilling its role of providing identified references upon request, it is not important whether the facility under evaluation actually possesses the requested documents – only that its response time and certainty of retrieval be at acceptable levels. Time and certainty can, of course, be affected by physical location, but the location is not important *per se.* Also, in its role of providing subject-matter searching, the physical location of the documents is important only to the extent that it affects access time and probability of identification. However, in the provision of browsing service, location is of the utmost importance.

At least, the location at which the user can perceive (see, listen to, view a facsimile of) the document is important. One might call this location the "browsing station." In a library it is the stacks; in a system which provides cathode ray tube displays, it is the viewing station.

The features of a browsing system which seem worth measuring are:

(1) Nearness to users, in the elapsed time sense.

(2) Composition of the file (coverage of subject matter, age of documents by subject category, languages included, and so on).

(3) Organization of the file.

A measure of the first feature is the average length of time it takes a potential user (as defined by the objectives of the system) to reach the browsing station. If queues form at the browsing station, the average waiting time should also be measured.

One does not actually "measure" the composition of the file, but simply compares its composition with the avowed objectives of the system to serve certain components of the potential user population.

The third feature, organization of the file, affects browsability favorably if items of interest to users are associated physically, and negatively if they are widely dispersed. File locations are not flexible, however, so what is good for one segment of the potential users may be bad for another. Again, one must rely on the objectives of the system to determine whether the primary target user group is being adequately served. Also, identification and separate location of current materials, or of materials associated with current projects, must be considered a favorable attribute of the typical browsing collection.

While much of the above information can be obtained from examination of the system, the user (or potential user) may serve as the best source of information on browsing effectiveness. An interview with him to determine how much he uses the system for browsing, how much he uses competing systems, and what he likes and dislikes about both will provide most of the information required for evaluation of effectiveness.

3.6 Interactive systems

An interactive system is one in which the response time is short enough that the screening of output, modification of requests, and receipt of new output are all part of a continuous process which avoids breaking the user's trend of thought. Another typical aspect of the interactive system is the ability to make stepwise judgments concerning output. For example, on the basis of the number of documents which meet a set of specifications, one may wish to modify the specifications before screening any of the documents. One may also request titles (and sometimes abstracts, keywords, or other surrogates) prior to selection of the full-text documents desired. Thus, some of the measures suggested in the previous section may be inappropriate.

Clearly, interaction is a matter of degree, and all systems possess some interactive capability.[1] Generally, however, an interactive system is one with special equipment such as inquiry and display stations which materially shorten response time and increase the flexibility of response. In any case, the search is easily identifiable by the nature of the system. For these systems, meaningful measures are the following:

(1) User time per search.

(2) Number of documents identified for depth screening.

(3) Number of these found relevant.

(4) Number of identified references available in the file (in case search file contains citations not in hard copy file).

(5) Overall judgment (satisfactory or unsatisfactory) and reasons for dissatisfaction, if any.

A simple recording form for the user will provide most of this

[1]A distinction is made between (1) a truly interactive system in which the system actually interacts with the searcher by providing pseudo search suggestions, and (2) a real-time search that yields nearly spontaneous search responses at a remote terminal.

information. In addition, it seems desirable to interview the user, as suggested in the previous subsection, in order to obtain information about his use of alternative systems.

3.7 System identification in the active mode by selective dissemination and current awareness

Current awareness refers to those activities which may be undertaken to make users aware of potentially useful documents, regardless of whether such documents are in the system file. Examples are circulation or distribution of indexes, contents pages of journals, and abstracts. Selective dissemination implies two processes:

(1) Selection of items with the needs of the particular user or group of users in mind.

(2) Actual distribution of titles, abstracts, or full-text copies of documents.

In current awareness programs, the system plays only a partially active role, since the user must predesignate the items of interest to him. (Usually, the procedure for ordering is greatly simplified.) However, in selective dissemination, the system may play a completely active role, distributing document representations (such as titles and abstracts) without requests and then distributing full-text copies upon request.

The wide spectrum of current awareness and selective dissemination programs makes generalization about evaluation difficult.

By letting the current awareness report serve as an order form, one can easily record the use made of this system. Of course, the awareness program has a cumulative effect which, it is hoped, is reflected in reduction of retrospective search time. That is, one would hope that with an effective current awareness program the user would more often know the document exists before requesting it than would be the case without the program. Thus, there should be a larger percentage of requests for specific documents and a smaller percentage of requests for retrospective searches.

The only way to determine whether current awareness really improves retrospective search is to design a long-term experiment, in which one set of (preferably matched) groups of potential users is given the service and another set is not. Comparison of their behavior over a period of years should provide the data needed. Such an experiment is not likely to be conducted, however, because of the pressure of systems management to enlarge its user population and the pressure from excluded groups to make use of a potentially useful service.

One must make some compromise between desirability and practicality. As a minimum, one can record the following for a sample of time:

For current awareness

(1) Number of documents requested as a result of the service.
(2) Number of documents found useful upon examination.
(3) Number of items (titles, etc.) to which user was exposed.
(4) User time spent in screening awareness literature.
(5) User's overall judgment as to satisfaction or dissatisfaction (with reasons given for the latter).

Item 1 divided by Item 3 is a special kind of precision ratio and Item 2 over Item 1 is another.

For selective dissemination

(1) Number of surrogates disseminated.
(2) Number of full-text documents disseminated.
    (a) After examination of surrogate
    (b) Directly
(3) For a sample.
    (a) Number of 2a found useful
    (b) Number of 2b found useful
    (c) Ratio of 3a to 2a
    (d) Ratio of 3b to 2a
(4) Ratio of 2a to 1.
(5) User time spent in screening 1.
(6) User time spent in screening 2a.
(7) User time spent in screening 2b.
(8) User's overall judgment as to satisfaction or dissatisfaction with reasons given for the latter).

The reader will recognize the ratios as a special kind of precision ratio.

An example is presented here to illustrate the macroevaluation of current awareness systems. The example is an experiment conducted for an operating system, the National Technical Information Service (NTIS), that announced availability of new research reports by several means, two of which were the Press Release (PR) and the Fast Announcement Service (FAS). The principal objective of the experiment was to determine the relative contribution each of these announcement modes made to the number of requests for the research reports, which is a gross way to estimate the effectiveness of the two announcement modes.

One hundred new reports were chosen randomly and assessed by probable future demand.[2] The reports were then assigned to four sample categories such that each of the four categories would have about the same average demand if no special announcement (PR or FAS) were made. These four categories were then assigned one of the following announcement modes:

(1) Press Release only.
(2) Fast Announcement only.
(3) Both Press Release and Fast Announcement.
(4) Neither Press Release nor Fast Announcement.

The results of predicted total retrieval were as follows:

	PR	No PR
FAS	128.3	117.0
No FAS	95.6	62.3

It was concluded that both announcement modes contributed substantially to demand since no PR or FAS yielded only 62.3 requests. There was some indication, however, that the FAS was more effective and that both announcement modes might be reaching the same audience, since the two modes announced together (128.3) did not yield much more demand than the FAS alone (117.0). The question which then arose was whether the cost of the PR mode was low enough to warrant the few additional requests it created. It was decided that it was not.

[2]Assessment of each report was by a model (*10*) that predicted future demand by such variables as price, subject categories, size, and source.

A more extensive experiment was then conducted in which five NTIS announcement modes were considered together by an extension of the experimental design described above. This experiment, which is described in Earl *et al.* (*4*) and in Bjorge *et al.* (*2*), yielded the relative contribution each mode (and combination of mode) made to demand and income to NTIS, as well as the cost of each mode and cost of demand created by that mode. As a result, one mode was dropped, another mode was used more extensively, and a third mode was modified substantially.

3.8 Evaluation of published recurring bibliographies

An important information product in document transfer systems is published recurring bibliographies which may be used for either current awareness when initially sent or retrospective searching purposes at a later point in time. Lancaster (*13*) has devised detailed procedures for evaluation of these publications with these two purposes in mind. He suggests that the current awareness purpose of published recurring bibliographies be evaluated by measuring the following properties of the index:

(1) Its *coverage.*
(2) Its ability to yield relevant literature (*recall*).
(3) The amount of *effort* necessary to discover relevant literature (*time* or *precision*).
(4) Its *novelty* factor (i.e., its ability to yield new references).

Thus, a user's performance requirements are as similar for the current awareness purposes as for the searching requirements stated previously. A full discussion of procedures using synthetic searches and real-life usage (including survey instruments) is given in Lancaster (*13*).

3.9 Estimation costs in macroevaluation

The economic macroevaluation of systems assumes the capability of assigning costs to documentation functions in enough detail and with enough precision that comparisons among alternatives will be useful for decision making. Generally, one encounters costs from two sources. First are costs which result from expenditures by the entity which administers the proprietary system being evaluated. Such expenditures are for salaries, supplies, purchase of documents, postage, telephone, buildings, equipment, and so on. Some expenditures, such as for salaries, are directly translatable into costs in the period during which the expenditure was made. Other expenditures, such as for buildings and equipment, are properly charged to costs by amortization over a number of periods.

The second source of cost is incurred outside the proprietary system being evaluated. Also, while it is ultimately paid for by some entity, it is often difficult or impossible to identify both the amount of the cost and the time at which the cost was incurred. Examples are costs of not having reference documents available to the researcher and costs of delay in receiving requested documents.

No one has found a completely satisfactory way of assigning costs which lie outside the system under evaluation. Some speculation about the possible magnitude of such costs may be useful in comparing systems, however. For example, in a long-term research project, a waiting period of several days for delivery of a wanted document may only be a minor annoyance and may be identified with, say, 1 hour or 4 hours of a senior researcher's time during which he reschedules his research program in view of the known waiting time. In other cases, failure to produce a desired reference quickly may result in the reference not being used at all, with either duplication of research work or decrease in the quality of the research. Assignment of costs in such cases is much more speculative, but even then some upper bounds might be placed. For example, one might speculate that failure to use a reference would, at most, waste a month of the researcher's time.

The most difficult costs of all to assign are "costs to society." For example, what is the cost to society when a cancer researcher fails to find references to the research of a biochemist who has published in an obscure journal? There is no answer, and we suggest that speculation about it is not productive in the typical evaluation study. There is a level in the hierarchy of budgeting at which such speculation can result in finding support, but at this level decisions tend to be based on social goals rather than on costs.

Viewed in another way, there are basically three ways in which the value of a document transfer system will accrue to society:

(1) *Reduced duplication of effort* – the system should result in less duplication of research.

(2) *Reduction of search time* – the system should reduce the unproductive time devoted to information transfer activities.

(3) *Research efficiency* – the system should help practitioners and scientists engaged in research perform their work more effectively.

Reduced duplication of effort – It is not known how much research effort is duplicated due to inadequate information communication. However, Martyn (*15*) estimated from a survey of 88 general research projects in the United Kingdom that 10 percent of the funds allocated to those projects might have been saved had relevant information been found earlier. Based on this finding, he estimated that an equivalent of over $14 million may have been spent unnecessarily in the United Kingdom because published information was not discovered earlier. If approximately 5,000 manuscripts are submitted to a system annually and if each of these manuscripts represents, conservatively, a $25,000 effort funded by the government and other organizations, this input alone represents over $125 million annually.

Reduction of search time – The American Chemical Society reports (*1*) that industrial chemists spend nearly 12 hours per week in literature searching and current awareness reading. Their report indicates that through improved information services the time spent by chemists in literature screening could be reduced from 7.5 hours (before the improved services) to 1 hour (with improved service) for a comparable information return. They estimate that information services yield a savings of $2,500 annually per researcher. Studies by Case Institute of Technology (*3, 5*) suggest that chemists devote approximately 33 percent of their time to scientific communications. A 10-percent savings of this time would annually yield nearly $1,400 per scientist. One may assume, therefore, that a system could save each user a substantial amount per year for information activities.

Research efficiency – Research plays a fundamental part in nearly every major problem area faced by the nation. It is not easy to weigh the effect of science and technology on these problems, so that it is difficult, if not impossible, to determine the value of better research to society. However, it is clear that, if improved research, say for psychology (*7*), can prevent further riots, reduce accidents, decrease crime and violence, cause more people to become employable, improve space exploration, and better education, efforts to improve research must result in an enormous payoff to the nation.

Examples of the cost of areas in which psychology, as an example, plays an important role are as follows:

(1) Cost of crime (1965) – \$20,980,000,000.
Law enforcement (1962) – \$3,172,000,000.
Correction (1965) – \$940,000,000.
(2) Cost of psychiatric care in hospitals (1966) – \$14,198,000,000.
Cost of patients in mental hospitals (1966) – \$12,480,000,000.
(3) Vocational training (1967) – \$659,000,000.

It is clear that if improved effectiveness in psychological research can save even one-tenth of 1 percent of the cost to society in these areas, the payoff to society from these areas alone would be over \$50 million.

Another way in which improved effectiveness in psychological research can benefit society is by cutting the taxpayer's expenditure in psychological research. For example, in 1968 the Federal budget for psychological sciences totaled \$124 million and for social science research, \$209 million. If the improved effectiveness can reduce costs by 10 percent, the taxpayer will receive well over \$12 million additional research on his investment.

Our principal concern in this chapter is with expenditure-type costs, because it is this kind of cost which the evaluation is under pressure to produce. Further, we can contribute something to the methodology of such cost determination, but we make the assumption that our ability to speculate on subjective costs is no better than that of anyone else.

3.9.1 COSTS FROM BUDGET AND EXPENDITURE RECORDS

Budget and expenditure records provide summary data which are sometimes useful. However, two weaknesses in using such data as the source of cost estimates are that (1) budgets do not always match expenditures, and (2) budget categories are frequently for "labor," "materials," "contract items," etc., which are not easily translatable into documentation functions.

The first weakness can be overcome by tabulating expenditures, rather than by taking budgeted amounts. The second can only be overcome by reclassifying and tabulating expenditures, making such allocations as necessary to attribute costs to functions. Such procedures are frequently useful. For example, by this technique, the National Lending Library for Science and Technology is able to report total labor cost per item loaned, total literature and binding costs, and so on. These are highly aggregative measures, however, and the requirements for cost data are frequently for the purpose of suboptimization of a portion of the system. Budget and expenditure data have almost no value for this purpose.

3.9.2 COSTS FROM PERSONAL INTERVIEWS

An approach which is relatively inexpensive, and at the same time sufficiently accurate for many management decisions, is the following:

(1) Determine costs of documents, microfilms, supplies, binding, postage, and contract items by analysis of expenditure data. Many expenditures will have to be allocated. For example, photocopy machine rental may have to be apportioned between circulation and cataloging functions on the basis of estimates of the relative number of copies made for each functional category. These proportions in turn can be estimated from sampling studies.

(2) Determine space-occupancy costs on the basis of actual rent if space is acquired by rental; otherwise as the market price for rental of equivalent space in the community.

(3) Figure an overhead to be applied as a percentage of direct labor to include:

(a) General overhead of the institution of which the proprietary system is a part; for example, general university overhead when the system being evaluated is the university library.

(b) Salaries of administrative and clerical personnel whose activities cannot meaningfully be allocated to documentation functions.

(c) Fringe benefits and payroll taxes.

(d) Heat, light, telephone, equipment rental, maintenance, depreciation, and other determinable aggregate costs not allocable to functions.

(4) Allocate direct labor to functions by personal interviews with the staff. (The rest of this subsection discusses this methodology.)

One first defines a set of mutually exclusive and comprehensive tasks, each of which can be identified with one of the functions being evaluated. For this purpose, identification is a function and searching is a task.

The extent of detail in the specification of tasks is dependent upon what use is made of the cost figures. In a recent study, the ordering and processing of books (*14*) was divided into 80 tasks. Another study, designed to compare costs of owning serial publications with costs of borrowing, identified only about 25 tasks. What one attempts to do is to define tasks which can be aggregated in different ways to make up the alternative procedures under investigation. For example, the tasks "type revised index card, withdraw old index card, replace with new index card" may all be replaced by the "type corrections" if the system is mechanized with remote terminal input and output.

Once the functions to be evaluated and the tasks which comprise each are identified, one next determines the departmental structure of the system being studied. People work in identifiable organizational units, but may work on several functions comprising a variety of tasks. For example, tasks which are identifiable with the acquisitions function may be accomplished in the acquisitions department, the accounting department, the shipping department, and the typing pool. For convenience, one can think of a table in which the functions are listed down the left-hand side of the sheet and the departments across the top. Totals at the bottom of the table are direct labor costs by department and totals at the right-hand edge are direct labor costs by function.

The direct labor costs which are entered in the cells of the table can be estimated in various ways. We are concerned here with obtaining such costs by interview. For each department one can construct a table similar to that shown in Table 3.2. This form is similar to one used in actual practice.

The period of analysis is usually one week. In some organizations time allocations must be obtained for an entire department by interviewing the supervisor, while in other organizations the members of the department must be interviewed individually. In all cases, the number of hours typically worked in the week must be obtained. This is the amount entered at the foot of the table and can be checked on a

Table 3.2 Form for Allocation of Direct Labor to Library Functions for Analytical Purposes

Function	Item	Department______								Totals
		Employee initials								
		JAC	LAS	RV	NJ	ORD	KER			
	Rate									
Acquisitions	hrs cost									
Check-in	hrs cost									
Cataloging	hrs cost									
Binding	hrs cost									
Marking	hrs cost									
Claiming	hrs cost									
Gifts and exchanges	hrs cost									
Circulation and reference	hrs cost									
Other	hrs cost									
Total	hrs cost									

sample basis against payroll records. Then, the total reported hours must be allocated over the functions of interest. In order to do this, it is desirable to prepare a checklist of tasks under each function by way of defining the function and preventing oversights of tasks which the employee may consider unimportant. The checklist can be shown to the employee, or the interviewer can actually guide the respondent through the list, checking off the tasks which are performed.

If the tasks themselves, rather than the functions of which they are a part, are the focus of interest, the interview technique may not provide sufficient accuracy. Here, we assume that the employee can state with sufficient precision how many hours per week are spent on the tasks making up each function. The interviewer should check to see that they add up to the total and should probe the respondent further to accomplish that end.

The rate which appears on the first line of the table should be obtained from payroll records rather than by interview. Frequently, employees can be classified and the average or median wage rate within each class can be used in cost extensions. This work, of course, is performed away from the interview site.

The procedure outlined above works well when the following conditions hold:

(1) The functional categories of interest are few enough and broad enough that an employee can readily recognize which one he is performing when he is doing a given task.

(2) Employment is reasonably stable, with no unusual amount of leave-taking, hiring, or reductions in staff during the study period.

(3) Typically, employees work exclusively in a given functional category, but at most they work in a few, say four or five, categories and then in substantial blocks of time.

Application of the methodology presents problems, but some of them can be controlled by checking the data. For example, there may be a tendency to overlook part-time employees in preparing Table 3.2; this error can be prevented by checking against the payroll. When personnel are on leave, one of the following procedures can be used:

(1) If their tasks are not being done by someone else, the department supervisors should report what the employees do in a typical week.

(2) If they are replaced by temporary personnel, the activities of the temporary personnel can be reported. The resulting bias is likely to be small unless the number on leave is unusually high.

(3) If there has been a great deal of shifting of tasks to accommodate leaves, a different study period should be chosen.

Time for coffee breaks and other personal needs can be split up proportionately over the principal tasks performed. The important thing is that all of the hours paid for should be accounted for on the recording sheet.

There is always a question of whether to ask what the employee does in a typical week or what he actually does during the current week. Experience shows that neither has a clearcut advantage over the other. In general, if a single week is available for the study, it is considered better to ask for activities during a typical week. When one does so, he must recognize that people tend to report those things which they think they should be doing rather than what they are actually doing. If the study period covers several weeks, it is generally considered preferable to ask for actual allocation of time.

3.9.3 DIRECT LABOR ALLOCATION BY USE OF DIARIES

One of the most obvious weaknesses of the interview method described in the above subsection is that employees may not remember accurately how they distributed their time over a given week. This weakness will be more acute if the number of tasks or functional categories is large and if there is a substantial amount of task switching.

A frequently used technique is the employee diary in which the employee records each task and the time at which the task was completed. A listing of all tasks of interest in the study is given to each employee and some instruction is given in the method of recording. A recording sheet might take the form shown in Figure 3.3.[3] Another column might be inserted for recording minutes spent on each task, but, since processing is likely to be done by computer, one will usually only need to key in the task identification and clock time.

While diaries help to solve the problem of recall, there is a real risk that they will modify the behavior of the employee. The novelty, as well as the knowledge that their work is being watched, even though indirectly, may cause employees to record what they understand their job *should be* rather than what it is. The problem can be alleviated partly by having them keep diaries for a period, say 2 weeks, before test recording begins. The employee, of course, is not aware of the change. The tendency to work harder can be partly controlled by not requiring coffee breaks, lunch periods, or other personal time to be recorded. The only thing recorded is the time at which the task changes, so that if an employee is opening mail starting at 9:00 A.M., takes a 20-minute coffee break at 10:00, and continues opening mail

[3] It is noted that summarization of the data collected in the diaries of Figure 3.3 produced the summary data required for Table 3.2.

Name ______________________

Department______________________

Date ______________________

Task identification	Time ended	Task identification	Time ended
Time began work	8:30 A.M.		
7	9:15		
11	10:00		
10	10:15		
11	12:00		
20	12:30		
7	5:00		

Figure 3.3 Example of diary-type recording form.

until 10:55, the only times recorded are 9:00, the time at which the previous task was completed, and 10:55, the time at which the mail-opening task was completed. If it is important to identify the various categories of personal time and idle time (time spent waiting for tasks), it must be done by some technique other than diaries. A suggestion is given in the next section.

3.9.4 DIRECT LABOR ALLOCATION BY USE OF INDIVIDUALLY TIMED TASKS

Another way of obtaining measures of the length of time required to accomplish a given task is to time employees by use of stop watches. Here it can be assumed that bias is extreme, and the technique is most useful in determining which of several alternative ways of doing a task will minimize the average time of accomplishing it. The technique may have some merit in establishing work standards, but has almost no value in estimating behavior in the real world.

Another disadvantage of the technique is that it meets with resistance from employee organizations – such stiff opposition that typically it cannot be used.

When one can obtain the cooperation of employees, and when the objective is to analyze the string of tasks making up a job, the technique can have real merit. An example of its successful use is given in Leonard (*14*).

3.9.5 DIRECT LABOR ALLOCATION BY USE OF POINT OBSERVATIONS

The most precise way of allocating time to tasks is by taking observations, randomized over time, of the activities being undertaken at the instant of observation. Some conditions are obvious:

(1) The employee must not be aware that the instant of observation is approaching.

(2) The observer must be familiar enough with the tasks being performed that he can identify them without inquiry.

(3) The observations must be made unobtrusively – possibly by the supervisor who is present by virtue of his or her job.

The concept of point observations (taken at a point in time) as a device for allocating time is a very simple one. If an employee is observed doing a given task a given percentage of the time (a given percentage of the observations), he is assumed to spend that percentage of his total time performing the task. There is sampling error, of course. One can let $\bar{x}$ be the guessed proportion of time devoted to a task, let the standard deviation be estimated by $\sqrt{\bar{x}(1 - \bar{x})}$, resulting in a coefficient of variation of $\sqrt{\bar{x}(1 - \bar{x})}/\bar{x}$. Then the tables of sample sizes given in Chapter 12 may be used to select a sample with the precision desired.

A tally sheet for recording data similar to that shown in Figure 3.4 can be constructed. This tally form records the number of persons working at each task in the department at the time of observation. One can also construct a similar recording form for each individual. The latter procedure permits allocation of an individual's time, while the former only permits allocation of the total time of the department.

One problem in allocating personal services by instantaneous observation is that observers forget to take measurements at the specified times, substituting measurement at a later time. Sometimes this defect can be controlled by taking observations at times spaced apart by a constant interval, say every half-hour. In taking such observations, it is important that the cycle be changed every day so as not to reflect natural periodicities in the work patterns.

The U.S. Post Office Department has been successful in using a buzzer which sounds at randomly spaced intervals as a device for identifying the time at which to take observations on mail being sorted. Another device is an alarm clock connected to a light rather

TALLY FORM

Department____________________ Date____________________

Observer____________________

Tasks	Times																

Figure 3.4 Sample of tally sheet for work measurement by point observations in time.

than a bell, so as to attract the attention of only those being observed.

In spite of the problems encountered in selecting the proper time to record, the point method has excellent potential in work sampling.

3.10 An example of cost and pricing for multiple information products

Insofar as an information system resides in a market-like environment, all of the economic and marketing implications of this environment must be considered. However, unlike the situation in most marketing environments, the distribution and sale of information products and services are interrelated and the functions involved in document transfer may be performed in many ways. One will be faced with several decisions concerning marketing of new services and modification of old. These decisions include questions of pricing, promotion and advertising policies, and channels of distribution, and must be based on considerations of cost, income, demand, and the effect of the decisions on other components of the system.

The schema in Figure 1.3 depicted the functions and processes of the system in a marketing environment. It was indicated that processes necessary to accomplish the composition, reproduction, acquisition and storage, identification, location, and presentation functions lead to improvements in such things as accessibility, quality, accuracy, speed, and timeliness of document transfer from authors to users. These improvements are made in order to increase user satisfaction, which in turn motivates use of the system. This motivation, however, is also partially determined by the price one must pay to use the system and by promotion, sales, and advertising procedures. The price the user must pay involves not only charges for products and services but also what it costs him in his own time. For example, if a retrospective search results in retrieval of 5,000 items, he is not likely to be satisfied since he must pay such a high price in his own time to screen out those documents which do not interest him.

In order to make decisions concerning marketing factors, one must design and implement an internal costing system. This system must have the capability of identifying unit costs that can be subdivided into fixed and variable costs. Information products and services typically have a high fixed cost and relatively low marginal cost. For example, the fixed cost for producing a journal article may be as illustrated in Figure 3.5. When one plots the marginal cost against usage, the curve drops as shown in Figure 3.6. It is important to establish marginal cost over a likely range of demand for each of the products and services.

A cost accounting system must also have the ability to identify direct and indirect cost where the indirect cost involves such items as administration and overhead. Furthermore, it is necessary to isolate indirect costs, such as the preparation of magnetic tapes for photocomposition, so that these costs can be allocated to all of the derivative products that will come from these tapes.

Net income is determined by the cost of producing the informa-

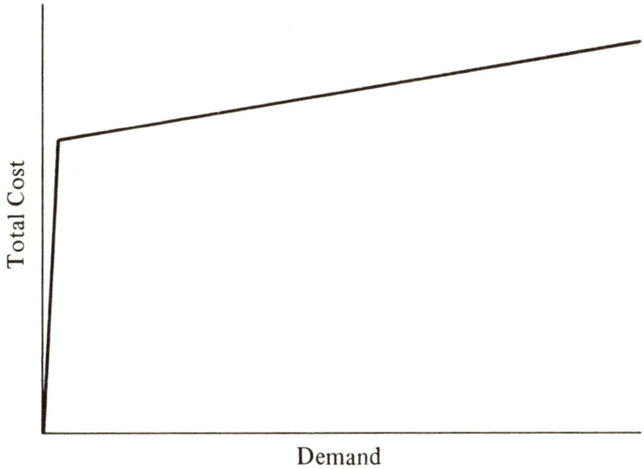

Figure 3.5 Total cost and demand for typical information products and services.

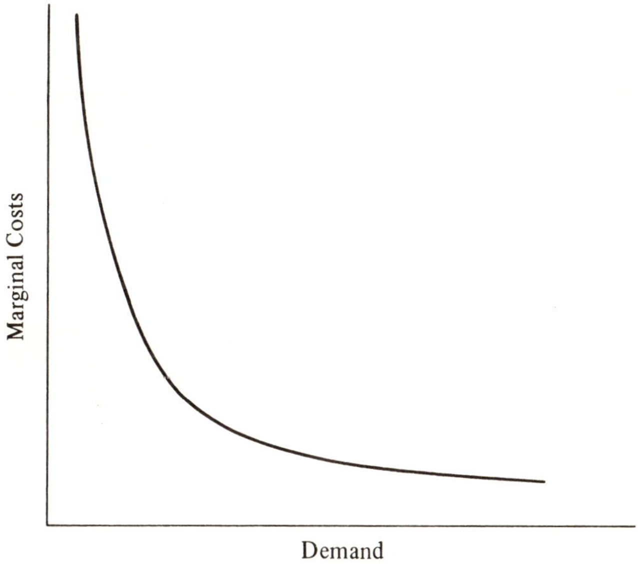

Figure 3.6 Marginal costs and demand for typical information products and services.

tion products and services and by revenue from demand. The income derived from demand is found by multiplying demand by price per unit. However, since information products and services yield a direct value to society as a whole and not just to individual users, there is justification for society's partially funding these important operations through such agencies as the National Science Foundation. This kind of funding can best be accomplished through research and development venture capital to make a system operational and take it to a point at which it is self-sustaining. It is clear that not all systems are likely to be developed by a private organization, since the capital outlay would extend over a long period and the return on investment would probably not accrue in sufficient time to make the return worthwhile.

As was indicated in Figure 1.3, demand is determined by the influence of the services themselves, promotion, and price. The relative importance of these factors depends largely on the characteristics of the market for the information products and services. There are two classes of market that one will serve: individuals and institutions. Each of these two classes has substantially different resources available for purchasing services. For example, an individual subscriber may be able to spend only \$50 to \$100 per year, whereas an institution may spend anywhere from \$1,000 to \$20,000 per year. This means that the two markets may present substantially different demand curves. One would expect the institutional market to have a relatively inelastic demand curve (demand not highly sensitive to changes in price), as shown in Figure 3.7. On the other hand, the market consisting of individuals probably would have an elastic (highly sensitive to price changes) demand curve, as shown in Figure 3.8. This means that one will have to define the market carefully for each service and establish a corresponding pricing policy. Fixed and direct cost might be allocated as a component of the price in such a way that a major portion would be allocated to those products and services with an inelastic demand and the remainder to those with an elastic demand.

One of the weaknesses in marketing information products and services has been a lack of appreciation for promotion, advertising, and sales. One reason for this attitude is a general feeling among professional societies that advertising, in particular, is unprofessional. However, it is important that new products and services be made known to those who can benefit from them. On the other hand, one should be careful not to create false sales that will result in failure to use the system again. Another important factor to consider is training

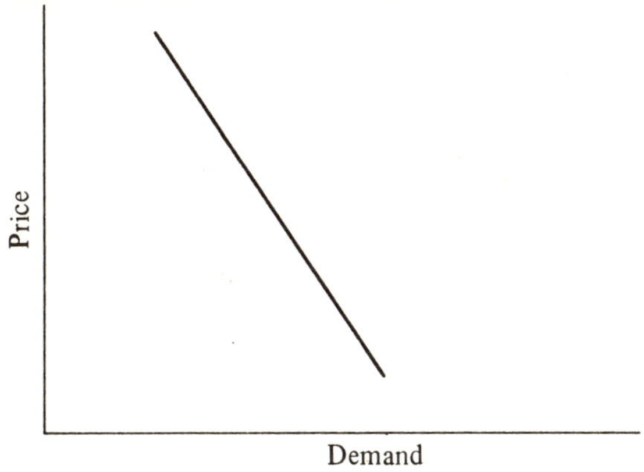

Figure 3.7 Typical inelastic price/demand curve.

in the use of the new services. This training could range from explaining the use of the system through promotion briefs to preparing a training film to be shown at professional meetings and universities.

Finally, one must consider the distribution channels involved in the transfer of documents from authors to users. These channels are somewhat difficult to define. For example, articles can be stored in a user's office, in a local library (in the form of hard copy or microfilm), by the author in the form of reprints, or perhaps at a central source such as the Center for Research Libraries. Identification can involve

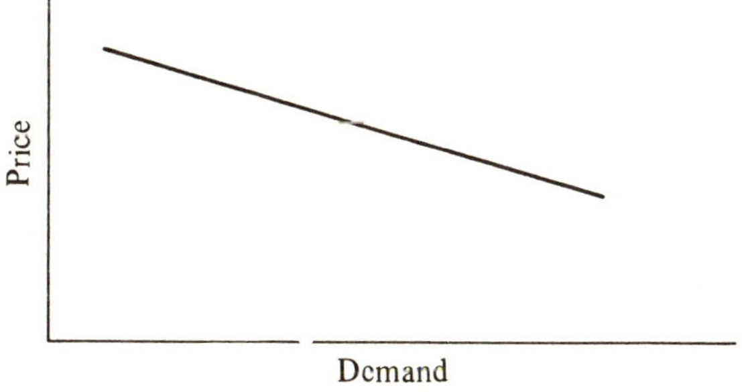

Figure 3.8 Typical elastic price/demand curve.

several alternative processes, including use of the journals themselves or use of a retrospective search system. Several combinations of these could and probably do occur.

The myriad channels of distribution may be depicted by a matrix consisting of alternative processes and levels for the six basic transfer functions. One could apply this matrix in the form of a stochastic model of market change, determine the relative frequency of each of the distribution channels, and establish the importance of these channels with regard to cost/benefits. Thus, the stochastic model could be used to diagnose the system in order to highlight gaps and weaknesses and to determine the effect of one product on another. Development of new products and services will undoubtedly affect the demand for and usefulness of other products and services. A highly effective identification system, for example, could result in lower usage of journal subscription channels. The same holds true for local library channels, where it may become easier for the user to obtain articles than it would be through his present journal subscription.

Demand is also affected by the amount that an individual or local institution can pay, a factor which must be weighed carefully when each new product or service is designed and marketed. One should also consider carefully the possibility of charging a combination fee to users and society registrants. For example, instead of limiting the fee to pay for journal publications, the dues might be extended to cover current awareness publications, bibliographies, and even retrospective search.

The example given below demonstrates the general relationship among cost, demand, and pricing of information products and services. In particular, it illustrates the importance of allocating fixed costs optimally among multiple products and services, and attempts to establish an optimal strategy from theoretical cost models for (1) retrospective search, (2) a current awareness tool, (3) magnetic tapes from input, and (4) recurring bibliographies. One important fixed cost is input cost, especially the cost of the magnetic tapes for photocomposition of bibliographic information. However, this input cost can be allocated to a number of bibliographic products and services. The question is, how should it be allocated among the four information products and services mentioned above?

Two facets must be considered in allocating costs. One of these is the interaction between cost and elastic or inelastic demand. Generally, the products for the individual market should have an elastic demand, whereas those for the institutional market, such as bibliographies or retrospective search, should have a more or less inelastic demand. In allocating costs, more should be allocated to the products with inelastic demand because their market will not be so sensitive to price changes. For example, if the cost of inputting the magnetic tapes was $10 per abstract and if there were two products, one elastic and one inelastic, to which this cost could be allocated, the allocation should not be $5 to each. A more realistic distribution would perhaps be $7 to the inelastic product and $3 to the elastic. The precise allocation would have to be governed by a study of the demand curve (or, at least, a simulated likely demand curve) for each product in order to determine an optimal pricing system.

The second facet to be considered in allocating costs is amortization. For some of the products and services, set-up costs can be amortized over several years rather than over a single year. For example, the cost of inputting the magnetic tapes for a retrospective search system could be amortized over a 5- or 10-year period because the information might be used for that length of time. On the other hand, amortization would not be feasible for a current awareness service, since its usefulness does not extend beyond a year.

Another consideration for cost allocation is competition among products; i.e., products in the same system may be competing with each other for markets and in price. An efficient current awareness program, for example, will reduce the necessity for a retrospective search service.

A model of the cost of retrospective systems has been developed by Westat under contract to the American Psychological Association (7). This model includes the following subsystems:

(1) User/system interface.

(2) Input (full text versus index terms) and number of items input.

(3) Search length based on achieving various levels of recall.

(4) Search modes.

(5) Screening processes.

(6) Method of presentation.

For this model we have assumed an on-line system consisting of manual indexing for input, a thesaurus to use for input as well as searching, user requests processed through an intermediary by telephone or in writing, and searches that, on the average, retrieve 80 percent of the relevant items. No screening is performed on search output, and abstracts of identified documents are sent to the user. We also assume that 25,000 documents are added to the file for search each year and that these will be purged from the files after 4 years. Thus, the total file will be 100,000 documents, and each year's input can be amortized over a 4-year period.

After careful examination of many different retrospective search systems, a generalized cost model was developed. This model will permit one to evaluate future, as well as present, systems.

The total cost of any given retrospective search system is composed of three types of costs:

(1) Fixed costs associated with each subsystem.

(2) Variable costs dependent on the number of items input to the system.

(3) Variable costs dependent on the number of searches conducted.

Simply stated

$$C = C' + C''X_1 + C'''X_2$$

Taking these three separately, one can analyze component costs of any system or subsystem with regard to size of the file, range of demand or system usage, and size of term list.

3.10.1 FIXED COSTS

There are fixed costs associated with each subsystem. These include such items as staff, space rental, computer rental, and fixed computer storage charges (C_1). Once a commitment is made for a specific computerized search system, these costs will be incurred, even if the system is only used once.

Another fixed cost element is the rent, staff, and screening devices (C_2) that may be used to display the full text of an abstract or document representation in screening search output. Fixed costs associated with input (C_3) include such items as thesaurus development, staff, tape conversion, and update costs. Other fixed costs are rent and sundry items associated with user/system interface (C_4) and mailing search output to the users (C_5). The fixed cost element is then

$$C' = C_1 + C_2 + C_3 + C_4 + C_5$$

3.10.2 VARIABLE COSTS

The variable costs that are dependent on file size or number of items input to the system (X_1) are composed of a cost per item of indexing, abstracting, keyboarding, and any other input processing. These costs can be allocated among various services that also use the input products (C_6), i.e., current awareness announcement, retrospective search, recurring bibliographies, and so forth. File loading costs include costs that vary with number of terms ($X_5 C_7$). The entire component can be expressed as

$$C'' = C_6 + X_5 C_7$$

Another type of variable cost is the cost dependent on the number of searches conducted per year (X_2), or the demand for the retrospective search system. This is the most complicated of the elements of the model, being composed of three parts: fixed costs per search, costs dependent on the number of items retrieved (X_3), and costs dependent on the number of items sent to the user (X_4). The fixed elements of the cost are the set-up costs for mailing titles to users (C_8) and the cost of the user/system interface, i.e., the intermediary (C_9). For our purposes we consider two alternative methods of user/system communication: written and oral requests.

There are three costs dependent on the number of items retrieved in any search (X_3): the computer costs of retrieving (C_{10}) and printing out the item (C_{11}) and the costs of screening each item retrieved (C_{12}). The cost dependent on the number of items mailed per search (X_4) is the cost of actually mailing the titles or abstracts to the user (C_{13}). The entire component can be expressed as

$$C'' = C_8 + C_9 + X_3(C_{10} + C_{11} + C_{12}) + X_4 C_{13}$$

Combining the elements of the cost model, we have

$$C = C_1 + C_2 + C_3 + C_4 + C_5 + X_1(C_6 + X_5 C_7)$$
$$+ X_2 [C_8 + C_9 + X_3(C_{10} + C_{11} + C_{12}) + X_4 C_{13}]$$

where

X_1 = number of items input (100,000),
X_2 = number of searches conducted (4,000),

X_3 = number of items retrieved per search (126),
X_4 = number of items mailed per search (22),
X_5 = number of terms in authority list (1,000),
C_1 = fixed cost associated with computing (\$131,000),
C_2 = fixed cost associated with screening (\$32,000),
C_3 = fixed cost associated with input (\$22,000 ÷ 4),[4]
C_4 = fixed cost associated with user/system interface (\$2,000 ÷ 4),
C_5 = fixed cost associated with mailing results (\$1,000 ÷ 4),
C_6 = total input cost per item (\$0.575),
C_7 = total file loading cost per item per term (\$0.00015 ÷ 4),
C_8 = fixed cost of mailing per search (\$0.00),
C_9 = fixed cost of user/system interface per search (\$15.00),
C_{10} = computer retrieval cost per item retrieved (\$0.05),
C_{11} = computer printing cost per item retrieved (\$0.008),
C_{12} = screening cost per item retrieved (\$0.125),
C_{13} = mailing cost per item mailed (\$0.10), and
C = total annual cost (\$391,532).

This general equation can be used to estimate costs of potential search systems as well as to compare the cost/effectiveness trade-off of system alternatives. Typical costs are given in parentheses for the retrospective search system using batch processing (*11*). Total cost (C) is found as follows:

$$
\begin{aligned}
C &= \$131{,}000 + \$32{,}000 + \$5{,}500 + \$500 + \$250 \\
&\quad + 100{,}000\,[\$0.575 + (1{,}000)(\$0.0000375)] \\
&\quad + 4{,}000\,[\$0.00 + \$15.00 + (126)(\$0.05 + \$0.008 + 0.125) \\
&\qquad + (22)(\$0.10)] \\
&= 169{,}250 + 61{,}250 + 161{,}032 \\
&= \$391{,}532
\end{aligned}
$$

The average cost per search is then \$97.90 (\$391,532/4,000), cost per retrieved document is \$4.45 (\$97.90/22) and, assuming 21 relevant documents retrieved, the cost per relevant item retrieved is \$4.66.

The following costs are allocated to the four information products mentioned above: indexing, \$3.50 per item; thesaurus, \$40,000; and input, \$10 per item. The percentage of these costs allocated to retrospective search is amortized over a 4-year period. Updating costs

[4] Some costs are divided by 4 to account for a 4-year amortization.

at $5,700 and other costs at $0.50 per item are allocated entirely to the retrospective search, with 4-year amortization.

The total costs per search are given in Table 3.3. These costs were found by allocating input costs by 25 percent, 50 percent, and 75 percent to retrospective search. Cost per search for these three levels of allocation is given for 1,000 through 6,000 searches per year in increments of 1,000. Clearly, the number of requests has little bearing on cost-per-search above a demand of 4,000-5,000. We recognize that these costs may not hold true for all search systems. However, systems based on batch processing or on-line search of index terms or full text seem to have cost/demand relationships similar to those shown above.

Table 3.3 Cost per Retrospective Search over Demand at 1,000, 2,000, 3,000, 4,000, 5,000, and 6,000 Searches per Year, with Input Allocated at 25%, 50%, and 75%

Percent allocation	Demand 1,000	2,000	3,000	4,000	5.000	6,000
25	$ 133	$ 90	$ 76	$ 69	$ 65	$ 61
50	155	101	83	74	69	65
75	177	112	90	79	73	69

A crude cost model was derived for the sales of magnetic tapes as a derivative product of the photocomposition tape input. Costs estimated from the model are based on percentage allocation of the tape input, $10,000 other fixed costs, and $100 per annual tape sales of 25,000 items. These costs are given for three levels of allocation (0 percent, 25 percent, 50 percent) in Table 3.4 over a demand of 10, 25, 50, 75, and 100.

Table 3.4 Cost per Tape Sale over Demand of 10, 25, 50, 75, and 100 Sales per Year, with Input Allocated at 0%, 25%, and 50%

Percent allocation	Demand 10	25	50	75	100
0	$ 1,110	$ 500	$ 300	$ 233	$ 200
25	7,350	3,000	1,550	1,067	825
50	13,600	5,500	2,800	1,900	1,450

Although these costs have not been considered as carefully as the others, cost/demand curves for tape sales should be approximately as given.

A cost model was also derived for analysis of a current awareness publication (*9*); it includes number of items per year, number of times each item appears, number of items per page, frequency of publication, alternative printing policies, and pricing strategy. This cost model is as follows:

$$C = C_{12}S + \frac{C_{11}X_3}{X_2} + \frac{C_{10}X_3X_4}{X_1X_2} + C_{13}X_5S + \frac{C_8X_3X_4S}{X_1X_2}$$

$$+ C_9X_5S + C_6X_5S + C_7X_5$$

where

X_1 = item density (i.e., number of items per page),
X_2 = number of sections (1-50),
X_3 = number of items input annually (24,000),
X_4 = number of times each item appears (3),
X_5 = number of issues per year (24),
C_6 = marginal cost of cover ($0.0234),
C_7 = set-up cost of cover ($15),
C_8 = marginal cost of printing each impression ($0.00425),
C_9 = cost of binding each copy ($0.08),
C_{10} = page set-up costs ($5 printing, $8.50 photocopy),
C_{11} = input costs per item ($0.30 computer tapes, $0-10 allocated for keyboarding),
C_{12} = subscription fulfillment costs ($1.87 per subscription per year),
C_{13} = copy mailing and handling costs ($0.09 per copy), and
S = number of subscribers (demand).

Note that C_{11} in this model accounts for the input costs, including the costs of keyboarding magnetic tapes. It is assumed in this example that the current awareness publication includes nearly 50 such categories which are available and disseminated to users. Table 3.5 gives the cost for 0 percent and 25 percent allocation of the tape input cost for subscription demands of 50, 100, 500, 1,000 and 2,000.

Table 3.5 Cost per Annual Subscription for a Current Awareness Publication over Demand of 50, 100, 500, 1,000, and 2,000 Subscribers, with Input Allocated at 0% and 25%

Percent allocation	Demand 50	100	500	1,000	2,000
0	$19	$12	$6.20	$5.50	$5.10
25	44	25	8.70	6.75	5.73

These figures are thought to accurately represent typical costs for a current awareness publication. It is noted that the 25 percent input allocation seems to dominate costs up to 500 annual subscriptions. For that reason, and since the demand may be elastic, only 0 percent and 25 percent allocation are considered. Also, it is assumed in the cost calculations that all 50 subject categories will have a similar demand, although this is probably not realistic. However, the cost model can easily accommodate a probable distribution of demand. Furthermore, one can readily determine from the model a break-even number of subscriptions, below which one probably would not wish to fulfill.

The same model can be applied to recurring bibliographies, for which a special cover is used and a total of four categories are available and disseminated. The cost with 0 percent and 25 percent allocation is given in Table 3.6 for subscription demands of 50, 100, 500, 1,000, and 2,000. Again, the 25 percent input allocation costs dominate the entire range of demand.

Optimal allocation to these four information products and ser-

Table 3.6 Cost per Annual Subscription of Recurring Bibliographies over Demand of 50, 100, 500, 1,000, and 2,000 Subscribers, with Input Allocated at 0% to 25%

Percent allocation	Demand 50	100	500	1,000	2,000
0	$194	$101	$26	$17	$12
25	507	257	57	33	20

vices can be established in two ways. The first way assumes that we choose a price for each of these products and services such that we maximize net income. Standard economic theory tells us that this price is the price at which marginal costs and marginal revenue are equal. In order to determine what marginal revenue is, we must assume a demand curve such as shown in Figure 3.9, with cost curves for retrospective search at 25 percent, 50 percent, and 75 percent input allocation plotted against demand. We find that the marginal cost in each instance is approximately $45 to $50 per search. Assuming the demand shown in Figure 3.9, we find that the price at which the

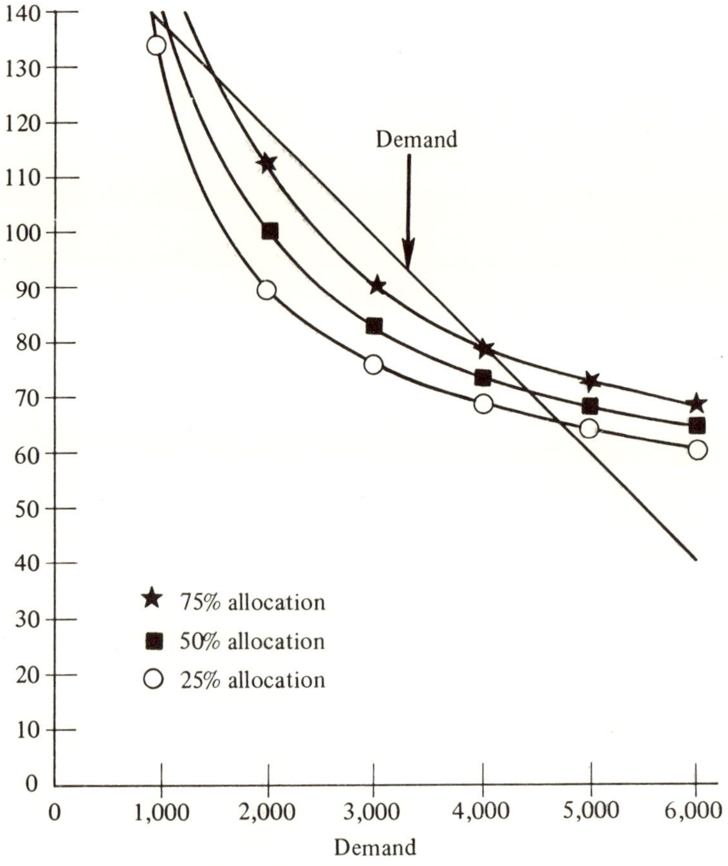

Figure 3.9 Price/demand and cost/demand (at 25%, 50%, and 75% input allocation) for retrospective search services.

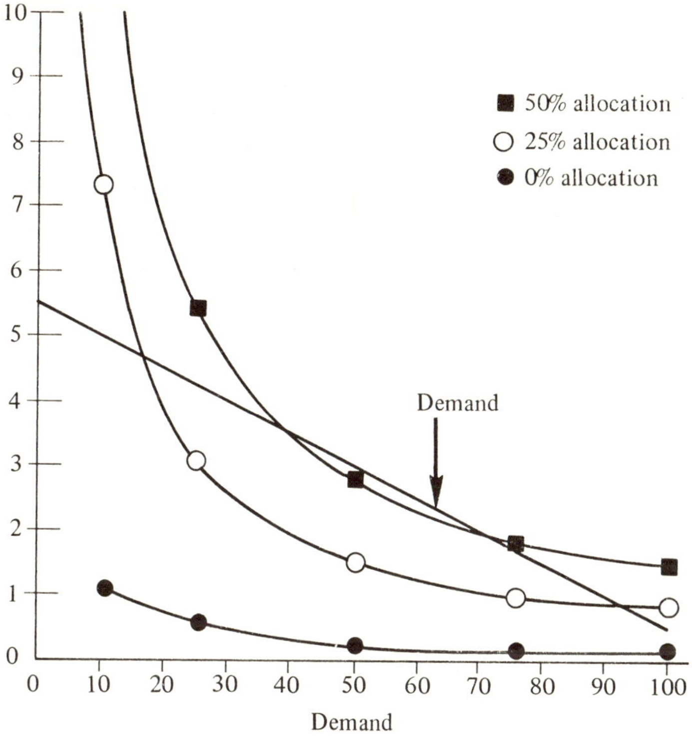

Figure 3.10 Price/demand and cost/demand (at 0%, 25%, and 50% input allocation) for magnetic tape sales.

marginal revenue yields about the same amount is slightly under $100, in which case we should have a demand of 3,000. Thus, we assume $100 to be the optimum price for all three cost curves.

If one is interested in breaking even rather than in maximizing the net income, we find that the break-even points are at $66, $71, and $79 for allocation of 25 percent, 50 percent, and 75 percent, respectively. The demand curve given in Figure 3.9 assumes a more or less inelastic relationship with price. Of course, we have no way of knowing what the true demand curve is, but will assume the inelastic curve for this example.

Price/demand and cost/demand curves are plotted for the sale of magnetic tapes (Figure 3.10). The three curves show cost versus demand at 0 percent, 25 percent, and 50 percent allocation. A rather inelastic demand curve is assumed for illustrative purposes. The marginal cost for tapes is found to be in the \$1,000 range; the marginal revenue that produces an equivalent amount is calculated to be about \$3,000. It is noted, assuming the demand curve above, that the 50 percent allocation barely yields a positive net income between the range of \$2,000 and \$3,400.

Figure 3.11 gives curves for a current awareness publication with 50 classification sections. Again, a rather elastic demand is assumed since current awareness publications may be sent to a number of individual subscribers, who are concerned with price. In this case, the marginal cost ranges from about \$4.75 to \$5 and the price necessary to achieve this marginal revenue is about \$9 per subscription.

Figure 3.12 gives the demand and cost curves for recurring bibliographies, where we find that the marginal cost is in the \$4 to \$8 range and that a price of \$30 will achieve an equivalent marginal

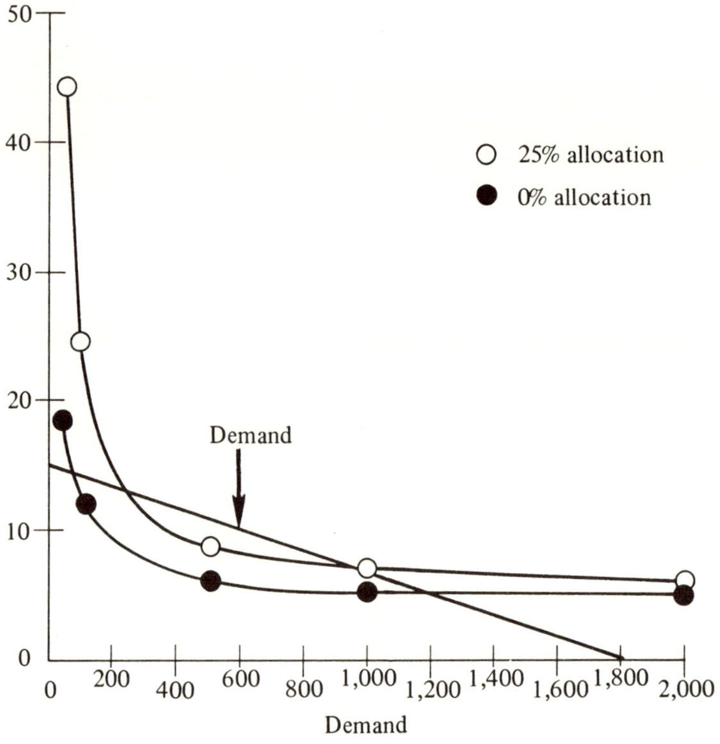

Figure 3.11 Price/demand and cost/demand (at 0% and 25% input allocation) for a current awareness publication with 50 sections.

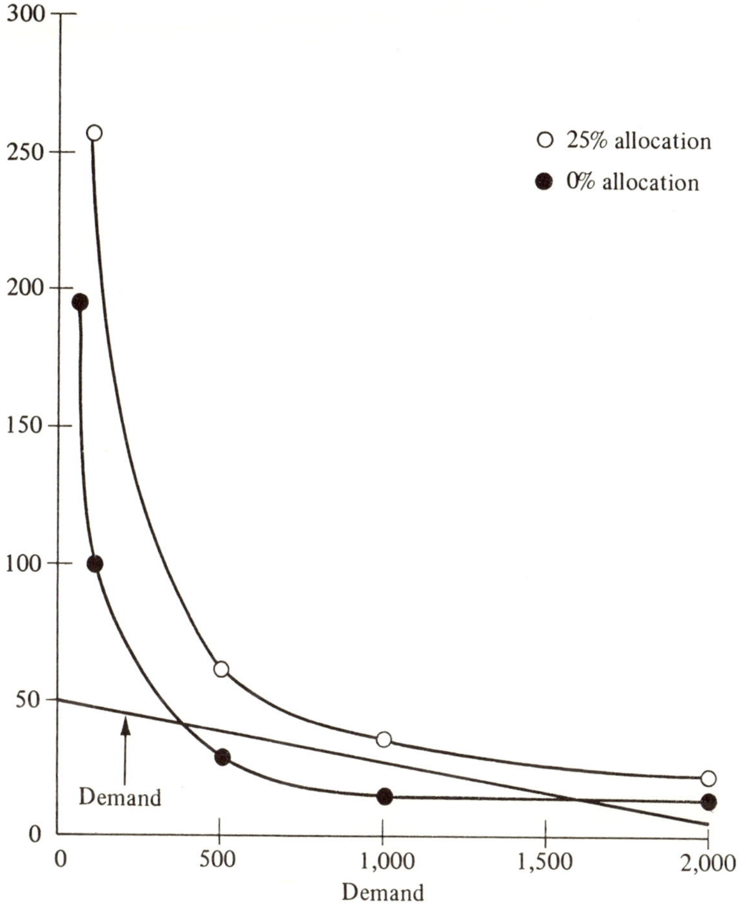

Figure 3.12 Price/demand and cost/demand (at 0% and 25% input allocation) for recurring bibliographies.

revenue. The demand curve for recurring bibliographies is considered to be rather elastic since this product will probably not be as popular as some of the others.

Let us assume that we wish to maximize net income and that the prices stated above will hold for the four information products and services. We find that, with six different allocation schemes, we arrive at the widely varying net income shown in Table 3.7, where the total net income ranges from \$196,400 to \$307,720. The optimum pricing/cost strategy based on the six allocations in that table is to allocate

100 percent of the input cost to retrospective search, and none to tape sales, current awareness, or the recurring bibliographies.

However, as mentioned previously, one must consider the effect of one product on another. In this case, we may find that the sale of tapes will seriously affect retrospective search demand. This possibility should be considered carefully when making a decision concerning the costing and pricing strategies.

Another criterion for choosing price for cost allocation is based on the risks involved in not choosing the correct price. For example, if we assume 25 percent allocation to the retrospective search and mistakenly choose a price that is 10 percent below the break-even price (i.e., instead of pricing at $66, we price at $60, yielding approximately 6,000 demand), a loss of nearly $120,000 will occur. On the other

Table 3.7 Net Income over Various Input Cost Allocations for Retrospective Search, Tape Sales, Current Awareness, and Recurring Bibliographies

Information products and services	Percent allocation					
Retrospective search	25	50	50	50	75	100
Tape sales	25	50	25	25	25	0
Current awareness	25	0	0	25	0	0
Recurring bibliographies	25	0	25	0	0	0
	Net income					
Retrospective search	$ 72,000	$ 51,000	$ 51,000	$ 51,000	$ 30,000	$ 9,000
Tape sales	70,000	12,000	70,000	70,000	70,000	134,000
Current awareness	72,000	126,000	126,000	72,000	126,000	126,000
Recurring bibliographies	-17,600	38,720	-17,600	38,720	38,720	38,720
	$196,400	$227,720	$229,400	$231,720	$264,720	$307,720

hand, there is a wide range of prices (from \$66 to \$140) which have positive net income. This means that one should tend toward a higher price for retrospective searching. It is also noted that, for 75 percent allocation, the range of profitable prices is \$80 to \$129, which is still a very loose range, but pricing below the break-even point may yield severe losses. Note also that, if the price is too high, there is a break-even point (on the upper left-hand part of the curve) at which losses can occur – about \$129 for the 75 percent allocation and about \$141 for the 25 percent allocation. Thus, if the price is higher in either one of these two cases, a loss will also be incurred; however, this loss is somewhat less than the loss at the other end of the curve, since a lower demand is involved.

In the other three services with relatively elastic curves, we find that the reverse is true. That is, losses incurred by charging too much are nearly the same as losses incurred by not charging enough. For example, if one charges \$5,000 at 25 percent allocation for the magnetic tapes, a \$20,000 loss would be incurred. On the other hand, if the charge were \$500, which is below the break-even point, the severity of the loss would be \$30,000.

If the shape of the price/demand curve is not known, the best strategy is probably to choose a price close to the knee of the cost/demand curve, unless there is evidence from other information systems that the price is too high or that the demand necessary to break even at that point is too high. It may be best to price high initially and adjust downward later, if necessary. The reverse may be quite difficult. The cost/demand curves can be very useful in resolving these kinds of problems.

One other decision that can be affected by this kind of analysis concerns the order in which new products are introduced and the screening points at which one can decide not to continue with a new product, at least in its present form. It is suggested that the least risky products – current awareness publications and recurring bibliographies – be introduced initially. If a risky product such as retrospective searching is not found to be effective from the marketing standpoint, one must quickly develop new products to use the expensive input processes or adopt a less costly process.

The example above is not given to suggest specific cost allocations or prices for information products and services, but rather to provide a general framework within which one can fit actual costs and make judgments about them.

References

1. American Chemical Society, "ACS Report Rates Information System Efficiency." *Chemical and Engineering News*, Vol. 47, No. 31 (July 28, 1969), pp. 44-46.
2. Bjorge, S. E., Urbach, P. F., Earl, P. H., King, D. W., Wiederkehr, R. R. V., "An Experiment to Determine the Effectiveness of Various Announcement Media on CFSTI Sales." In: *Proceedings of the American Society for Information Science Annual Meeting, Columbus, Ohio, 20-24 October 1968.* New York, Greenwood Publishing Corp., Vol. 5, 1968, pp. 327-329.
3. Case Institute of Technology, Operations Research Group, *An Operations Research Study of the Dissemination and Use of Recorded Scientific Information.* Report to Office of Scientific Information, National Science Foundation, under Grant No. G-8434. December 1960, pp. 171-503.
4. Earl, P. H., King, D. W., Wiederkehr, R. R. V., *The Determination of the Effect of Announcement Media on CFSTI Sales.* Formal Report Submitted to Clearinghouse for Federal Scientific and Technical Information. Bethesda, Md., Westat Research, Inc., December 1967.
5. Halbert, M. H., Ackoff, R. L., *An Operations Research Study of the Dissemination of Scientific Information.* Report to Office of Scientific Information, National Science Foundation. Case Institute of Technology, Operations Research Group, February 1958. PB 144 328.
6. Helmkamp, J. G., "Managerial Cost Accounting for a Technical Information Center." *American Documentation*, Vol. 20, No. 2 (April 1969), pp. 111-118.
7. King, D. W., *Cost/Benefits Analysis.* A Study Conducted for the American Psychological Association. Bethesda, Md., Westat Research, Inc., November 1969.
8. King, D. W., *Evaluation During File Development of the Glass Technology Coordinate Index File.* Bethesda, Md., Westat Research, Inc., November 1967.
9. King, D. W., Brown, A. M., *Some Comments on Marketing AIP Information Products and Services.* A Study Conducted for the American Institute of Physics. Bethesda, Md., Westat Research, Inc., July 1970.
10. King, D. W., Bryant, E. C., Daley, J. M., Searls, D. T., *A Decision Model for Determining Document Printing Quantities.* Bethesda, Md., Westat Research, Inc., February 1965. PB 167 175.
11. King, D. W., Caldwell, N. W., *Study for the Cost-Effectiveness of Retrospective Search Systems.* A Study Conducted for the American Psychological Association. Bethesda, Md., Westat Research, Inc., July 1970.
12. Lancaster, F. W., *Evaluation of the MEDLARS Demand Search Service.* Bethesda, Md., National Library of Medicine, January 1968.
13. Lancaster, F. W., *Procedures for the Evaluation of Published Recurring Bibliographies.* Bethesda, Md., Westat Research, Inc., 1969.
14. Leonard, L. E., Maier, J. M., Dougherty, R. M., *Centralized Book Processing. A Feasibility Study Based on Colorado Academic Libraries.* Metuchen, N. J., Scarecrow Press, 1969.

15. Martyn, J., "Unintentional Duplication of Research." *New Scientist,* Vol. 21, No. 377 (February 1964), p. 338.
16. Orr, R. H., Pings, V. M., Pizer, I. H., Olson, E. E., "Development of Methodologic Tools for Planning and Managing Library Services. I: Project Goals and Approach; II: Measuring a Library's Capability for Providing Documents." *Bulletin of the Medical Library Association,* Vol. 56, No. 3 (July 1968), pp. 235-267.
17. Shumway, R. H., "Some Estimation Problems Associated with Evaluating Information Retrieval Systems." *In: Evaluation of Document Retrieval Systems: Literature Perspective, Measurement, Technical Papers,* Chapter 3.1. Bethesda, Md., Westat Research, Inc., December 31, 1968.
18. Urbach, P., *Measuring User Reaction to the Clearinghouse Fast Announcement Service.* Clearinghouse for Federal Scientific and Technical Information, January 31, 1967.

Chapter Four
Microevaluation of Identification Systems

4.1 Introduction

The principal reason for microevaluation is diagnosis. No system works perfectly, and gross (or macro-) evaluation can only show how well the system works overall. The black box concept of macroevaluation provides almost no identification of failing components or why they fail. Such identification and diagnosis are precisely the goals of microevaluation. In microevaluation, one must abandon the concept of a black box and think instead of a system of components, each of which interacts with others. The term "components" must be interpreted in the broadest possible sense, however. "Facets of the system" might be more descriptive.

The real interest here is in a categorization of focal points for evaluative scrutiny. At the broadest level, these focal points are frequently identified as:

(1) Indexing, cataloging, and other input activities.
(2) File organization.
(3) Retrospective searching.
(4) Current awareness and selective dissemination.
(5) Screening and other output activities.

These are all *processes* as contrasted to *things* (documents, hardware, filing equipment, and so on).

The intellectual activities of the user may properly be considered a part of the system when the user is administratively responsible to the same entity that governs the other information activities. In that case, he can be required to take training or in other ways to be responsive to the wishes of system management. Some intelligence systems and part of the U.S. Patent Office are examples in which this view of the user may be appropriate. In general, however, it seems advisable to consider the user as an outsider who can judge the system in terms of its responsiveness to his needs. If properly done, microevaluation should reveal the identity of the failing components and the reasons for such failures. Because of its importance to document transfer systems, we consider first the evaluation of the retrospective search and the activities which relate directly to it.

4.2 Errors in retrospective searching

It is convenient to think of a relatively complete searching process and to identify all of the tasks associated with it. In specific cases, however, some of the tasks may be absent or may be combined with other tasks.

We assume initially that the user is not a part of the system, so the system begins to operate when a request is submitted in verbalized form. The request is interpreted by a coder (possibly) and is encoded into the search language, possibly through interaction with the requester. The encoded query is matched against the indexed file. The indexed file has previously been indexed on the basis of words, phrases, concepts, and so on, which express the contents of the separate documents in the file. The contents of documents which pass the query-file matching test are screened (possibly) for relevance and those passing the test are submitted to the user. This completes one iteration of the search and may be repeated as often as necessary.

A careful analysis of the above steps shows that errors can creep into the system in the following ways:

(1) The person who encodes the request may misinterpret it (coder interpretation error).

(2) The system language may be so restrictive that the request encoded into that language may not reflect the same content as the verbalized request.

(3) The file may contain indexing errors.

(4) The screener may make errors in selecting documents from the output which match the verbalized request.

Of course, blunders can occur all along the way. There is also the very real possibility that the requester may ask for one thing when he really wants something else. For the moment, however, we leave this possibility out of the system; it is discussed in some detail in a subsequent chapter.

Even though system relevance response and user relevance judgment are determined independently, they are usually highly correlated (in a statistical sense). This is because all of the usual retrieval processes involve a form of the user's question. For example, an intermediary interprets a user's question (initially stated in natural language), he translates that question into a system query (stated in terms available to the system), the system matches the query and indexed documents in terms available to the system, and an intermediary screens documents from the system output based on his interpretation of the user's question. All of these forms of the user's question are related to documents in the file in a manner similar to user relevance judgment and should be highly correlated to user relevance judgment. The relationships are given in the schema of Figure 4.1.

The user relevance judgment, which is the relationship between a user search question and an individual document, is shown in the upper right-hand corner. Continuing clockwise around the schema (in the form of spokes) are the following:

(1) *User relevance judgment*, which is the degree of relationship between the user question and a document.

(2) *Intermediary relevance judgment*, which is an intermediary's judgment of the degree of relationship between the user's question and a document.

(3) *Query relevance judgment*, which is an assessment of the degree of relationship between a query and an individual document (i.e., does the document actually contain the concepts required by the query?).

(4) *System relevance response*, which is the system's assessment of the relationship between a query and a document. The system response is often a computer printout that implies a value of 1 for those documents identified and 0 for others.

(5) *Screened system relevance response*, which corresponds to an intermediary's judgment of the relation between the user's question and a document.

All five relationships can be multi-valued or dichotomous. Furthermore, all of the corresponding scores can be plotted against one another to form relationships that are analogous to the well-known 2 × 2 table that was given in Chapter 2. Just as accuracy was defined in Chapter 2, the corresponding relationships of the question forms and documents provide four accuracy measures, including *interpretation accuracy, query accuracy, input accuracy,* and *screen accuracy*, as indicated in the schema. A lack of accuracy in each case contributes to the deterioration of overall system accuracy, and the relative contribution can be measured along each link in the chain. Thus, system accuracy, when properly segmented, serves as a mechanism for diagnosing a system and its sources of failure.

If one plots user relevance judgment against intermediary rele-

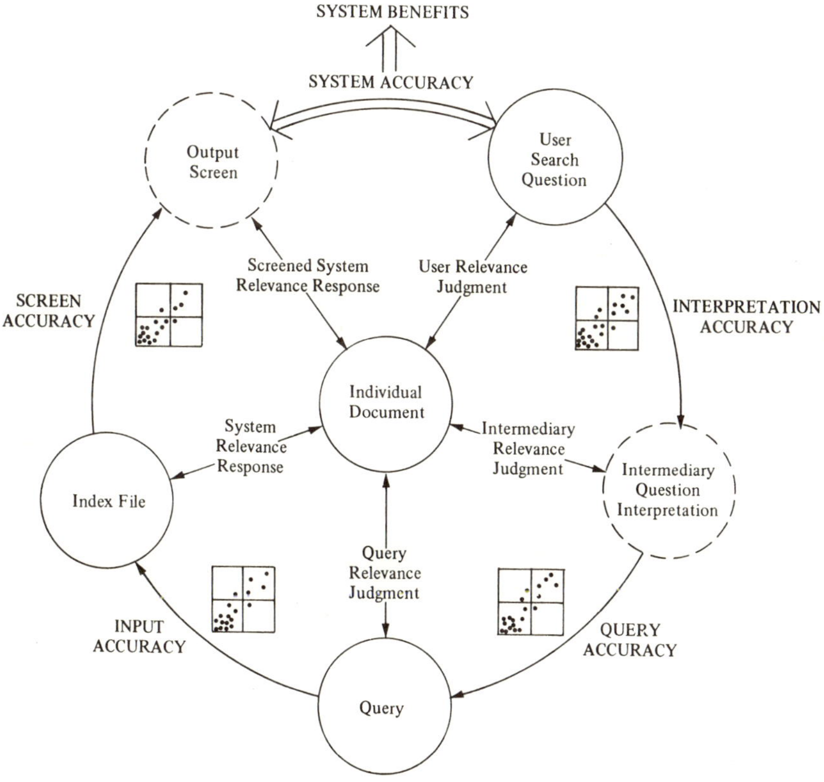

Figure 4.1 Schema presenting system accuracy and relationships that contribute to it.

vance judgment, a relationship similar to that shown in Figure 4.1 may be found, or a 2 × 2 relationship may occur when the judgments are dichotomous. Clearly, there will be some deviation between the two judgments of relevance. Interpretation accuracy is the correlation between the two judgments. Some researchers, including Lancaster (*12*) and O'Connor (*13*), feel that question interpretation by the intermediary contributes substantially to the deterioration of system accuracy. O'Connor points out that the deviations may be attributed to disagreements concerning the questions as well as judgments of the documents. The important thing, however, is to isolate the degree to which interpretation contributes to system accuracy and to investigate further if results indicate that faulty interpretation yields unsatisfactory system accuracy.

Query accuracy can also be found from the relationship between intermediary relevance judgment and query relevance judgment in the manner shown in Figure 4.1 or the 2 × 2 dichotomous relationship. If one plots query relevance judgment against user relevance judgment, the resulting relationship confounds the effects of question interpretation (by the intermediary) and query formulation. The two effects may need to be isolated to pinpoint ways of improving the system if accuracy is not satisfactory. There is ample evidence that query formulation can be a considerable source of difficulty (*11, 12*).

As mentioned previously, query relevance judgment is the score of a document against the query formulated in system language. System relevance response is the system's assessment of the relationship between a user's question (now in the form of a query) and a document. It is produced by matching the index file and the document for terms (or associated terms) stated in the search query. Deviations from a perfect correspondence can also be plotted in the same manner as those above that can be attributed to: (1) lack of agreement in interpretation of terms between indexers and searchers, (2) inadequate term list and structure, (3) indexing errors, and (4) depth of indexing. A number of studies have been addressed to indexing processes since system accuracy is clearly dependent on input accuracy. A good review of indexing research is given by St. Laurent (*15*).

When an intermediary screens the system output, he bases his decision on his interpretation of the user's question. This judgment should be the same as the intermediary relevance judgment mentioned previously (if judged by the same person), except that a decision made by a screener (sometimes the user) is often based on establishing the relationship between an interpretation of the user's question and a document representation (titles, key words, abstracts, etc.) rather than the full text of the document. Thus, some failure can be attributed to screening due to (1) the screener's interpretation of the user's question and (2) the fact that a document representation may be used as a proxy for the full text of a document (*5, 8, 17*).

Each source of failure can be isolated and accuracy can be measured for interpretation, query, input, and screening. However, the primary interest is the overall accuracy of the relationship between system relevance response and user relevance judgment, as defined in Chapter 2. The problem is that all possibilities must be considered. For example, a relevant document may be missed due to interpretation error, but this document may be identified by search query for the wrong reason. The only feasible way to account for all combinations of occurrences is by mathematical model. Such a model is described in the following section. A worked example of this model is given in Section 4.4.

4.3 A system model for retrospective searches

The sources of error given in the previous section can be described as a set of conditional probabilities. These probabilities can be displayed meaningfully in 2 X 2 tables as in Figure 4.2. The following notation will be used consistently:

V_r, relevant with respect to verbalized request;
$V_{\bar{r}}$, nonrelevant with respect to verbalized request;
C_r, relevant with respect to coder's interpretation;
$C_{\bar{r}}$, nonrelevant with respect to coder's interpretation;
E_r, relevant with respect to encoded request;
$E_{\bar{r}}$, nonrelevant with respect to encoded request;
R_r, relevant with respect to system's response;
$R_{\bar{r}}$, nonrelevant with respect to system's response;
S_r, relevant with respect to screener's judgment; and
$S_{\bar{r}}$, nonrelevant with respect to screener's judgment.

Conditional probabilities will be designated by the standard notation $P(A|B)$, which is read "the probability of A, given B." Thus, $P(C_r|V_{\bar{r}})$ means "the probability that a document is relevant to the coder's interpretation, given that it is not relevant to the verbalized request."

Whether one can express relationships among the components of a retrospective searching system as probabilities, and the context within which such probabilities have meaning, requires some elaboration. Let us consider a probability such as $P(R_r | V_r)$, that is, the probability that a document relevant to the verbalized request (V_r) will be retrieved (R_r). If one chooses a request at random from the stream of

	Relevance with respect to coder's interpretation	
Relevance with respect to verbalized request	$C_{\bar{r}}$	C_r
V_r	$P(C_{\bar{r}} \| V_r)$	$P(C_r \| V_r)$
$V_{\bar{r}}$	$P(C_{\bar{r}} \| V_{\bar{r}})$	$P(C_r \| V_{\bar{r}})$

	Relevance with respect to encoded request	
Relevance with respect to coder's interpretation	$E_{\bar{r}}$	E_r
C_r	$P(E_{\bar{r}} \| C_r)$	$P(E_r \| C_r)$
$C_{\bar{r}}$	$P(E_{\bar{r}} \| C_{\bar{r}})$	$P(E_r \| C_{\bar{r}})$

	Relevance with respect to response by system	
Relevance with respect to encoded request	$R_{\bar{r}}$	R_r
E_r	$P(R_{\bar{r}} \| E_r)$	$P(R_r \| E_r)$
$E_{\bar{r}}$	$P(R_{\bar{r}} \| E_{\bar{r}})$	$P(R_r \| E_{\bar{r}})$

	Relevance with respect to screener's interpretation	
Relevance with respect to verbalized request	$S_{\bar{r}}$	S_r
V_r	$P(S_{\bar{r}} \| V_r)$	$P(S_r \| V_r)$
$V_{\bar{r}}$	$P(S_{\bar{r}} \| V_{\bar{r}})$	$P(S_r \| V_{\bar{r}})$

Figure 4.2 Conditional probabilities used in retrospective search models.

requests entering the system, presumably it would be possible to say whether any document in the system was relevant or nonrelevant to that request. Also, one can observe whether such a document is retrieved or is not retrieved by the system. The relative frequency with which relevant documents[1] are retrieved by the system should approach stability as the number of observations is increased. Since an observation is identifiable with a document, such stability should occur either if many documents are matched against a single request or if a few documents in each of many searches are matched against their separate search requests. If the ratio generated by the latter method does, in fact, approach stability as the number of requests increases, the value approached as a limit will be referred to as "the probability of retrieval by the system, given relevance to the verbalized request," that is, $P(R_r|V_r)$. In practice, one is always working with relative frequencies, since the limiting values are unknown. It is convenient in model construction, however, to work with the conceptual limits and to call them probabilities.

One can construct a model of the retrospective search system which has the following features:

(1) It shows the following summary figures:

(a) The probability that a relevant document will be retrieved.

(b) The probability that a nonrelevant document will be retrieved.

(2) It shows the activities which are the principal sources of error. This identification is provided by the display of Figure 4.2. Ideally, of course, all entries in these tables should be zeros and ones, with the ones in the lower left-hand and upper right-hand corners. The amount of departure from this ideal indicates the extent of departure from perfection.

(3) The effect of error-prone components on the total output of the system can be obtained. For example, it is possible to show what effect coder interpretation errors have on system performance.

(4) It shows how specified improvement in any component will affect system output.

Mathematically, the model can be described as a finite Markov chain with absorbing states. Section 4.5 provides mathematical notes

[1] Relevant to the verbalized request.

for those who are interested, but need not be read in order to apply the model to an actual evaluation.

The model constitutes a simple application of the rules of probability in order to determine the following probabilities:

$$(1)\quad P(E_r|V_r) = P(E_r|C_r)\,P(C_r|V_r) + P(E_r|C_{\bar{r}})\,P(C_{\bar{r}}|V_r)$$

$$(2)\quad P(E_r|V_{\bar{r}}) = P(E_r|C_r)\,P(C_r|V_{\bar{r}}) + P(E_r|C_{\bar{r}})\,P(C_{\bar{r}}|V_{\bar{r}})$$

$$(3)\quad P(R_r|V_r) = P(R_r|E_r)\,P(E_r|V_r) + P(R_r|E_{\bar{r}})\,P(E_{\bar{r}}|V_r)$$

$$(4)\quad P(R_r|V_{\bar{r}}) = P(R_r|E_r)\,P(E_r|V_{\bar{r}}) + P(R_r|E_{\bar{r}})\,P(E_{\bar{r}}|V_{\bar{r}})$$

$$(5)\quad P(S_r, R_r|V_r) = P(S_r|V_r)\,P(R_r|V_r)$$

$$(6)\quad P(S_r, R_r|V_{\bar{r}}) = P(S_r|V_{\bar{r}})\,P(R_r|V_{\bar{r}})$$

The notation $P(S_r, R_r|V_r)$ indicates the probability that the system has classified the document as relevant *and* that the screener has also classified it as such, given that the document is, in fact, relevant with respect to the verbalized request. The conditional probabilities listed above can be summarized in 2 X 2 tables as shown in Figure 4.3. Since each row adds to unity, one can easily fill in the additional items.

Note that the last 2 X 2 table in Figure 4.3 is simply a distribution of the last column of the preceding table. In addition to the probabilities given above, we have:

$$(7)\quad P(R_{\bar{r}}|V_r) + P(S_{\bar{r}}, R_r|V_r) + P(S_r, R_r|V_r) = 1$$

$$(8)\quad P(R_{\bar{r}}|V_{\bar{r}}) + P(S_{\bar{r}}, R_r|V_{\bar{r}}) + P(S_r, R_r|V_{\bar{r}}) = 1$$

The *expected number* of documents in each of the cells is simply the probability in the cell times the number of documents in the file which are relevant (or nonrelevant) with respect to the verbalized request. Methods for estimating the cell probabilities and a worked example are given in the next section.

Some important features of the model are the following:

(1) It provides a means for tying together the influences of the various components of the searching system, so that measures of performance of the searching subsystem are derived from measures of performance of the components.

(2) It permits one to determine the effect of a change in performance of a component on the performance of the subsystem.

(3) The conditional probabilities used as performance measures can be identified with the customary measures of recall and precision as follows:

(a) $P(S_r, R_r | V_r)$ is the theoretical recall ratio for the system.

(b) Let N_r be the number of documents in the file relevant to a verbalized request and $N_{\bar{r}}$ the number nonrelevant. Then, the theoretical precision ratio is:

$$\frac{N_r \cdot P(S_r, R_r | V_r)}{N_r \cdot P(S_r, R_r | V_r) + N_{\bar{r}} \cdot P(S_r, R_r | V_{\bar{r}})}$$

	Cumulative through encoding stage	
Relevance with respect to verbalized request	$E_{\bar{r}}$	E_r
V_r	$P(E_{\bar{r}} \| V_r)$	$P(E_r \| V_r)$
$V_{\bar{r}}$	$P(E_{\bar{r}} \| V_{\bar{r}})$	$P(E_r \| V_{\bar{r}})$
	Cumulative through system output	
Relevance with respect to verbalized request	$R_{\bar{r}}$	R_r
V_r	$P(R_{\bar{r}} \| V_r)$	$P(R_r \| V_r)$
$V_{\bar{r}}$	$P(R_{\bar{r}} \| V_{\bar{r}})$	$P(R_r \| V_{\bar{r}})$
	Cumulative through screening	
Relevance with respect to verbalized request	$S_{\bar{r}}$	S_r
V_r	$P(S_{\bar{r}}, R_r \| V_r)$	$P(S_r, R_r \| V_r)$
$V_{\bar{r}}$	$P(S_{\bar{r}}, R_r \| V_{\bar{r}})$	$P(S_r, R_r \| V_{\bar{r}})$

Figure 4.3 Cumulative probabilities through various stages of the retrospective search.

(4) The model results in measures of *effectiveness* rather than *efficiency*, since no costs are introduced. A later section shows how costs can be used to influence management decisions.

4.4 A worked example of the retrospective searching model

Figure 4.4 provides a worksheet by which the estimates of conditional probabilities can be reduced to summary measures of performance. The tilde (~) over the noted probabilities indicates that they are probabilities estimated from a sample. Methods of estimation are given later.

A. Errors in interpreting verbalized request

Verbalized request	Coder's interpretation $C_{\bar{r}}$	C_r
V_r	(1) $\tilde{P}(C_{\bar{r}}\|V_r)$ = 0.2000	(2) $\tilde{P}(C_r\|V_r)$ = 0.8000
$V_{\bar{r}}$	(3) $\tilde{P}(C_{\bar{r}}\|V_{\bar{r}})$ = 0.9900	(4) $\tilde{P}(C_r\|V_{\bar{r}})$ = 0.0100

B. Errors in encoding the request (deficiencies in language)

Coder's interpretation	Encoded request $E_{\bar{r}}$	E_r
C_r	(5) $\tilde{P}(E_{\bar{r}}\|C_r)$ = 0.2000	(6) $\tilde{P}(E_r\|C_r)$ = 0.8000
$C_{\bar{r}}$	(7) $\tilde{P}(E_{\bar{r}}\|C_{\bar{r}})$ = 0.9700	(8) $\tilde{P}(E_r\|C_{\bar{r}})$ = 0.0300

Figure 4.4 Worksheet for computing outputs from the retrospective searching model.

C. Errors due to indexing

Encoded request	Retrieved by system: $R_{\bar{r}}$	Retrieved by system: R_r
E_r	(9) $\tilde{P}(R_{\bar{r}}\vert E_r)$ = 0.3400	(10) $\tilde{P}(R_r\vert E_r)$ = 0.6600
$E_{\bar{r}}$	(11) $\tilde{P}(R_{\bar{r}}\vert E_{\bar{r}})$ = 0.9987	(12) $\tilde{P}(R_r\vert E_{\bar{r}})$ = 0.0013

D. Errors due to screening

Verbalized request	Screened output: $S_{\bar{r}}$	Screened output: S_r
V_r	(13) $P(S_{\bar{r}}\vert V_r)$ = 0.4000	(14) $P(S_r\vert V_r)$ = 0.6000
$V_{\bar{r}}$	(15) $P(S_{\bar{r}}\vert V_{\bar{r}})$ = 0.7000	(16) $P(S_r\vert V_{\bar{r}})$ = 0.3000

E. Probability of encoding relevance for documents relevant and nonrelevant with respect to the verbalized request

(1) 0.2	X	(7) 0.97	=	(17) 0.194	
(2) 0.8	X	(5) 0.2	=	(18) 0.1600	
		(17) + (18)	=	(19) 0.3540	$P(E_{\bar{r}}\vert V_r)$
		1.000 - (19)	=	(20) 0.6460	$P(E_r\vert V_r)$
(3) 0.99	X	(7) 0.97	=	(21) 0.9603	
(4) 0.01	X	(5) 0.2	=	(22) 0.002	
		(21) + (22)	=	(23) 0.9623	$P(E_{\bar{r}}\vert V_{\bar{r}})$
		1.000 - (23)	=	(24) 0.0377	$P(E_r\vert V_r)$

Figure 4.4 Worksheet for computing outputs from the retrospective searching model. (Continued)

F. Probability of system response for documents relevant and nonrelevant with respect to the verbalized request

(19) 0.3540	X	(11) 0.9987		=	(25) 0.3535	
(20) 0.6460	X	(9) 0.34		=	(26) 0.2196	
		(25)	+ (26)	=	(27) 0.5731	$P(R_{\bar{r}} \mid V_r)$
		1.000	- (27)	=	(28) 0.4269	$P(R_r \mid V_r)$
(23) 0.9623	X	(11) 0.9987		=	(29) 0.9611	
(24) 0.0377	X	(9) 0.34		=	(30) 0.0128	
		(29)	+ (30)	=	(31) 0.9739	$P(R_{\bar{r}} \mid V_{\bar{r}})$
		1.000	- (31)	=	(32) 0.0261	$P(R_r \mid V_{\bar{r}})$

G. Probability of screened selection for documents relevant and nonrelevant with respect to the verbalized request

(14) 0.6000	X	(28) 0.4269		=	(33) 0.2561	$P(S_r, R_r \mid V_r)$
	(28) 0.4269		- (33)	=	(34) 0.1708	$P(S_{\bar{r}}, R_r \mid V_r)$
(16) 0.30	X	(32) 0.0261		=	(35) 0.0078	$P(S_r, R_r \mid V_r)$
	(32) 0.0261		- (35)	=	(36) 0.0183	$P(S_{\bar{r}}, R_r \mid V_{\bar{r}})$

H. Summary

Verbalized request		Not retrieved	Retrieved
Relevant documents			
Prior to screening	(27)	0.5731	
After screening	(34)	0.1708	(33) 0.2561
Nonrelevant documents			
Prior to screening	(31)	0.9739	
After screening	(36)	0.0183	(35) 0.0078

I. Measures of recall and precision

Recall, Item (33)		0.2561
Precision		
Number in file identified as relevant	(N_r)	20
Total nonrelevant documents in file	$(N_{\bar{r}})$	19,980
Total retrieved $N_r \cdot$ (Item 33)	5.12	
plus $N_{\bar{r}} \cdot$ (Item 35)	155.84	
equals	160.96	
Precision ratio = $\frac{N_r \cdot \text{(Item 33)}}{\text{total retrieval}}$	0.318	

Figure 4.4 Worksheet for computing outputs from the retrospective searching model. (Continued)

The basic probability estimates are given in Sections A through D of the worksheet, and all subsequent probability estimates are derived from them. The worksheet is designed so that the computations can be done easily by a clerk with a hand calculator.

Examination of the hypothetical data in the table cells shows that errors in interpreting the verbalized request and in encoding the request are substantial. Suppose one wishes to determine the effect on performance of reducing coder interpretation errors to zero. This might be done either by teaching users to do their own encoding or by providing a better means of communication between users and coders, perhaps by meetings or telephone calls. Note that at this point there is some confusion between the coder's attempt to mirror what was said in the verbalized request and his attempt to determine what the user *meant* to say. The confusion will be resolved subsequently.

Numerically, one is interested in determining the effect of replacing the probability estimates in Section A of Figure 4.4 by zeros and ones, as follows:

	$C_{\bar{r}}$	C_r
V_r	0	1
$V_{\bar{r}}$	1	0

Using these figures and proceeding again through the computations in the worksheet yields the following summary (Section H):

Verbalized request		Not retrieved		Retrieved
Relevant documents				
Prior to screening	(27)	0.3917		
After screening	(34)	0.2433	(33)	0.3650
Nonrelevant documents				
Prior to screening	(31)	0.9789		
After screening	(36)	0.0148	(35)	0.0063

Thus, if one were able to eliminate coder error, he would improve the retrieval of relevant documents by 10 percentage points (from 25.61 to 36.50) and also reduce the retrieval of nonrelevant documents from 0.78 percent to 0.63 percent.

As an alternative, one might consider redesign of the term list (or its associated thesaurus or dictionary) so as to improve the relationship between the encoded request and the coder's interpretation (Section B of Figure 4.4). By experimentation, he might estimate that the probabilities of Section B could be changed to:

	$E_{\bar{r}}$	E_r
C_r	0.1	0.9
$C_{\bar{r}}$	0.8	0.2

Working through another iteration of the solution would show the following summary results:

Verbalized request		Not retrieved		Retrieved
Relevant documents				
Prior to screening	(27)	0.4981		
After screening	(34)	0.2008	(33)	0.3011
Nonrelevant documents				
Prior to screening	(31)	0.8624		
After screening	(36)	0.0963	(35)	0.0413

Improvement in retrieval of relevant documents is not as great as in the first alternative, but the filtering out of nonrelevant documents is somewhat better. Which of these alternatives (or others which might be proposed) should be selected would depend upon the relative importance of missing documents compared to obtaining unwanted documents and upon the relative costs of the alternatives. More will be said later about the selection of alternatives.

The validity of the model can be checked from the data by computing from the original data,

$\tilde{P}(R_r|V_r)$ = proportion of the "verbalized relevant" set retrieved, and

$\tilde{P}(R_r|V_{\bar{r}})$ = proportion of the "verbalized nonrelevant" set retrieved,

and comparing directly against $\tilde{P}(R_r|V_r)$ and $\tilde{P}(R_r|V_{\bar{r}})$ as computed in items (28) and (32). This check on validity should always be made.

Figure 4.4 is a worked example of the retrospective searching model using a combination of four specific alternatives. These alternatives are as follows:

Intermediary interpretation	- by letter - by telephone
Searching	- eight-term queries - four-term queries
Indexing	- single indexer - single indexer with review
Screening	- none - by titles

Each of these alternatives may be varied to produce different combinations and correspondingly different summary figures of effectiveness. It should also be noted that each alternative has certain implications in the cost area which must be considered in making efficiency evaluations.

In order for us to be able to decide upon an optimum overall retrospective search system, we must investigate all possible combinations of alternative subprocesses, including intermediary interpretation, searching, indexing, and screening. Table 4.1 gives two alternatives for intermediary interpretation, searching, indexing, and combinations for screening. Also included in Table 4.1 are effectiveness probabilities and costs. Thus, in this simple example, we can consider a total of 16 combinations ($2 \times 2 \times 2 \times 2$) of alternatives in view of their cost/effectiveness trade-off.

In Figure 4.4, it is assumed that the user submits his request to an intermediary by letter and that the request involves a fixed cost of $2,000 plus a variable cost of $11.25 per search to the system. It would be equally plausible to substitute oral communication by telephone between the system and user in place of written communication, thereby raising the variable cost to $15.00 per search. While the second alternative causes an increase in expense, it may also be found to increase the probability of correct coder interpretation [$P(C_r|V_r)$] from 0.80 to 0.90 and to lower the likelihood of coder misinterpretation [$P(C_r|V_{\bar{r}})$] from 0.01 to 0.005. Thus, system effectiveness may be improved, although at an increased cost.

Alternatives are also available with regard to the searching query. The example presumes eight terms per query, which has $131,000 fixed cost, plus a $0.058 per item retrieved variable cost for the system. If the number of search terms is held to less than four, there still remains the $131,000 fixed cost; however, the cost increases since the

Table 4.1 Alternative Retrospective Searching Processes: Effectiveness Probabilities and Costs

Alternatives	Effectiveness probabilities		Other variables[a]	Fixed costs	Variable costs
Intermediary interpretation					
(1) By letter	$P(C_r \mid V_r) = 0.80$	$P(C_r \mid V_{\bar{r}}) = 0.010$		$C_4 = \$500$	$C_9 = \$11.25$/search
(2) By telephone	$= 0.90$	$= 0.005$		$= \$500$	$= \$15.00$/search
Searching					
(1) 8 terms/query	$P(E_r \mid C_r) = 0.80$	$P(E_r \mid C_{\bar{r}}) = 0.03$		$C_1 = \$131{,}000$	$C_{10} + C_{11} = \$0.058$/item retr.
(2) Less than 4 terms/query	$= 0.85$	$= 0.05$		$= \$131{,}000$	$= \$0.058$/item retr.
Indexing					
(1) Single	$P(R_r \mid E_r) = 0.66$	$P(R_r \mid E_{\bar{r}}) = 0.0013$	$X_1 = 20{,}000$ items	$C_3 = \$\ 5{,}500$	$C_6 + C_7 X_5 = \$0.50$/item
(2) With review	$= 0.76$	$= 0.0016$	$= 20{,}000$ items	$= \$11{,}000$	$= \$0.95$/item
Screening					
(1) No screening titles mailed	$P(S_r \mid V_r) = 1.00$	$P(S_r \mid V_{\bar{r}}) = 1.00$		$C_2 = \$0$ $C_5 = \$250$	$C_{12} = \$0$ $C_8 = \$0.20$/search $C_{13} = \$0.002$/item sent
(2) Screen on titles titles mailed	$= 0.80$	$= 0.15$		$C_2 = \$0$ $C_5 = \$250$	$C_{12} = \$0.04$/item retr. $C_8 = \$0.20$/search $C_{13} = \$0.002$/item sent

[a] $X_2 = 10{,}000$ searches, $X_5 = 1{,}000$ terms.

items retrieved increase in each instance. Also, one would expect that alternative 2 would require substantial additional screening and processing costs. Encoding accuracy $[P(E_r|C_r)]$ shifts from 0.80 under the first alternative to 0.85 under the second, while the probability of correcting interpretation error in the encoding process $[P(E_r|C_{\bar{r}})]$ moves from 0.03 (alternative 1) to 0.05 (alternative 2).

The next opportunity to vary alternatives is provided by the indexing process. The example given earlier involves merely a single indexing attempt at a fixed cost of $5,500 and a variable cost of $0.50 per item, which yields a 0.66 probability of retrieval given a relevant encoded request $[P(R_r|E_r)]$, and a 0.0013 probability of retrieval given a nonrelevant encoded request. It is possible then to substitute the alternative of providing an indexing review which would raise the fixed cost to $11,000 and variable cost of $0.95 per item, but at the same time change $P(R_r|E_r)$ to 0.76 and $P(R_r|E_{\bar{r}})$ to 0.0016. Thus, effectiveness increases as well as cost.

In this example, the screening process offers two alternatives: no screening and screening on titles. The associated probabilities of correct favorable screening $[P(S_r|V_r)]$ on titles are 1.0 and 0.80, respectively, while the probabilities of unfavorable screening error $[P(S_r|V_{\bar{r}})]$ are 1.0 and 0.15. In this case all the fixed costs remain the same for the first alternative as for the second. The variable costs associated with screening are $0 for no screen and $0.04 per item retrieved for screening on titles. A second type of expense is the cost for presentation to the user; it is $250 fixed cost, $0.20 per search, and $0.002 per item sent.

Thus, through use of the retrospective searching model (Figure 4.4), the system evaluator is able to arrive at an overall figure for system effectiveness which combines the effects of various combinations of alternatives for system components. The costs given in Table 4.1 can be incorporated into the overall cost model given in Chapter 3.

$$C = C_1 + C_2 + C_3 + C_4 + C_5 + X_1(C_6 + X_5C_7) + X_2[C_8 + C_9 + X_3(C_{10} + C_{11} + C_{12}) + X_4C_{13}]$$

where:

X_1 = number of items input,
X_2 = number of searches conducted,
X_3 = number of items retrieved per search,
X_4 = number of items mailed per search,

X_5 = number of terms in authority list,
C_1 = fixed cost associated with computing,
C_2 = fixed cost associated with screening,
C_3 = fixed cost associated with input,
C_4 = fixed cost associated with user/system interface,
C_5 = fixed cost associated with mailing results,
C_6 = total input cost per item,
C_7 = total file loading cost per item per term,
C_8 = fixed cost of mailing per search,
C_9 = fixed cost of user/system interface per search,
C_{10} = computer retrieval cost per item retrieved,
C_{11} = computer printing cost per item retrieved,
C_{12} = screening cost per item retrieved,
C_{13} = mailing cost per item mailed, and
C = total annual cost.

By considering the costs of the various combinations of alternatives, the evaluator is able to make judgments concerning the relative efficiency of certain alternative combinations. The results for the 16 combinations are given in Table 4.2.[2] These results are given by recall, number of relevant retrieved, number of nonrelevant retrieved, total retrieved, total costs (10,000 searches), cost per search, and cost per relevant document retrieved. We feel that cost per relevant document retrieved provides the best single figure of merit in this case. The costs above are without regard to the user; that is, they include only system costs. A second set of figures is given which includes user costs. This example is discussed later in this chapter.

Table 4.2 shows the results of 16 combinations of four alternatives, including both retrieval and cost figures as they would apply to the system and the system user. The alternatives in this table are coded by the numbers given in Table 4.1. For example, alternative combination 2121 represents alternative 2 for intermediary interpretation (telephone), alternative 1 for searching (eight-term query), alternative 2 for indexing (with review), and alternative 1 for screening (no screen).

If retrieval effectiveness alone is considered, the evaluator might quickly narrow his consideration to alternative combinations 2122 or 2112. These combinations show that 8.8 and 7.7 relevant documents

[2]As an exercise, it is suggested that one look at the raw figures in Table 4.1 and guess which system alternative will yield the best results before looking at the results in Table 4.2.

Table 4.2 Alternative Retrospective Searching Processes: Effectiveness Measures and Costs

Alternative combinations	Recall	No. rel. retr.	No. retr. (X_3)	No. mailed (X_4)	Total system cost	System cost/ search	System cost/ rel. retr.
1111	0.43	8.6	528	528	$ 578,550	$ 57.86	$ 6.73
1112	0.34	6.9	528	85	780,890	78.09	11.32
1121	0.49	9.8	613	613	644,050	64.41	6.57
1122	0.39	7.8	613	98	878,950	87.90	11.27
1211	0.46	9.2	798	798	740,550	74.06	8.05
1212	0.37	7.4	798	126	1,046,310	104.63	14.14
1221	0.52	10.4	921	921	828,850	82.89	7.97
1222	0.42	8.3	921	145	1,181,730	118.17	14.24
2111	0.48	9.6	481	481	587,850	58.79	6.12
2112	0.38	7.7	481	80	772,230	77.22	10.03
2121	0.55	11.0	556	556	647,350	64.74	5.89
2122	0.44	8.8	556	91	860,450	86.05	9.78
2211	0.51	10.2	745	745	746,250	74.63	7.32
2212	0.41	8.2	745	118	1,030,710	103.07	12.58
2221	0.59	11.7	861	861	830,350	83.04	7.10
2222	0.47	9.4	861	137	1,160,270	116.03	12.34

may be expected out of a total retrieval of 91 and 80 documents, respectively. Many of the other combinations may be rejected swiftly due to excessive numbers of documents retrieved; others may be rejected because of excessively small proportions of relevant documents retrieved.

If the evaluator broadens his consideration to include system costs, alternative combination 1111 indicates a $57.86 cost per search, whereas combinations 2111, 1121, and 2121 indicate costs of $58.79, $64.41, and $64.74, respectively. On the other hand, the system costs per relevant document retrieval would favor combination 2121 with a cost of $5.89 as opposed to 2111, 1121, and 1111 with costs of $6.12, $6.57 and $6.73, respectively. If system costs are considered without regard for retrieval effectiveness, combinations 1111, 2111, 1121, and 2121 all appear to be excellent choices. In general, we would conclude from this example that the written or telephone request has little bearing on the cost/effectiveness outcome. However, it does appear that searching on eight terms per query is a superior approach to searching on less than four terms per query. The indexing strategy also appears to have little effect on the cost/effectiveness outcome. This process will be investigated in more detail in the next chapter, however, where it will be shown that the searching/indexing interface is more complex than indicated in this example. It would appear that screening at the level in this example is not justified on a cost/effectiveness basis. However, our decision might be different when we consider the cost incurred by the user of the system. Note for the example that the four choices mentioned above all result in sending over 480 documents to the user, which yields a large expense to him. Here, there are two cases to be considered – one with the user as a part of the system and the other with the user as entirely independent of the system. A great deal more is said in Chapter 6 about screening processes and in Chapter 7 about user costs.

It should be emphasized that the choice of any particular combination of alternatives will depend largely on the objectives of the system and specific parameter limitations placed on its operation. For example, a poison treatment center would be much more interested in retrieving, as swiftly as possible, *all* relevant information concerning a particular poison than in whether each search cost $80 or $120, as long as the costs remained within reasonable limits. On the other hand, a university library would be more interested in retrieving a limited amount of the relevant information available (say 50 percent) while keeping the cost involved to a minimum and without particular concern for the response time. No matter how the particular system is constituted or how alternative combinations are derived, examination of the relative merits of the overall system is greatly facilitated by the stochastic model described in this chapter and one can establish the effects of various changes in view of the entire system more clearly.

The next section of this chapter is devoted to some of the more esoteric mathematical considerations of the model discussed above. Section 4.6 discusses ways of estimating probabilities for the retrospective searching models. The next three chapters are devoted to evaluation of the processes that enter into the model and methodology for estimating the effectiveness probabilities.

4.5 Mathematical notes on the retrospective searching model[3]

The retrospective searching model can be described as a finite Markov chain with absorbing states. The fact that the cell probabilities (except for the screening process) are conditional only upon the previous step makes it possible to structure the model as a matrix of transition probabilities, as in Figure 4.5. The cell entries are those used in the example of Figure 4.4. Absorbing states are $R_{\bar{r}}$ and R_r. In canonical form, the matrix of Figure 4.5 can be written:

$$\left[\begin{array}{c|c} Q & B \\ \hline O & I \end{array}\right]$$

where

Q = the matrix of transitions from nonabsorbing to other nonabsorbing states,
B = the transitions from nonabsorbing to absorbing states,
I = the identity matrix, and
O = the zero matrix.

Then, by the theory of finite Markov chains (7), the *fundamental matrix* is given by $(I - Q)^{-1}$. The results of most interest are the probabilites of $R_{\bar{r}}$ and R_r, given relevance or nonrelevance with re-

[3]This section need not be read as a prerequisite to applying the model. It is presented as a more concise explanation for those with training in stochastic processes.

	$V_{\bar{r}}$	V_r	$C_{\bar{r}}$	C_r	$E_{\bar{r}}$	E_r	$R_{\bar{r}}$	R_r
$V_{\bar{r}}$	0	0	0.99	0.01	0	0	0	0
V_r	0	0	0.20	0.80	0	0	0	0
$C_{\bar{r}}$	0	0	0	0	0.97	0.03	0	0
C_r	0	0	0	0	0.20	0.80	0	0
$E_{\bar{r}}$	0	0	0	0	0	0	0.9987	0.0013
E_r	0	0	0	0	0	0	0	0
$R_{\bar{r}}$	0	0	0	0	0	0	1	0
R_r	0	0	0	0	0	0	0	1

Figure 4.5 Matrix of transition probabilities for the retrospective searching model

spect to the verbalized requests. The first row of $(I - Q)^{-1}B$ yields $P(R_{\bar{r}}|V_r)$ and $P(R_r|V_r)$, while the second row yields $P(R_{\bar{r}}|V_{\bar{r}})$ and $P(R_r|V_{\bar{r}})$. The screening probabilities can be applied to $P(R_{\bar{r}}|V_{\bar{r}})$ and $P(R_r|V_{\bar{r}})$ to complete the quantification of performance.

4.6 Estimation of probabilities in the retrospective searching model

Estimation of the conditional probabilities is a simple matter in concept, but there are severe practical difficulties. In the first place, the concept of *relevance* is an elusive one. Verbalized requests prepared by two different users might read identically, yet the users' judgments of the relevance of documents to those requests might be quite different. In this text a plan has been devised which permits one to identify separately the user's inability to verbalize his requirement accurately. The methodology will be presented later. Here, however, we assume that, once the search requirement has been stated, it is appropriate to measure system performance against the stated requirement rather than against some modification of the requirement which was not verbalized by the user.

This approach implies that the user who stated the request cannot judge whether a sample document is relevant to that request because he may unconsciously test against a part of the requirement which is unstated. This point of view may seem revolutionary and not in accord with the objective of designing systems to satisfy users' needs. The point is important, however, and the rule must be adhered to. This is not to say that the user must be left out of the evaluation picture – only that he must be left out *at this point.*

In the estimation of performance probabilities, it is necessary to have one or more samples of documents, and for each of these samples one must be able to categorize each document in the sample as either "relevant to the request" or "not relevant to the request."[4]

We have said that the requester should not make the judgment, but who should? It seems advisable to have a judge (or judges), knowledgeable in the subject matter, make the determination. There is no implication that a judge will make the same determination as the requester, nor should there be. If a committee of judges makes the decision, one can adhere to an arbitrary rule for settling disagreements.

A naive approach to estimation is to take a random sample of documents from the file, to classify them as relevant or nonrelevant with respect to the request, and then to make similar judgments with respect to the other components in the system. The difficulty with this approach, of course, is that it is likely to contain no relevant documents, making further separations of relevant documents impossible.

In addition, one cannot use as a sample of relevant documents those produced by the system under test because of the obvious bias toward documents which the system is capable of producing. One approach, which has been used successfully by Lancaster (*10*), King (*9*), and others, is to ask the requester to list any documents which he knows are relevant to his requirements at the time he is stating his request. These documents have been used as the basis for computing the recall ratio, that ratio being the fraction of the known relevant documents which the system retrieves. They can also be used for the estimation of probabilities required in the model proposed here.

Shumway (*18*) has shown that, if one can assume that the known relevant documents are as likely to be produced by the system as any other relevant documents, then the maximum likelihood estimate of the recall ratio is the fraction of known relevant documents retrieved. Also, an estimate of total relevant documents in the file is given by the total relevant documents retrieved (both previously identified and not previously identified) divided by the estimated recall ratio.

Clearly, one must be able to identify a set of relevant documents which can be used in the test. In the absence of any better method, one can simply ask the user to provide a list of known relevant documents. These, of course, must be screened by an independent judge

[4] Actually, one can insert other classes, such as "marginally relevant," with only slight effect upon the complexity of the required computations.

against the verbalized request and must be considered not relevant unless they pass this test. Otherwise, one may require the system to produce documents against a requirement which has not been fed into the system.

Test performance can be improved if additional resources are put into the identification of relevant documents. However, such identification must be done independently of the system being tested. One approach is to have someone, not on the technical staff of the system, search bibliographies for entries which seem to fit the verbalized requirement. A particularly good source may be references cited in known relevant documents listed by the user. A judge must then screen all items so produced to make sure they match the verbalized request. Those not matching should be discarded.

The sample of nonrelevant documents is easy to obtain. One simply takes a random sample of the file and has it screened against the verbalized request by the judge. Those not matching the request are retained and those matching are added to the sample of known relevant documents. The screening of the random sample provides valuable information which should be retained for future use. When aggregated over a number of searches, the proportion of documents relevant to the verbalized request provides an estimate of the proportion relevant in the average search (to be elaborated further) and hence permits one to state, within limits of statistical error, the average number of relevant documents per request.

Determination of sample sizes will be discussed later, as will the selection of sample search requests and the aggregation of data over searches. With respect to a given search, the estimation procedure can be followed easily from the following example with hypothetical data.

Assume that, independently of the search system, 10 documents which match the verbalized request have been identified. Assume also that 50 nonrelevant documents have been selected. These 60 documents are put in scrambled order and are assigned identifying numbers. Those 10 which are relevant are identified on a master record of the number assignments, but this information is not made available to anyone in the test who is required to make relevance judgments.

We assume that there is an analyst (coder) whose job is to put the request in system language. We have him do so *before seeing the 60 test documents.* We then present the 60 documents to him and ask him to classify them as relevant or nonrelevant *with respect to the verbalized request*, not to the query which he has encoded. Suppose the results are as follows:

Predetermined status	Coder's judgment Not relevant ($C_{\bar{r}}$)	Relevant (C_r)	Total
Relevant (V_r)	2	8	10
Not relevant ($V_{\bar{r}}$)	45	5	50

On the basis of this evidence alone, we conclude:

$$\tilde{P}(C_r|V_r) = 8/10 = 0.8000$$

$$\tilde{P}(C_r|V_{\bar{r}}) = 5/50 = 0.1000$$

Now, the 60 documents are matched against the encoded request by an impartial judge. The encoder should not do this matching because of his previous exposure to the documents and his bias toward matching against what he *thinks* the encoded request says rather than against what it really says. Suppose the results are as follows:

Coder's judgment	Encoded request Not relevant ($E_{\bar{r}}$)	Relevant (E_r)	Total
Relevant (C_r)	4	9	13
Not relevant ($C_{\bar{r}}$)	35	12	47

Then, estimates of conditional probabilities are:

$$\tilde{P}(E_r|C_r) = 9/13 = 0.6923$$

$$\tilde{P}(E_r|C_{\bar{r}}) = 12/47 = 0.2553$$

One effective, but costly, procedure is to have the test documents re-indexed by "experts" at this point. The new indexing is then matched against the encoded request to determine "relevance." Perhaps a sample of the test documents can be re-indexed for this purpose, making it possible to construct a more traditional indexing experiment (e.g., see reference 9). In any case, the difference in classification (relevant or nonrelevant) between matching against the subject matter (this step) and matching against the indexing (next step) should be analyzed to determine cause of failure.

Next, one matches the encoded query against the indexing of the 60 documents exactly as they appear in the file. The distinction between this test and the one above is important. In the above test, we matched the document itself against the encoded query to determine whether each document would have been produced by the research system if it had been indexed perfectly. Note the importance of withholding the "true relevance" status from the judge. Now, we are interested in determining the effect of indexing errors on retrieval, so the match is made against the actual indexing. Assume the following results:

Judgment against encoded request	System judgment		
	Not relevant ($R_{\bar{r}}$)	Relevant (R_r)	Total
Relevant (E_r)	6	15	21
Not relevant ($E_{\bar{r}}$)	23	16	39

Then, estimates of conditional probabilities are:

$$\tilde{P}(R_r|E_r) = 15/21 = 0.7143$$

$$\tilde{P}(R_r|E_{\bar{r}}) = 16/39 = 0.4103$$

At this point another set of test documents comes into the picture. This is the set of documents produced by the system, but not previously contained in the set of predetermined nonrelevant documents. These documents must be screened against the verbalized request by the same person who makes the original determination to set up the samples of relevant and nonrelevant documents. Suppose 25 such documents are produced, of which 2 are determined to be relevant. That is, the total retrieval is 16 + 15 + 2 + 23 = 56 documents, of which 31 are in the test group, and 25 are identified by the retrieval. The new test group consists of 85 documents. They are presented to a screener. Suppose the results are as follows:[5]

[5] A more complete discussion of the estimation of screening effectiveness is presented in Chapter 6.

Status with respect to verbalized request	Screener's judgment		
	Not relevant ($S_{\bar{r}}$)	Relevant (S_r)	Total
Relevant (V_r)	1	11	12
Not relevant ($V_{\bar{r}}$)	60	13	73

Then,

$$\tilde{P}(S_r|V_r) = 11/12 = 0.9167$$

$$\tilde{P}(S_r|V_{\bar{r}}) = 13/73 = 0.1781$$

In aggregating estimates over several searches, one must decide whether to average the conditional probabilities or whether to compute the conditional probabilities from aggregated frequencies. Both procedures have some inherent weaknesses. If one tries to average conditional probabilities estimated from individual searches, he encounters the problem of what to do with zero denominators. The problem is very real, as experienced by Lancaster (*10*). It is, of course, possible to establish arbitrary rules, but even so the variation among estimates tends to be wide.

More stability derives from combining frequencies so that an aggregate numerator is divided by an aggregate denominator. This procedure has the effect of giving more weight to those searches with large numbers of documents relevant to the verbalized request, that is, to more general searches. It answers the question, "What is the probability that if a *document* is relevant to X it will be judged relevant to Y?," while averaging individual probabilities answers the question, "What is the probability that for a *search* a document relevant to X will be judged relevant to Y?" The former relates the probability to the document over all searches, while the latter relates the probability to the document for an "average" search. Both are meaningful concepts to management, but the latter interpretation is probably more natural to the user. He is likely to want to know how well he can expect the system to perform on a given search. This procedure was used by Lancaster (*10*) in obtaining average recall and precision ratios and has much to recommend it for this application. An average of ratios is algebraically biased in that the average ratio times the average denominator will not yield the average numerator. In spite of the weaknesses of the average of ratios, it is recommended for use in estimating probabilities in information retrieval applications.[6] This procedure introduces additional instability into the estimates, but avoids dominance by a few searches with high total retrievals.

A compromise which is strongly recommended when it can be applied is to classify searches by degree of specificity, thus developing one model for specific searches, another for quite general searches, and perhaps a third for searches of intermediate specificity. There is some evidence that users can predict the number of documents which satisfy their requirements. If so, such estimates can be used to categorize the search. Within a search category, the average of aggregated frequencies should be used to estimate probabilities.

4.7 Some sample design problems in the estimation of conditional probabilities

We have already seen that some sampling problems arise in the selection of test documents for a given search. We now consider these problems in more detail, plus the related problems associated with selection of search questions and test personnel. Sample size and the aggregation of observations are inherent in all of these problems.

The traditional approach to sample size determination requires one or the other of the following:

(1) A statement of the precision required (for example, determine recall ratio within 5 percent, with confidence probability 0.95).

(2) A statement of the resources available (for example, $25,000 to do the evaluation).

Given the first specification, one chooses a sample size to yield the required precision at minimum cost; given the second specification, one chooses a sample size to yield the maximum precision for the fixed cost.

In practice, however, sample determination is not that simple. Several estimates are usually required, perhaps on a number of different characteristics. What is optimal for one estimate may be far from optimal for another. Also, variances which form the basis for

[6] A statistical approach to correct methodology is to examine the error of estimation in relation to the true value of the estimated ratio, applying the Markov theorem on weighted least squares to select an averaging device. An extensive discussion is inappropriate here.

optimization are usually unknown and frequently estimable to only very rough approximations.

The design of an evaluation of a retrospective search system is likely to proceed along the following lines:

(1) The evaluation is either proposed or directed to be done.

(2) A tentative budget is proposed.

(3) The budget is allocated over supervisory salaries, consultant fees, data collection, data analysis, and other identifiable costs.

(4) The amount for data collection is translated into terms of number of searches which can be run on the basis of some rough ideas about the number of documents to be looked at, by whom, at the various search stages.

(5) The results of 4, above, are translated roughly into terms of expected precision.

(6) If the expected precision is satisfactory, the planning progresses. If not, compromises are made or the evaluation does not proceed.

Evidently, steps 4 and 5 provide the only opportunity for sample size manipulation, so it is important to examine the principles involved. Let us examine sources of variation in the estimates of probabilities we want to obtain. Some of the principal sources are as follows:

(1) Searches differ from one another.

(2) The test documents for each search differ, with respect to content and indexing.

(3) Judges differ, and the same judge may make different decisions at different times.

(4) Encoders and screeners differ.

Some of these sources of statistical variation (error) are more important than others. Since we want to estimate the probability (relative frequency) with which certain judgments will coincide *for a search drawn at random from the total population of searches*, it is clear that the differences among searches enter into every estimate of statistical error. That is, if we used all documents in the file, and the consensus of all encoders, all judges, and all screeners, there would still be large differences between results from search to search. Searches are the most important source of variation. Therefore, an effective sample design will require a large number of searches. For a fixed cost, this means examining a small number of documents for each search – but how "large" and how "small"? In general, the solution should depend upon the relative variability of documents and searches, and the relative cost of adding another document or adding another search.

However, there are some constraints which simplify the decision-making process. One is that the number of known relevant documents is small in the typical system. If this were not the case, one might assume that no retrospective searching would be done, except possibly for bibliographic purposes. Lancaster (*10*) found in 299 test searches of medical literature that the average number of documents pre-identified as relevant by the user was 6.5. He found the range to extend from 3 to 27 documents, with over 50 percent falling between 3 and 8, inclusive. These documents included known relevant documents as well as documents identified by independent searching. One can assume that the number of documents relevant *to the verbalized request* would be somewhat greater, if any significant amount of independent "hand" searching were done.

Lancaster's average recall over the 299 searches was 57.7 percent, with a standard error (computed by the present authors from his data) of 1.9 percent. These estimates are based upon a simple unweighted average of the ratios. Using the sum of the retrievals over the sum of the bases yields an estimate of 58.9 percent, with a standard error of 2.1 percent. Neither of these results is very encouraging from the standpoint of evaluation cost, since 299 requests covering 1,939 test documents represents a substantial evaluative investment.

King (*9*) found slightly higher variability in estimating recall ratios from data where the average value of the base was 3.2 documents.

The excessive dispersion of the data leads one to suspect that diverse populations are being averaged together. It is possible that one could classify searches in a meaningful way (perhaps by specificity) so as to reduce the variance. Further computation with the Lancaster data indicates that no great gain can be expected from classifying searches according to the number of pre-identified relevant documents, but the procedure might well pay dividends in other applications.

Whether or not diverse populations are being averaged does not necessarily invalidate the recall ratio (as used by Lancaster) or a conditional probability estimate (as suggested here) as measures of system performance. If performance varies widely from search to search, then this variability should be reflected in the evaluation procedures. It may be a fact of life that large samples are required for accurate evaluation of system performance.

In the first steps of the estimation procedure outlined in the previous section, one obtains the relative frequency with which documents will be judged relevant by the coder for the two cases: (1) previously judged relevant to the request and (2) previously judged nonrelevant to the request. One uses the outcome of this judgment to categorize the documents for the second test, and so on. Thus, there is a mixing of the original relevance status in each succeeding step after the first. Since one may assume that for estimation purposes it is no more important to form judgments about nonrelevant documents than about relevant documents, one may as well approximately equalize the initial samples of relevant and nonrelevant documents.

That is, if one has been able to identify seven documents in advance which are relevant to the request, he may as well select a sample of nonrelevant documents of about the same size. He should not exactly equalize the sample sizes in every case, because doing so would provide the judge with information which could influence his choices. It is better to introduce some variation in sample sizes, so that on the average the two classes of sample documents contain approximately the same numbers.

The standard deviation (see Chapter 11) per search from the Lancaster data appears to be about 0.33, the average number of documents per search is about 6.5, and the recall ratio is about 0.58. The King data show a standard deviation of 0.43 on 3.25 documents per search, with a recall ratio of 0.59. Using the Lancaster data, the coefficient of variation is 0.33/0.58 = 0.57. This figure, along with the reliability specifications, can be used as entries in Table 12.1 in order to determine sample size. For example, if one wishes to determine a conditional probability within 5 percent of its "true" value with 90 percent confidence, he will need approximately 365 searches[7] of the kind conducted by Lancaster. Since the average number of documents in Lancaster's searches was 6.5, and we want to make estimates for both relevant and nonrelevant documents, we would require an average of 13 documents per search, or 13 × 365 = 4,745 documents altogether.

The Lancaster data show that the standard deviation decreases by 0.01 for each additional document in the base in the neighborhood of

[7]By linear interpolation in Table 12.1.

6.5 documents. There is danger, of course, in extrapolating this effect beyond, say, 20 documents.

Sample size requirements seem discouragingly high, but there is substantial evidence that they are realistic for the kind of study undertaken by Lancaster. There is a possibility, however, that variances (and hence sample sizes) can be smaller for the kind of estimation recommended here. The difference is that Lancaster's judgment of relevance was supplied by the user, so that the user's inability to verbalize his requirement exactly, for whatever reason, would introduce greater variability in the responses. Here, however, we are judging relevance to a verbalized request, thus eliminating peculiar user requirements. Under these conditions we should expect less variation in the relative frequencies from which the probability estimates are derived. Since sampling in document retrieval systems takes place over time, data can be generated on the basis of a rough estimate of required sample size, with the final determination of sample size left open until a substantial body of data has been collected. Thus, one can take advantage of the smaller variations which may be encountered in systems with greater stability than those investigated here. For planning purposes, the results derived here may be satisfactory.

Another major problem in the design of a retrospective searching evaluation is the selection of searches (or verbalized requests). There is no entirely satisfactory substitute for real searches generated by real users in the normal course of their work. A systematic sample of such searches from the stream of incoming requests should be used if possible. The evaluation procedure is such that one should be able to augment the normal staff by a judge, or judges, and not slow down service to users by the evaluation process. Also, if records are available, a sample can be drawn from searches already completed.

Let us review again the procedures required in the evaluation.

Figure 4.6 shows the steps in searching, without special attention to evaluation, along the left-hand margin and the procedures required for evaluation in the middle of the page. At the right-hand margin are spaces for recording the estimated man-hours per search for various classes of evaluation personnel.

If evaluation is to be done concurrently with normal searching activity, then the following conditions must be met:

(1) The test set (step T_1) must be obtained quickly, so that step T_4 can be accomplished in time to merge outputs from normal searching and the test searching (T_5) and so that all output can be screened

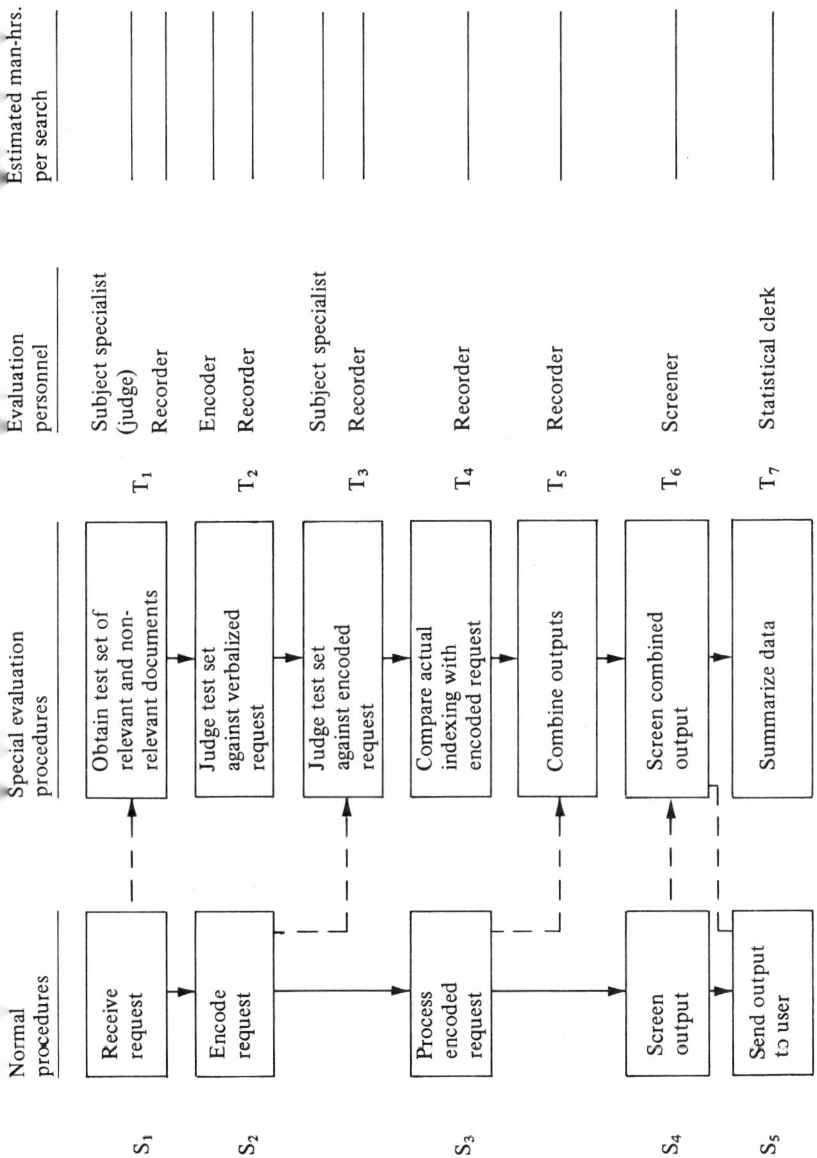

Figure 4.6 Planning diagram for retrospective search experiment.

(T_6) and submitted to the user. Some of the additional resources required in T_1 might well be charged against operations rather than against evaluation, since the output will be improved to the extent that additional relevant documents will be located. If it is impossible to devote time to independent searching in T_1, then one must use only that set of documents pre-identified by the user (after screening for relevance to the verbalized request).

(2) The encoder must have enough time available to judge test sets against the verbalized request. This activity need not be done in sequence, however, so the work may be done on a "time available" basis.

(3) The screener must have enough time available to screen the extra output which is created by processing the test set. Typically, this will be a small increment of output because of the (hopefully) heavy overlap in relevant documents between the test set and the normal system output.

(4) The combined output must be judged by the person making the judgment in step T_1. Since the documents in the test set have already been judged, only the incremental output of the system need be judged. Again, this need not be done in sequence, but should be done while the judge's acquaintance with the verbalized request is fresh in his mind.

(5) The judgments in T_1 and T_3 are best done by different persons to avoid carryover bias due to previous acquaintance with the documents.

Note that only two of the regular technical staff members of the search system need to become involved – the encoder and the screener. Two subject specialists on the evaluation staff are required and the rest of the data collection is of a clerical nature.

Within each organization being evaluated, one must determine whether the additional evaluation work can be done "on-line" as requests are processed, or whether a separate evaluation study must be done with an entirely separate staff. The latter approach is not recommended if there is an alternative, because one is then evaluating a simulation of the system rather than the system itself. The weakness reveals itself in (1) simulation of real requests, (2) simulation of the encoder's behavior, and (3) simulation of the screener's behavior. The literature contains many discussions of the problems of simulating system behavior and little more can be contributed here. If it *must* be done, then conclusions must be qualified accordingly.

Ideally, one would like to draw a random sample of judges, a random sample of encoders, and a random sample of screeners. In practice, one generally is seriously limited by the availability of such persons – one must get along with those that are available. When there is more than one person available for each task, however, the searches should be assigned at random to those technicians who are available. This procedure increases the generalizability of the conclusions, but, at best, one must qualify generalizations to the limitations of the sampling process.

4.8 Estimates of sampling error in retrospective search evaluation

Earlier, it was shown that variation from search to search may be expected to be high. Just how high is a function of the particular system under evaluation and the environment within which it operates.

There are two distinct, but related, problems in the estimation of sampling error. First, the estimates of conditional probabilities will vary from search to search. There are eight such conditional probabilities (see Figure 4.2). The variance of each of these can be computed by the standard formula:

$$s^2 = \frac{\Sigma(z_i - \bar{z})^2}{n - 1}$$

where

z_i = the ratio found in the ith search,
$\bar{z}$ = the average over all searches, and
n = number of searches investigated.

The standard deviation is the square root of the variance and the standard error is:

$$s_{\bar{z}} = \sqrt{s^2 | n}$$

Estimation of the effect of errors in estimating the probabilities on the overall estimates of system performance is a more difficult problem. Two quantities are of primary interest. They are:

(1) Probability that a document, relevant to the verbalized request, will be retrieved, $P(R_r | V_r)$.

(2) Probability that a document, not relevant to the verbalized request, will be retrieved, $P(R_r | V_{\bar{r}})$.

An approximation to the variance of $P(R_r | V_r)$ is as follows:

$$\text{var}\,\tilde{P}(R_r|V_r) = [\tilde{P}(R_r|E_r) - \tilde{P}(R_r|E_{\bar{r}})]^2\ [\tilde{P}(E_r|C_{\bar{r}})^2\ \text{var}\,\tilde{P}(C_r|V_r)$$
$$+ \tilde{P}(E_r|C_r)^2\ \text{var}\,\tilde{P}(C_r|V_r) + \tilde{P}(C_r|V_r)^2\ \text{var}\,\tilde{P}(E_r|C_r)$$
$$+ \tilde{P}(C_{\bar{r}}|V_r)^2\ \text{var}\,\tilde{P}(E_r|C_{\bar{r}})] + [\tilde{P}(C_r|V_r)\,\tilde{P}(E_r|C_r) = \tilde{P}(C_{\bar{r}}|V_r)$$
$$\tilde{P}(E_r|C_{\bar{r}})]^2\ \text{var}\,\tilde{P}(R_r|E_r) + [1 - \tilde{P}(C_r|V_r)\,\tilde{P}(E_r|C_r) - \tilde{P}(C_{\bar{r}}|V_r)$$
$$\tilde{P}(E_r|C_{\bar{r}})]^2\ \text{var}\,\tilde{P}(R_r|E_{\bar{r}})$$

where each of the variances on the right-hand side of the equality sign is the square of the standard error, as defined above. The standard error of $\tilde{P}(R_r | V_r)$ is then the square root of var $\tilde{P}(R_r | V_r)$.

The expression appears frightening because of the complex notation, but actually it is easy to compute. The notation can be simplified by using the numerical identifiers given earlier; for example, $\tilde{P}_4 = \tilde{P}(C_r | V_{\bar{r}})$. Then,

$$\text{var}\,\tilde{P}(R_r|V_r) = (\tilde{P}_{10} - \tilde{P}_{12})^2\ [(\tilde{P}_6^{\,2} + \tilde{P}_8^{\,2})\ \text{var}\,\tilde{P}_2 + \tilde{P}_2^{\,2}\ \text{var}\,\tilde{P}_6$$
$$+ \tilde{P}_1^{\,2}\ \text{var}\,\tilde{P}_8] + (\tilde{P}_2\tilde{P}_6 + \tilde{P}_1\tilde{P}_8)^2\ \text{var}\,\tilde{P}_{10}(1 - \tilde{P}_2\tilde{P}_6 - \tilde{P}_1\tilde{P}_8)^2$$
$$\text{var}\,\tilde{P}_{12}$$

The variance of the other estimate of primary interest can be written:

$$\text{var}\,\tilde{P}(R_r|V_{\bar{r}}) = (\tilde{P}_{10} - \tilde{P}_{12})^2\ [(\tilde{P}_6^{\,2} + \tilde{P}_8^{\,2})\ \text{var}\,\tilde{P}_4 + \tilde{P}_4^{\,2}\ \text{var}\,\tilde{P}_6$$
$$+ \tilde{P}_3^{\,2}\ \text{var}\,\tilde{P}_8] + (\tilde{P}_4\tilde{P}_6 + \tilde{P}_3\tilde{P}_8)^2\ \text{var}\,\tilde{P}_{10} + (1 - \tilde{P}_4\tilde{P}_6 - \tilde{P}_3\tilde{P}_8)$$
$$\text{var}\,\tilde{P}_{12}$$

If one of the stages is not in the system, the variances applying to that component are zero, and the conditional probabilities are replaced by zeros and ones. For example, suppose one omits the comparison of the coder's interpretation with predetermined relevance status. Then,

$\widetilde{P}_1 = 0,\ \widetilde{P}_2 = 1,\ \widetilde{P}_3 = 1,\ \widetilde{P}_r = 0$ and $\operatorname{var}\widetilde{P}_2 = \operatorname{var}\widetilde{P}_4 = 0.$

$$\operatorname{var}\widetilde{P}(R_r|V_r) = (\widetilde{P}_{10} - \widetilde{P}_{12})^2 \operatorname{var}\widetilde{P}_6 + \widetilde{P}_6{}^2 \operatorname{var}\widetilde{P}_{10} + (1 - \widetilde{P}_6) \operatorname{var}\widetilde{P}_{12}$$

$$\operatorname{var}\widetilde{P}(R_r|V_{\bar{r}}) = (\widetilde{P}_{10} - \widetilde{P}_{12})^2 \operatorname{var}\widetilde{P}_8 + \widetilde{P}_8{}^2 \operatorname{var}\widetilde{P}_{10} + (1 - \widetilde{P}_6) \operatorname{var}\widetilde{P}_{12}$$

4.9 Notes on extensions to nondichotomous cases

In the model presented in the preceding sections, we have assumed that judgments could always be made dichotomously. In some ways this corresponds to reality. For example, the user must eventually decide whether or not to cite a reference. There are instances, however, in which the "use" of a document is not so clear-cut. A document may be useful as background material even though it is not used directly. Therefore, some evaluators prefer three categories of relevance which, although the exact language varies, convey the meanings of "highly relevant," "moderately relevant," and "nonrelevant."

The general model presented in matrix form in Section 4.3 will accommodate any number of relevance categories in any of the judgments. In practice, however, there are some real limitations based upon sample sizes. That is, with three relevance classes one needs 50 percent more observations than with two categories in order to obtain essentially the same degree of precision.

If one is restricted to hand calculation, the computations become somewhat more tedious. For example, if there are three categories of relevance with respect to the verbalized request denoted by V_r, V_m, $V_{\bar{r}}$ ("m" stands for "moderate" relevance) and two categories of coder interpretation, then one can write:

$$P(E_r|V_r) = P(E_r|C_r)\,P(C_r|V_r) + P(E_r|C_m)\,P(C_m|V_r) + P(E_r|C_{\bar{r}})\,P(C_{\bar{r}}|V_r)$$

$$P(E_r|V_m) = P(E_r|C_r)\,P(C_r|V_m) + P(E_r|C_m)\,P(C_m|V_m) + P(E_r|C_{\bar{r}})\,P(C_{\bar{r}}|V_m)$$

$$P(E_r|V_{\bar{r}}) = P(E_r|C_r)\,P(C_r|V_{\bar{r}}) + P(E_r|C_m)\,P(C_m|V_{\bar{r}}) + P(E_r|C_{\bar{r}})\,P(C_{\bar{r}}|V_{\bar{r}})$$

One simply uses the standard rules for multiplication and addition of conditional probabilities to make the extensions to any number of classes.

It is recommended that, if one is considering many classes, he make the small investment of time necessary to apply the matrix processes described earlier in this chapter.

Often, the output of the mechanized part of the system is not a listing of presumably relevant documents, but an ordered listing of what is presumed to be the 50 (or 100, or 200) "most relevant" documents. The order of listing is from most relevant to least relevant, and a "relevance score" is attached to each item in the listing. Under these circumstances, one can select a cutoff point, designating all documents with higher relevance scores as "relevant" and all others as "nonrelevant." The evaluation can then proceed as above. The value selected for the cutoff can affect one's assessment of the effectiveness of the system, of course, but for diagnostic purposes this procedure may be adequate.

We now consider the case in which one of the judgments represents a continuous variable (or at least has a great many classes) and the other has a few classes. As an illustration, suppose we wish to compare the relevance score assigned by the system (R) against the initial judgment of highly relevant (V_r), moderately relevant (V_m), and not relevant ($V_{\bar{r}}$). One could construct a scatter diagram similar to that shown in Figure 4.7.

By aggregating over many searches, one can obtain a frequency distribution of R for each of the classes $V_{\bar{r}}$, V_m, and V_r. Then selecting any cutoff R_o, and using relative frequencies as an estimate of probabilities, it is easy to arrive at the values:

$$\tilde{P}(R > R_o | V_{\bar{r}}),\ \tilde{P}(R > R_o | V_m) \text{ and } \tilde{P}(R > R_o | V_r)$$

Similar probabilities can be computed for the classes of encoder's judgment, that is, $\tilde{P}(R > R_o | E_{\bar{r}})$ and $\tilde{P}(R > R_o | E_r)$. The number of classes against which to compare is arbitrary, and, of course, one could as easily estimate $P(R_1 < R < R_o | V_r)$. The procedure is quite general.

By varying the cutoff score, R_o, one can easily show how well the system will perform in identifying the documents in the various classes of relevance with regard to the verbalized request. That is, from Figure 4.7 it may be seen that raising R_o will yield fewer nonrelevant documents, but also fewer moderately relevant and relevant documents. Lowering R_o will produce the reverse effect.

A special case arises in matching the file against a request which calls for documents containing term A, *and* term B, *and* term C, and so on. Frequently, such requests are placed in a way which permits one to determine the documents which match all of the terms, all but

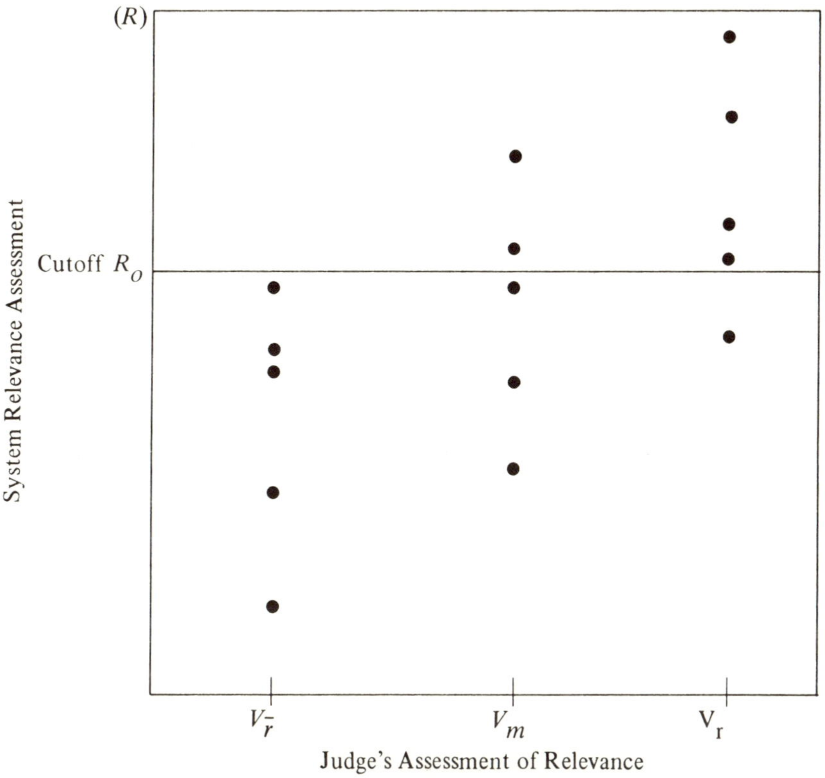

Figure 4.7 System relevance assessment plotted against judge's assessment of relevance to the verbalized request, hypothetical data.

one, all but two, and so on. This procedure has the effect of assigning a system relevance score to every document in the file, the score being the number of terms matched. One can also work out more complex score-assignment plans. In particular, normalization to account for number of terms in the request is frequently done. In any case, such system outputs can be handled by the procedures outlined above.

4.10 Summary measures of effectiveness in retrospective searching

So far, we have discussed evaluation of the retrospective searching system from the time the user submits his request until documents (or identifications or surrogates) are returned to him. The procedures outlined above evaluate the system in terms of its response to the verbalized request. They do not fault the system if the verbalized request fails to convey the user's real requirement. The primary reason for this viewpoint is that diagnosis of the search system is difficult, if not impossible, if one confounds (in the statistical sense) the defects of the system and the sins of the user.

It is obvious, however, that the primary objective of the system is to serve the needs of the user, and evaluation of effectiveness is incomplete until the user's judgment has been imposed on the output. Let U_r and $U_{\bar{r}}$ denote relevance and nonrelevance to the user, respectively; then, for a system with screening, we are interested in $P(S_r, R_r | U_r)$, $P(S_r, R_r | U_{\bar{r}})$ and $P(R_{\bar{r}} | U_r)$. Without screening, one is interested in $P(R_r | U_r)$ and $P(R_r | U_{\bar{r}})$. These are summary measures, with little diagnostic importance, since they do not show the source of any failures.

To introduce diagnostics, one may set up the following 2 X 2 table:

Relevance to user	Relevance to verbalized request	
	$V_{\bar{r}}$	V_r
U_r	$P(U_r \| V_{\bar{r}})$	$P(U_r \| V_r)$
$U_{\bar{r}}$	$P(U_{\bar{r}} \| V_{\bar{r}})$	$P(U_{\bar{r}} \| V_r)$

The documents used in estimation of the above probabilities can be the same set of documents previously selected in terms of relevance or nonrelevance to the verbalized request. Departure of the estimated probabilities from zeros and ones indicates failure of the user to convey his requirements. Evaluative studies conducted in the past have revealed this failure to be an important source of error.

4.11 Overall measures

Many attempts have been made to arrive at a single "measure of merit" for retrospective searching systems, but no one has yet developed a universally acceptable measure. It is likely that no such measure exists. We do not require such a measure for the evaluation of an automobile, for example, so why must we require one for a system whose costs, benefits, and performance are less tangible?

At least since 1956 (*14*), principal attention has been centered on two measures which have come to be known as measures of recall and precision. Earlier it was shown how these measures are related to the conditional probabilities proposed here. It seems safe to assume that these measures have become well enough established that they will be used for a long time to come. Therefore, it is recommended that they be computed and reported in evaluative studies.

Measures of recall and precision, or modifications such as proposed by Salton (*16*), have become particularly important in judging the comparative effectiveness of systems where controlled changes have been imposed experimentally. One of the most useful adaptations of this technique is to vary the cutoff point along the relevance score, in systems which provide such scores, thus achieving a set of points which trace a curve on the precision-recall graph. A schematic is shown in Chapter 2. The same kind of curve can be obtained by varying the number of search terms used in a coordinate-indexed system or the level of specificity of the terms used. Hence, the technique is quite valuable for diagnostic purposes.

References

1. Bivona, W. A., *Selective Dissemination of Information. Vol 1: Pilot Test at U. S. Army Natick Laboratories.* Final Report. Reading, Mass., Dynamics Corp., May 14, 1967. AD 654 997.
2. Cleverdon, C. W., *The Critical Appraisal of Information Retrieval Systems.* Cranfield, Bedford, England, The College of Aeronautics, September 1968. (Paper prepared for the International Congress of FID, Moscow.)
3. Cornell University, Department of Computer Science, *Reports on Analysis, Search and Iterative Retrieval.* Scientific Report No. ISR-14 to the National Science Foundation. Ithaca, N. Y., October 1968.
4. Cornell University, Department of Computer Science, *Reports on Evaluation Procedures and Results 1965-1967.* Scientific Report No. ISR-13. Ithaca, N. Y., December 1967.
5. Dym, E. D., "Relevance Predictability. I: Investigation Background and Procedures." *In*: Kent, A., Taulbee, O. E., Belzer, J., Goldstein, G. D., eds. *Electronic Handling of Information: Testing and Evaluation.* Washington, D. C., John I. Thompson & Co.; London, Academic Press, 1967, pp. 175-185.
6. Jordan, J. R., "A Framework for Comparing SDI (Selective Dissemination of Information) Systems." *American Documentation*, Vol. 19, No. 3 (July 1968), pp. 221-222.

7. Kemeny, J. G., Snell, J., *Finite Markov Chains*. Princeton, N. J., D. Van Nostrand Company, Inc., 1960.
8. Kent, A., Belzer, J., Kurfeerst, M., Dym, E. D., Shirey, D. L., Bose, A., "Relevance Predictability in Information Retrieval Systems." *Methods of Information in Medicine (Methodik der Information in der Medizin)*, Vol. 6, No. 2, (April 1967), pp. 45-51.
9. King, D. W., *Evaluation During File Development of the Glass Technology Coordinate Index File.* Bethesda, Md., Westat Research, Inc., November 1967.
10. Lancaster, F. W., *Evaluation of the MEDLARS Demand Search Service.* Bethesda, Md., National Library of Medicine, January 1968.
11. Lancaster, F. W., *Information Retrieval Systems: Characteristics, Testing, and Evaluation.* New York, Wiley & Sons, 1968.
12. Lancaster, F. W., "Interaction Between Requesters and a Large Mechanized Retrieval System." *Information Storage and Retrieval*, Vol. 4, No. 2 (June 1968), pp. 239-252.
13. O'Connor, J., "Relevance Disagreements and Unclear Request Forms." *American Documentation*, Vol. 18, No. 3 (July 1967), pp. 165-177.
14. Perry, J. W., Kent, A., Berry, M. M., *Machine Literature Searching*. New York, Interscience Publishers, 1956.
15. St. Laurent, M. C., *A Review of the Literature of Indexer Consistency*. M. A. Thesis. University of Chicago, Graduate Library School, February 1967. (Studies of indexing depth and retrieval effectiveness.) Grant NSF-GN-380.
16. Salton, G., "A Comparison Between Manual and Automatic Indexing Methods," *American Documentation*, Vol. 20, No. 1 (January 1969), pp. 61-71.
17. Shirey, D. L., Kurfeerst, M., "Relevance Predictability. II: Data Reduction." *In*: Kent, A., Taulbee, O. E., Belzer, J., Goldstein, G. D., eds. *Electronic Handling of Information: Testing and Evaluation.* Washington, D. C., John I. Thompson & Co.; London, Academic Press, 1967, pp. 187-198.
18. Shumway, R. H., "Some Estimation Problems Associated with Evaluating Information Retrieval Systems." *In: Evaluation of Document Retrieval Systems: Literature Perspective, Measurement, Technical Papers,* Chapter 3.1. Bethesda, Md., Westat Research, Inc., December 31, 1968.
19. Wolfe, M. A., Herner, S., Herner, M., "SDI System for the U.S. Public Health Service, Office of Pesticides." *Journal of Chemical Documentation,* Vol. 7, No. 3 (August 1967), pp. 138-141.

Chapter Five
Evaluation of Indexing Processes and Indexing Language

5.1 Introduction

The literature of document retrieval contains many papers on evaluation of the quality of indexing. We have seen how one can obtain measures of the effect of indexing errors on retrieval by replacing $P(R_r|E_r)$ by 1.0 and $P(R_r|E_{\bar{r}})$ by 0 in the model presented in Chapter 4. This approach to evaluation has the advantage of not faulting the system for indexing errors which do not affect the retrieval. It is too gross, however, to reveal the sources of indexing error so that corrective procedures can be instituted. For this latter purpose, a specially designed indexing experiment can be very useful.

We consider first the case in which indexing is done by hand, that is, by humans as a result of cogitation. Our objective is to find out how well this activity is performed.

The first difficulty we encounter is that of defining what the indexer is expected to achieve. The *result* of his indexing is a set of tags assigned to the document for identification purposes. Presumably, they indicate what the document is about. Obviously, indexers will disagree concerning the assignment of index tags. When they do disagree, who is "right"? In some cases one can say with certainty whether a document does or does not contain an indexable feature; for example, a specific compound in a chemical document. In general, however, there is room for argument, so the definition of what tags "should" be assigned is difficult if not impossible. Perhaps the best one can do in such cases is to define as correct the judgment of a senior indexer who is familiar with the system, its objectives and users, and who has had an opportunity to consider the alternative viewpoints. This is equivalent to settlement by fiat, and does not face the problem of what to do when two judges differ, but it is a procedure which has been useful in practice.

One point of view is that the evaluator is less interested in accuracy of indexing than he is in consistency. The argument is that, if indexers are consistent in the assignment of tags, the user can learn to accommodate his search processes to indexing faults. This argument fails in the limit, of course, because assignment of no tags to any document would certainly be consistent, but not very useful to the user. Certainly, some minimum (but undefinable) level of accuracy is assumed.

In any case, most indexing studies are concerned with measuring either accuracy or consistency. We will discuss ways of arriving at estimates of each.

5.2 Selection of test procedures

Sometimes the purpose of an indexing study is simply to determine how accurate (or consistent) the current practice is. More often, however, one wishes to test new procedures designed to reduce costs, to increase effectiveness, or both. Some such possible procedures are to restrict indexing time per document, to index words in titles or first and last paragraphs only, to merge independent indexing by two indexers, to give indexers additional training, and to extend or restrict the number of terms selected. It should be noted, however, that if the basic structure of the term list is changed, such as by introduction of hierarchies, or introduction of links and roles, much more than an indexing experiment is required. Such an experiment will be required to test accuracy of indexing under the proposed change and to determine costs, but the effect of such a drastic change on the entire system must be estimated by doing experimental or pilot studies involving every component.

One should make every effort to narrow attention to a few test procedures prior to beginning the experimentation. About 20 years of experience with "nonconventional" indexing has filled the literature with case data, so that it should be possible for the systems designer to narrow his interest with reasonable confidence. The learning by indexers which is necessary before testing new procedures is time-consuming and expensive. It should not be undertaken lightly, particularly if normal workloads are demanding.

5.3 Selection of indexers

The statistical analyst would be happy if he could draw a random sample of indexers from a large population of possible indexers and then assign them randomly to the different indexing procedures. But in practice he will rarely have more than a half dozen to draw from. About all he can ask is that his experimental indexers be, in the view of system management, reasonably typical of the potential supply of available indexers.

While it is possible to design experiments to reveal the effect of differing levels of experience and education (see Chapter 13), to do so is frequently a hollow exercise because of the constraints on availability. One must make every effort to design the experimental situation to be as nearly like the real world of indexing as possible.

Once the experimental indexers are selected, they must be trained in any new procedures. This investment of their time is absolutely necessary, but is frequently overlooked. It is well known that the novelty of an experimental procedure will cause a participant to behave differently than he would under normal conditions. One approach is to instruct the indexers in the new procedures and then have them index documents for a period of time. One can record such data as number of index terms selected, time required to index, and number of questions asked of supervisors. When these statistics stabilize, one can assume that stability has been reached on the learning curve and may then proceed with the experiment. The participants should not know, however, when the training period stops and the experimental period begins.

5.4 Selection of documents

In the typical document transfer system, there is a stream of documents coming into the system and being indexed in the normal course of operation. This is the stream to be sampled for measurement of the accuracy of current indexing procedures and for comparison against experimental changes. Even a well-established system is likely to change over time, so it is desirable to select the test sample from those documents indexed recently. A satisfactory procedure for most purposes is to take a systematic sample of every k^{th} acquisition number during the most recent year, or 6-month period.

For consistency tests, one need only feed these documents back into the system as a part of the normal workload. One need not even make certain that they are indexed the second time by a different indexer, although identification of who did the indexing each time is important. It is assumed that adequate records are kept to make this determination possible. Separation of the documents into two sets, the first representing repeated indexing by the same indexer and the second, indexing by two indexers, will provide useful information on how consistency within indexers compares to consistency between indexers.

If additional procedures are to be tested, the test set of documents should be indexed by each of the test procedures; added precision is gained thereby. The only case in which this cannot be done is that in which the number of available indexers is so limited that each one must index by more than one procedure. In this case a fresh set of documents must be presented to the indexer for each procedure tested. Thus, if n documents are required for each test and k tests are to be conducted, a total of nk test documents must be selected from the file.

If one is attempting to obtain a measure of indexing error by comparing with the indexing of an expert, it is good practice to have the expert first index the documents independently and then to compare with the indexing under test. It has been found that errors of omission of terms occur even among experts; this procedure therefore helps to reduce such error.

5.5 Experimental design

Chapter 13 presents some principles of experimental design, and should be read as a prelude to designing an indexing experiment. The strong argument for simplicity in design is that one can more easily generalize the results to the real world. On the other hand, if one wishes to isolate the effects of training, experience, subject matter, language in which written, and so on, he must consider these effects as experimental factors which must be designed into the experiment. Thus, some kind of factorial arrangement will be required.

That such arrangements can limit one's ability to generalize can be demonstrated as follows. Suppose one-half of the indexers have high school diplomas and one-half have college degrees, and that each of these groups is divided into inexperienced and experienced categories. Averages can then be obtained for each of the four cells in the following array:

Indexing experience level	Education: High school	Education: College
Inexperienced	________	______
Experienced	________	______

The overall average can only be used as a generalization if one is referring to a system in which one-fourth of the indexers are inexperienced high school graduates, one-fourth are inexperienced college graduates, one-fourth are experienced high school graduates, and one-fourth are experienced college graduates – an unlikely combination of personnel. Generalization to the real world can only be made from the four cell means, weighting them by the proportions of those categories expected in the real world – a requirement which is frequently overlooked.

On the other hand, a random selection of indexers from those available in the system permits easy generalization to expected performance, but prevents one from drawing diagnostic conclusions about the effects of education, experience, and other influencing factors.

The proper course to take depends upon the objectives to be achieved.

5.6 Analysis of results

One generally will accumulate data on time required to index and perhaps other management-type data. Such data can easily be reduced to averages and the indexing methods can be compared on this basis. Standard errors (see Chapter 10) can also be reported to indicate one's confidence in the averages reported.

Our main concern here is in analyzing statistics which reflect the assignment of index tags. If the experiment is of substantial size, the reduction of experimental data to machinable form is a necessity. If the term list is short, say, no more than 200, one can identify each column of an 80-column punch card with a given index term, punching a zero if the term is not indexed in the given document and a one if it is. Three cards will then accommodate up to about 200 terms, plus identifying information.

Even with as few as a hundred or so terms, punching data in this manner is tedious. A much easier process is to punch the identifying numbers of index terms selected on a card or cards and to write a machine program for processing the data. If the operating system provides for machine entry of indexing, generally the identical format can be used to enter experimental indexings. In the analysis which follows, it has been assumed that machine processing of the entire data base as well as the test set is possible.

First the test set should be tabulated and its indexing should be compared with that of the entire data base. This can easily be done by reporting for each term (tag) its frequency of indexing in the file and in the test set as follows:

	Percent of documents assigned tag	
Tag identifier	In the file	In the data base
(1)	(2)	(3)

Any glaring departures from representativeness should thus be displayed. If the file has been changing rapidly, then one should compare with only the recent acquisitions.

Assume now that it is possible to determine correct indexing. One can then prepare the following table for each test procedure:

	Number of times assigned				Number of times not assigned when it should have been	
	Correctly		When it should not have been			
Tag identifier	No.	%	No.	%	No.	%
(1)	(2)	(3)	(4)	(5)	(6)	(7)

Column (5) provides an estimate of the probability of overindexing and Column (7) an estimate of the probability of underindexing. In practice, the latter error has been found to be more prevalent than the former. Underindexing leads to missed documents and overindexing to false retrievals, provided those terms are used in searching.

If coordinate searches are used, one can estimate roughly the effect of underindexing on retrieval as follows: Let $\widetilde{P}_i$ be the relative frequency with which term i is indexed when it should be, i.e., Column (3) divided by 100. Let N be the number of documents in the file which should be tagged with the given combination of index terms specified in a search. That is, if terms denoted by the numbers 17, 84, and 92 are coordinated in a search, then N is the number of documents which should have that combination, and thus be retrieved in a search. The expected retrieval, however, is $N\pi P_i$ where π stands for "the product of." For example, if $P_{17} = 0.6, P_{84} = 0.85, P_{92} = 0.80$, and 25 documents in the file should have been tagged with terms 17, 84, and 92, one would expect on the average to retrieve $25 \times 0.6 \times 0.85 \times 0.80 = 10.2$ of them. This formulation assumes independence of indexing errors and hence is an approximation to reality. However, it has been found to be a reasonably good approximation in some applications (*6*). A more detailed model and example of its use in predicting the effect of indexing on search results are given in Section 5.8.

A tabulation of terms used in searching from the historical records of the system, when compared against indexing errors, will give some indication of how important indexing deficiencies are. These indications can be checked against the results of the analysis presented in Chapter 4. The term-by-term comparison might appear as follows:

	Relative frequencies			
Tag identifier	Correct assignment	Under-assignment	Over-assignment	Number of searches in which used
(1)	(2)	(3)	(4)	(5)

Aggregate measures of indexing errors are provided by relative frequencies computed from aggregates over all terms. If the indexing structure is hierarchical, as is frequently the case, then an analysis as outlined above for each level of hierarchy is quite useful. It will also show to what extent searchers use the various hierarchies. The results of the indexing experiment should be given to searchers to help them in the choice of search terms.

If the objective of the indexing experiment is to measure consistency, then the independent indexing of the test set in the normal manner is compared with the test indexing. The following summary table will provide the information necessary to make administrative decisions:

	Number of times assigned		
Tag identified	By one indexer	By two indexers	By neither
(1)	(2)	(3)	(4)

5.7 Relationship between consistency and accuracy

Since consistency of indexing is easier to measure than accuracy, one may wish to set up consistency tests as a means of controlling the effectiveness of the indexing task. In theory, one could have consistent but highly inaccurate indexing, but in practice consistency and accuracy tend to be highly correlated. Cooper (*4*), however, feels that consistency should not be used as a measure for indexing effectiveness.

Consistency (or inconsistency) can be measured in several ways. Consider the following 2 × 2 table which summarizes for a given term the number of times it was assigned by neither, both, or only one of two independent indexers in a sample of N documents:

	Second indexer		
First indexer	Not assigned	Assigned	Totals
Not assigned	N_{00}	N_{01}	$N_{0.}$
Assigned	N_{10}	N_{11}	$N_{1.}$
Totals	$N_{.0}$	$N_{.1}$	$N_{..}$

A common measure of consistency is:

$$C = N_{11}/(N_{11} + N_{01} + N_{10}) \qquad (1)$$

If, in the above 2 × 2 table, we replace the second indexer by a judge whose indexing is presumed to be correct by fiat, we have:

	Correct indexing		
Indexer	Not assigned	Assigned	Totals
Not assigned	M_{00}	M_{01}	$M_{0.}$
Assigned	M_{10}	M_{11}	$M_{1.}$
Totals	$M_{.0}$	$M_{.1}$	$M_{..}$

This table can be described in terms of conditional probabilities as follows:

	Correct indexing	
Indexer	Not assigned	Assigned
Not assigned	P_0	P_1
Assigned	P_2	P_3
Total	$P_0 + P_2 = 1$	$P_1 + P_3 = 1$

Then, a measure of indexing accuracy which has been found useful is:

$$P_3 = M_{11} | M_{.1} \qquad (2)$$

This relative frequency, under certain definitions and assumptions about the population being sampled, can be identified with an estimate of the conditional probability that the index term will be chosen, given that it should be chosen. This is p as defined in the previous section. If one can assume that most indexing errors are errors of omission, then he would expect to find a strong correlation between $(P_3)^2$ and C as defined in equations (1) and (2).

This has been found to be the case in practice. For example, an indexing study in the Organometallics File of the U.S. Patent Office (2) showed that for 201 sample documents with the two measures matched for a sample of one-third of the terms, the correlation between $(P_3)^2$ and C was 0.95. In this case, it was possible to estimate $(P_3)^2$ by the equation:

$$(P_3)^2 = 1 + 1.02(C - 1) \tag{3}$$

If one assumes that P_3 is equal for two indexers and that $M_{1\,0} \mid M_{.0}$ is negligible, he can estimate P_3 from C by using

$$P_3 = \frac{2C}{1 + C} \tag{4}$$

Examples of the relationships between accuracy and consistency are given in Table 5.1 for 45 terms found in the U.S. Patent Office indexing experiment. The table demonstrates that the two measures are highly correlated.

It is easy to estimate relationships between accuracy and con-

Table 5.1 Comparison of Measures of Accuracy (P_3) and Consistency (C), 45 Terms, 201 Documents, and 2 Analysts, Organometallics File, U.S. Patent Office

Term	Number of documents	$(P_3)^2$	C	$\frac{2C}{1+C}$	P_3
1	13	1.00	0.88	0.94	1.00
2	55	0.68	0.71	0.83	0.83
3	49	0.60	0.60	0.75	0.78
4	30	0.61	0.72	0.84	0.78
5	10	0.49	0.40	0.57	0.70
6	58	0.79	0.76	0.86	0.89
7	41	0.59	0.54	0.70	0.77
8	59	0.79	0.79	0.88	0.89
9	59	0.65	0.68	0.81	0.80
10	87	0.68	0.75	0.86	0.82
11	27	0.37	0.32	0.48	0.61
12	51	0.77	0.80	0.89	0.88
13	124	0.90	0.88	0.94	0.95
14	49	0.77	0.72	0.84	0.88
15	95	0.79	0.77	0.87	0.89
16	39	0.65	0.73	0.84	0.81
17	46	0.77	0.75	0.86	0.88
18	45	0.85	0.83	0.91	0.92
19	24	0.44	0.41	0.58	0.67
20	43	0.72	0.81	0.90	0.85
21	48	0.71	0.74	0.85	0.84
22	90	0.69	0.66	0.80	0.83

Table 5.1 Comparison of Measures of Accuracy (P_3) and Consistency (C), 45 Terms, 201 Documents, and 2 Analysts, Organometallics File, U.S. Patent Office (Continued)

Term	Number of documents	$(P_3)^2$	C	$\frac{2C}{1+C}$	P_3
23	28	0.73	0.73	0.84	0.86
24	33	0.39	0.43	0.60	0.62
25	98	0.77	0.72	0.84	0.88
26	59	0.65	0.55	0.71	0.80
27	101	0.72	0.73	0.84	0.85
28	58	0.48	0.53	0.69	0.69
29	25	0.88	0.85	0.92	0.94
30	20	0.77	0.73	0.84	0.87
31	33	0.85	0.85	0.92	0.92
32	25	0.46	0.39	0.56	0.68
33	79	0.54	0.50	0.67	0.73
34	75	0.66	0.60	0.75	0.81
35	26	0.40	0.42	0.59	0.64
36	99	0.58	0.52	0.68	0.76
37	134	0.81	0.81	0.90	0.90
38	65	0.58	0.61	0.76	0.76
39	97	0.65	0.68	0.81	0.81
40	25	0.67	0.62	0.77	0.82
41	13	0.43	0.40	0.57	0.65
42	46	0.77	0.76	0.86	0.88
43	51	0.69	0.67	0.80	0.83
44	41	0.81	0.79	0.88	0.90
45	38	0.75	0.78	0.88	0.87
Averages (unweighted)		0.675	0.665	0.788	0.816

sistency experimentally. One simply conducts a test in the manner outlined above for measurement of consistency, and then relies on a judge (or committee of judges) with the two independent indexings before him (them) to determine what is the "correct" indexing. Both 2 × 2 tables presented above can be prepared for each index term, or a sample of them, with the measures P_3 and C computed for each. The resulting measures can be correlated in the usual manner and fitted by a regression equation (see Chapter 11). Such a study will show whether consistency is an adequate measure of accuracy for the file under study.

5.8 Description of mathematical retrieval models

Regardless of which measure one chooses for determining indexing effectiveness, the important question is how indexing effectiveness relates to searching effectiveness. If we wish to compare two indexing modes, we need to know the relationship between indexing accuracy (P_3 and P_2) and search accuracy in order to determine whether cost differences between the two indexing modes are warranted.

In Chapter 4, we showed how indexing accuracy is an important element in estimating search accuracy. We showed indexing accuracy by the following relationship:

		Relevance to encoded request		
		$E_{\bar{r}}$	E_r	Total
System relevance	R_r	a	b	$a + b$
response	$R_{\bar{r}}$	c	d	$c + d$
Total		$a + c$	$b + d$	$a + b + c + d$

where parameters of the overall search effectiveness model include:

$$P(R \mid E_r) = b \mid (b + d) \quad (5)$$

$$P(R_r \mid E_{\bar{r}}) = a \mid (a + c) \quad (6)$$

The question, then, is how to relate indexing accuracy to equations (5) and (6).

In an evaluation program, values of the cells above are expected values estimated by the average over number of search queries.

Mathematical models were developed to estimate average values in the retrieval profile. The principal objectives of these models were:

(1) To estimate the number of missed documents (d) and false drops (a) resulting from indexing errors at various levels.

(2) To estimate total retrieval ($a + b$) and missed documents (d) resulting from using various numbers of terms in search queries.

(3) To provide a better insight into search effectiveness under a variety of search strategies.

Consider a search query involving k terms in which *all* k terms must be indexed in retrieved documents. That is, the queries state that term 1 *and* term 2 *and* . . . term k must be retrieved. Let: (1) P_2 and P_3 be "true values" of relative frequencies averaged over all indexers, terms, and documents in the file, (2) n_2 and n_3 be the number of terms of the k terms in the search query to which values of P_2 and P_3 apply ($n_2 + n_3 = k$), and (3) Q_j denote the proportion of the file which should contain j of the k terms in a search query (it corresponds to the generality ratio given in Chapter 2). Then, assuming independence of indexing errors from term to term, expected values of the retrieval profile may be obtained from the following equations:

Total retrieval

$$a + b = (a + b + c + d) \sum_{n_2 + n_3 = k} P_2^{n_2} P_3^{n_3} Q_{n_3} \tag{7}$$

Missed relevant

$$d = (a + b + c + d)\, Q_k \,[1 - P_3^{k}] \tag{8}$$

False drops

$$a = (a + b + c + d) \sum_{n_3 < k} P_2^{n_2} P_3^{n_3} Q_{n_3} \tag{9}$$

Thus, one can obtain estimates for a and d by inserting parameters estimated from an indexing experiment (P_2,P_3) and a search experiment (Q_k). Estimates of the other cell entries in the retrieval profile can be found arithmetically so that $P(R_r | E_r)$ and $P(R_r | E_{\bar{r}})$ can be found directly from $a + b$, d, and a.

Note that if a single-term query were used, the values of P_3 and P_2 would correspond to $P(R_r | E_r)$ and $P(R_r | E_{\bar{r}})$, respectively. Since k = 1, the values of n_2, n_3, and the remainder of the equations would then be as follows:

Total retrieval

$$a + b = (a + b + c + d) \sum_{n_2 + n_3 = k} P_2^{n_2} P_3^{n_3} Q_{n_3}$$

$$= (a + b + c + d)\ [P_2^{0} P_3^{1} Q_1 + P_2^{1} P_3^{0} Q_0]$$

$$= (a + b + c + d)\ [P_3 Q_1 + P_2 Q_0]$$

$$= P_3\,[Q_1 (a + b + c + d)] + P_2\,[Q_0 (a + b + c + d)]$$

That is, total retrieval equals the proportion of documents indexed correctly times the number of documents in the file having the one-query term $[Q_1(a + b + c + d)]$, plus the proportion of documents indexed incorrectly (commissions) times the number of documents in the file not having the query term $[Q_0(a + b + c + d)]$.

False drops

$$a = (a + b + c + d) \sum_{n_3 < k} P_2{}^{n_2} P_3{}^{n_3} Q_{n_3}$$

$$= (a + b + c + d)[P_2{}^1 P_3{}^0 Q_0] \qquad \text{since } n_3 = 0 \text{ is less than } k = 1$$

$$= (a + b + c + d) P_2 Q_0$$

This corresponds, of course, to the second part of the equation for total retrieval.

Missed documents

$$d = (a + b + c + d) Q_k [1 - P_3{}^k]$$

$$= (a + b + c + d) Q_1 [1 - P_3{}^1]$$

That is, missed documents are the total number of documents in the file having the query term times the proportion of the documents not indexed given they should be $[1 - P_3]$.

The equations become somewhat more difficult when more than a single term is used in a search query.

An example (7) is given for three-term searches ($k = 0, 1, 2, 3$) to demonstrate how the models are applied. In the experiment from which the example is taken, 14 search queries contained three terms. These search queries were applied to the 58 documents in which correct indexing was determined. The number of documents that contained 0, 1, 2, 3 correct terms are given below:

	Number of correct terms found in document (k)			
Search number	0	1	2	3
1	36	14	7	1
2	46	8	4	0
3	44	14	0	0
4	56	2	0	0
5	23	23	7	5
6	23	23	7	5
7	26	31	1	0
8	23	19	7	9
9	14	27	11	6
10	25	33	0	0
11	35	15	8	0
12	11	24	22	1
13	25	29	4	0
14	45	13	0	0
Total	432	275	78	27
Q_k	0.532	0.339	0.096	0.033

In the first search (of the 58 documents sampled) 1 had all three terms, 7 documents had a combination of two out of the three terms, 14 documents had one of the three, and 36 documents did not have any of the three terms. When summed over 14 searches, we find that 53.2 percent of the file had none of the three terms posed on the average and 3.3 percent of the file had all three terms posed on the average.

The values of total retrieval, false drops, and missed documents are found from a true experiment. In that experiment, Q_k were as given above, $P_3 = 0.94$, $P_2 = 0.0001$, and the total number in the file was 22,000. Values for the equations are given below:

n_2	n_3	Q_{n_3}	$P_2^{n_2}$	$P_3^{n_3}$	$P_2^{n_2} P_3^{n_3} Q_{n_3}$
0	3	0.033	1.000	0.83	0.027
1	2	0.096	0.0001	0.88	0.85×10^{-5}
2	1	0.339	$(0.0001)^2$	0.94	approaches zero
3	0	0.532	$(0.001)^3$	1.00	approaches zero

The first row represents the circumstances where $n_3 = 3$, which means all three terms must be in the documents. We established above that 3.3 percent of the file should have been indexed by all three terms ($Q_3 = 0.033$). Of these, we find that only 83 percent will be retrieved due to indexing errors ($P_3{}^3 = 0.83$), so that the correct retrieval will be 2.7 percent of the entire file (0.83×0.033). Thus, correct retrieval (b) is $0.027 \times 22{,}000 = 594$ documents.

The second row represents the cases in which $n_3 = 2$, which means that any two of the three terms must be in the documents. Again we established above that 9.6 percent of the file was represented in this case. If the search query is A and B and C, this 9.6 percent represents documents that have terms A and B, A and C, or B and C. Thus, for false drops to be generated, term C must be committed in the first instance, term B in the second instance, and term A in the third instance. We know that this can happen in 0.01 percent of the documents ($P_2{}^1 = 0.0001$), so that the total proportion of the file to which this can happen is 0.0001×0.096. However, some of these documents may have been missed because the correct terms A and B, A and C, or B and C were missed due to omissions. We know that the chance of indexing two terms correctly is 88 percent ($P_3{}^2 = 0.88$), so that the total proportion of false drops is reduced by this amount. False drops (a) is $[0.0001 \times 0.96 \times 0.88] \times 22{,}000 = 0.2$. Thus, there will on the average be fewer than one false drop due to committed terms.

The third row represents the case in which $n_3 = 1$, which means that only A or B or C is in the document. For a false drop to occur, B and C must be committed together in the first instance, and so on. However, we find this event to be so rare, in this case (0.0000001), that it is not considered. Thus, the second row yields the essential number of false drops.

Finally, the sums:

$$\Sigma \quad P_2{}^{n_2} P_3{}^{n_3} Q_{n_3} = 0.027 + 0.85 \times 10^{-5} \approx 0.027$$

$$\sum_{n_3 < k} P_2{}^{n_2} P_3{}^{n_3} Q_{n_3} = 0.85 \times 10^{-5}$$

and

$$Q_k(1 - P_3{}^k) = 0.0056$$

In the experiment, retrieval equations (7), (8), and (9), and the total file size ($a + b + c + d$) took on several values since searches were performed within combinations of subclasses. Thus, $a + b + c + d$ had the following values: 22,000; 1,160; 440; 250; and 105 documents for All, 4, 3, 2, and 1 subclasses, respectively. Estimates of total retrieval, missed documents, and false drops are as follows:

Number of subclasses	Total number of documents $a + b + c + d$	Estimated total retrieval $a + b$	Estimated missed documents d	Estimated false drops a
All	22,000	594	123	0.2
4	1,160	31	6.5	0.01
3	440	12	2.5	0.004
2	250	6.8	1.4	0.002
1	105	2.8	0.6	0.001

Similarly, estimates may be found for other values of k. Values for $P(R_r|E_r)$ and $P(R_r|E_{\bar{r}})$ are 0.83 and 0.0001, respectively. These values can be incorporated into the stochastic search model described in Chapter 4. A complete description of search models incorporating combinations of both "and" and "or" logic may be found in Bryant *et al.* (*3*).

Another example is given to demonstrate the validity of the models given by equations (7), (8), and (9), and to show the effect of two indexing procedures on total retrieval.

The results from an experiment (*2*) with the Organometallics File of the U.S. Patent Office are given in Table 5.2.

One can see that the results given in Table 5.2 alone may not be sufficient to decide which indexing procedure is optimum or, indeed, if any or all procedures are acceptable. To make judgments of this kind, one needs to express certain file output characteristics in terms of indexing errors.

Comparisons are given for the Organometallics File of the U.S. Patent Office, where the parameters of the model were estimated from an indexing experiment with 24 documents and a search experiment was conducted with 201 documents. Both sets of documents were indexed in the same manner. The retrieval profile cell entries are given for queries involving 4, 8, and 12 terms in Table 5.3. This class of models provided good estimates for the retrieval profile in this instance.

Table 5.2 Relative Frequencies P_3 and P_2 and Time Required for Three Indexing Procedures in the Organometallics File of the U.S. Patent Office[a]

Indexing procedure	P_3	P_2	Av. total time per document, min.
Single indexer	0.89	0.0014	64.3
Single indexer reviewed	0.95	0.0002	111.6
Double indexer[b]	0.98	0.0033	128.6

[a]Sample size of 24 documents.
[b]Two independent indexings lumped together (set sum).

Documents were judged "relevant" if their indexing in the standard set met the search specifications. Thus, the retrieval profile reflects only the effect of indexing errors.

Equations (7) through (9) assume independence of indexing errors f.om term to term. In case this assumption is unwarranted, one can modify the equations to account for dependence. Evidently, the assumption of independence was not unwarranted in the illustration cited above.

Table 5.3 Comparison of Model Estimates and Observed Cell Entries for the Retrieval Profile of the U.S. Patent Office's Organometallics File of 3,625 Documents Prepared by a Double Indexer Procedure

	Number of terms per search					
	4 terms		8 terms		12 terms	
Retrieval profile cell entry	Model estimates	Sample	Model estimates	Sample	Model estimates	Sample
Total retrieval $(a + b)$	48.9	52.7	30.1	32.5	3.6	2.9
False retrieval (a)	3.6	5.1	1.4	2.9	0	0.7
Correct retrieval (b)	45.3	47.6	28.7	29.6	3.6	2.2
Missed documents (d)	12.7	9.4	18.4	16.6	3.8	5.0
Total relevant $(b + d)$	58.0	57.0	47.1	46.2	7.4	7.2

Table 5.4 Comparison of Time with Observed Cell Entries for the Retrieval Profile of 184 Search Queries in the U.S. Patent Office's Organometallics File of 3,625 Documents

	Indexing procedure		
Retrieval profile cell entry	Single indexer[a]	Double indexer[a]	Single indexer reviewed
Indexing time (min.)	64.3	128.6	111.6
Total retrieval $(a + b)$	22.7	34.5	26.7
False retrieval (a)	4.5	9.2	5.6
Correct retrieval (b)	18.2	25.3	21.1
Missed documents (d)	9.6	2.5	6.7
Total relevant $(b + d)$	27.8	27.8	27.8
$P(R_r \mid E_r)$	0.660	0.710	0.76
$P(R_r \mid E_{\bar{r}})$	0.0012	0.0026	0.0016

[a]These cell entries are averaged over all queries. The cell entries in Table 5.3 are for queries involving 4, 8, and 12 terms only.

The decision concerning the optimum indexing procedure is made in view of the "trade-off parameters" summarized for three indexing procedures in Table 5.4. Obviously, this information is more valuable than that found in Table 5.2. One can select the optimum indexing procedure with a given number of documents to be indexed, a given number of searches to be conducted per year, and some rough indication of the relative importance of cell entries in the retrieval profile.

The indexing and preliminary search experiments should yield information from which to establish an acceptable level of indexing accuracy by incorporating values of $P(R_r \mid E_r)$ and $P(R_r \mid E_{\bar{r}})$ into the stochastic models in Chapter 4, along with relative costs of the two procedures and their effect on retrieval.

5.9 Evaluation of indexing languages

The above sections have discussed the evaluation of indexing procedures, that is, the assignment of tags to documents. The tags themselves make up the *indexing language*, which also requires evaluation.

A first cut at evaluation of the indexing language was presented in the previous section. There, the probabilities $P(E_r \mid C_r)$ and $P(E_r \mid C_{\bar{r}})$

measure the ability of the language to encompass the encoder's interpretation of the request. They also may partly be attributable to outright blunders on the part of the encoder, but hopefully this source of error is small in comparison to the indexing language limitation.

Indexing languages vary primarily with respect to *specificity*, that is, with respect to how closely the characteristics of the concept being indexed match the descriptions of the class into which it is put (the tag), i.e., "chromium steel" is more specific than "steel" which is more specific than "metals." Given a hierarchical classification containing all three tags, the indexer may choose any of them. (Methods for evaluating his choice are presented in the previous sections.) However, if the indexing language does not contain a sufficiently specific term, the fault is that of the language itself rather than the indexer who is thus forced to index more generally than warranted by the subject matter.

Clearly, it is less expensive, on the average, to correct errors in indexing than to correct errors in indexing languages. The former involve procedural changes, while the latter involve major changes in the system. Moreover, in a large system, vocabulary changes are unlikely to have a significant effect on system performance for a considerable period of time.

Evaluation of indexing systems involves detailed analysis of the attempts to express the request in terms of the index language and of the errors in system response. The former matches the verbalized request statement with the encoded request and results in a listing of sources of failures. This listing should be quite specific. That is, "Dextrose was specified in the request, but there is no index category covering dextrose." Note, however, that if there is such a category, but it is missed by the searcher, then it is a searching error – not an error in the indexing language. In this case, one might investigate further to see whether the system entry vocabulary is at fault.

An important question is how failures due to indexing languages are reflected in the models given above. If the indexing language does not contain a sufficiently specific term, the values of Q_k in the models will undoubtedly increase since a generic term such as "metals" will be correctly found in more documents – even though such specific terms as "chromium steel" and "molybdenum" may actually appear in the documents. Even though P_3 and P_2 may not change and $P(R_r|E_r)$ and $P(R_r|E_{\bar{r}})$ may not change, the values of $P(E_r|C_r)$ and $P(E_r|C_{\bar{r}})$ will change.

Suppose we have the following simple example. The coder asks for "chromium steel" but uses "steel" due to limitations of the indexing languages. Also, assume a file of 1,000 documents – 20 of which have "chromium steel," another 40 have other specific descriptions of steel, and 10 documents have generic concepts of steel. Q_k under a specific indexing language would be 0.0200 and under the generic indexing language would be 0.0700, so that the models above would be affected. Also, $P(E_r|C_r)$ and $P(E_r|C_{\bar{r}})$ would be calculated as follows:

		Encoded request		
		$E_{\bar{r}}$	E_r	Total
Coder's interpretation	C_r	0	20	20
	$C_{\bar{r}}$	930	50	980
		930	70	1,000

Thus, $P(E_r|C_r) = 1.0$ and $P(E_r|C_{\bar{r}}) = 0.051$.

Also, Q_k is affected by the inherent relationship of terms used together in search queries.

The number of documents retrieved is dependent on the relationships of query terms found within documents. Usually, terms applied in a search query have an inherent relationship to one another that also occurs in the text of documents. For instance, the term "Inflammation" is commonly used in combination with a specific part of the body such as stomach, but it is rarely found with an organism attacked by a chemical agent such as Protozoan. Thus, search terms chosen by meaningful relationships would have a much larger retrieval than the same number of search terms picked randomly. The correlation of terms is taken into account in the retrieval models by parameters Q_k.

Lancaster (*8*) has pointed out that it is expensive to adopt a sophisticated index language for vocabulary control in document transfer systems. The more sophisticated the index language, on the whole, the more expensive it will be to apply and maintain.

One important economic consideration is the size of the vocabulary. The larger the number of index terms in the vocabulary (i.e., the greater the number of document classes that can be uniquely defined), the greater its specificity and the greater the precision capabilities of the system. However, a large vocabulary is costly to develop, costly to apply, and costly to update. The specificity of the vocabulary must be related directly to the specificity of the requests made to the system. It is certainly uneconomical to establish a vocabulary considerably more specific than the level of specificity required by the demands placed upon the system. This implies the strong economic necessity for conducting a careful analysis of representative requests at the stage of the system design.

On the other hand, the development of a rich, readily accessible *entry vocabulary*[1] is likely to reduce the costs of the indexing operation because it decreases the amount of intellectual effort involved in the indexing process. In the early stages of indexing documents into a new retrieval system, many intellectual decisions have to be made. As these decisions are recorded in the entry vocabulary, however, the intellectual burden on subsequent indexers is reduced. For example, a document on poiseuille flow comes up for indexing. There is no term for this in the authority list so that the indexer has to do some research to discover what is involved in this phenomenon. Finally, he decides how the topic is to be indexed, recording his decision in the entry vocabulary as:

Poiseuille Flow *use* LAMINAR FLOW *and* PIPE FLOW

The intellectual decision is now made and recorded. Subsequent indexers merely have to follow the direction given. The richer the entry vocabulary developed, the less the intellectual burden on the indexer, and the greater the economies in the indexing operation.

Another factor to be considered is that of the number and variety of index language devices included in the vocabulary to improve its recall and/or precision capabilities. In particular, various types of precision devices are expensive to apply in document transfer systems. Examples are links and roles, subheadings, and term weighting. To be economically justifiable, we must be able to show that the added input and manipulation costs involved in the use of these devices are offset by appreciable savings in screening time at output (i.e., by greatly improved precision).

[1] A set of words or phrases used by researchers, but which is more extensive than the list of index terms. A way of matching such words or phrases with index terms is an important part of the indexing and searching.

Of course, in the operation of a document transfer system, we have the option of using a carefully controlled index language carefully applied at the time of indexing, thus minimizing time and costs at the searching stage. Alternatively, we can adopt a rather free indexing, with little vocabulary control, and expend additional effort (e.g., by the use of sophisticated searching aids) at the output stage. This matter of the relative weight given to input effort as opposed to output effort is an extremely important one to consider in the economic evaluation of a document transfer system because it affects indexing policy and practice, the system vocabulary, and searching strategies and procedures. One factor to be considered is the volume of document input in relation to the volume of requests handled. In the situation in which many documents are indexed but comparatively few requests are handled, it would usually be sensible to economize at the input stage and to expend more time at output. In the opposite conditions (few documents, many requests), the reverse would be true. Another important factor to be considered is the need to save time at output (i.e., what are the response time requirements of system users?).

It appears that these questions can only be answered by experimentation. Further, since such experimentation involves essentially the redesign of systems, it is expensive. For this reason, this evaluation must usually be accomplished under foundation or large institution support, with some hope that the results will be generalizable to other environments.

5.10 Other considerations relating to indexing policies and procedures

Lancaster (*8*) has pointed out a number of other considerations worth investigating in relation to indexing policies and procedures, including:

(1) What should be the level of exhaustivity adopted in indexing (i.e., on the average, how many index terms should be assigned)?

(2) How much time should be expended, on the average, in the indexing of a document?

(3) What professional level of personnel should be used for the indexing operation?

(4) Is an indexing revision or checking operation worthwhile?

The most difficult problem relating to indexing policy is the decision as to the most appropriate level of exhaustivity to adopt (i.e., how many index terms to use on the average). The more exhaustive the indexing, the greater will be the recall potential of the system, but the number of false drops is likely to increase. In a particular unique environment of documents, index language, and requests, there will be an optimum level of exhaustivity of indexing. The problem is to find this optimum level (i.e., the point of diminishing returns). The reason for this problem is that each new term indexed from a document will increase the proportion of terms indexed given that they should be (P_3). However, each term added has a decreasing probability of being relevant from the standpoint of the use of the concept or the searcher's interpretation of relevance. Suppose, for example, that 50 concepts appear in a document that can be correctly indexed by the indexing language. If only 10 of these 50 concepts are indexed, the value of P_3 will be 0.20. However, in most instances, we find that after a few concepts are indexed, the remainder become subsidiary to the principal point of the document and the user may not feel that documents retrieved by the subsidiary concepts are relevant to his information requirements.

Lancaster (*8*) also brings out another point. Suppose we index a particular collection of documents at an average level of 15 terms per item, and test the retrieval performance of this system by the use of a representative sample of, say, 50 requests. Using the best possible searching strategies (determined retrospectively), we may find that, for this particular group of requests, at the indexing level adopted, the system is operating at $P(R_r|E_r) = 0.73$ or recall = 73 percent. By additional indexing experiments, holding constant the request, search strategies, and index language, we may find that an increase in exhaustivity to an average of 20 terms increases values of P_3 which in turn raises $P(R_r|E_r)$ to 0.90. However, we may find that we will need to raise the average exhaustivity level to 35 terms per article for values of P_3 to raise $P(R_r|E_r)$ to 0.95. Under these conditions, we might establish from our stochastic model of the previous chapter that the average of 20 terms per item is an optimum level to employ in this particular environment of documents, requests, and index language. In other words, after the 20-term level there may be evidence of diminishing returns after looking at the model with various values of P_3, hence $P(R_r|E_r)$, and we will need to raise the exhaustivity level as high as 35 terms (thus greatly increasing our indexing costs) in order to achieve a 0.05 improvement in $P(R_r|E_r)$ which may be proven to be insufficient by the stochastic model. We are able to plot a performance curve of exhaustivity level versus $P(R_r|E_r)$ as shown in Figure 5.1. From a plot of this kind, which can be translated into overall search effectiveness by the model in the previous chapter, we can establish a break-even point for indexing exhaustivity (i.e., a point beyond which the addition of further index terms, although adding appreciably to input costs, is not making any highly appreciable difference to the recall potential of the system).

We can approach what is essentially the same problem from a different direction by studying the effect of varying time expenditures on the indexing operation. The more time we expend in indexing, the better we expect P_3 and P_2 to be. However, there is likely to be a very definite leveling off after a comparatively short expenditure of time. If 90 percent of the correct retrieval tags are assigned in the first 10 minutes of indexing, but an additional 30 minutes are needed to find the extra 10 percent judged to be correct, we may reasonably conclude that 10 minutes per document is an optimum average indexing time, and we can establish our indexing quotas on this basis.

Another indexing problem is the matter of the professional level of the staff used in the indexing function. We would like to be able to use the lowest level of personnel that will give us acceptable results. Do we really need highly qualified subject specialists? This is often assumed, but the need has rarely been proved conclusively. In opera-

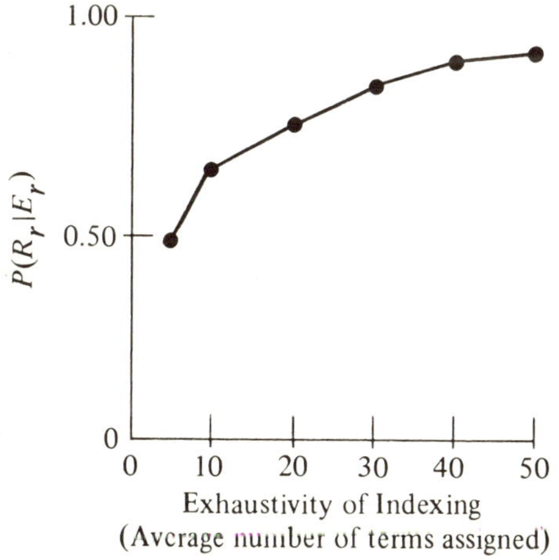

Figure 5.1 $P(R_r|E_r)$ **as a function of number of terms assigned.**

ting a document transfer system, we should be prepared to experiment with various levels of personnel. Perhaps nonsubject-specialists with good indexing experience will perform as well as those with subject expertise. If so, we would probably expect to pay these people rather less money, and thus we would make definite economies in system operation. Experimentation with personnel of varying backgrounds and experience can certainly be conducted while the system is being planned and designed. (See Chapter 13.)

One additional factor requires analysis in relation to the matter of indexing policy. This is the question of whether we need to "check" or "revise" the work of our indexers. Do we need senior indexers examining the work of the others? These procedures are costly in manpower and it is not known whether they uncover sufficient errors to make the whole operation worthwhile. Results of experiments on this operation were described in Table 5.2. These results and their costs can be incorporated into the stochastic model of the previous chapter to determine the ultimate search effectiveness resulting from checking. It could be found, for example, that only inexperienced indexers require review.

References

1. Atherton, P., King, D. W., Freeman, R. R., *Evaluation of the Retrieval of Nuclear Science Document References Using the Universal Decimal Classification as the Indexing Language for a Computer-based System.* New York, American Institute of Physics UDC Project, May 1, 1968.
2. Bryant, E. C., King, D. W., Terragno, P. J., *Analysis of an Indexing and Retrieval Experiment for the Organometallic File of the U.S. Patent Office.* Denver, Colo., Westat Research, Inc., August 1963. PB 166-488.
3. Bryant, E. C., King, D. W., Terragno, P. J., *Some Technical Notes on Coding Errors.* Bethesda, Md., Westat Research, Inc., July 1963. PB 166-487.
4. Cooper, W. S., "Is Interindexer Consistency a Hobgoblin?" *American Documentation*, Vol. 20, No. 3 (July 1969), pp. 268-278.
5. Hooper, R. S., *Development and Application of a Technique for the Evaluation of Document Retrieval Systems.* Washington, D. C., American University, May 25, 1967.
6. King, D. W., "Evaluation of Coordinate Index Systems During File Development." *Journal of Chemical Documentation*, Vol. 5, No. 2 (May 1965), pp. 96-99.
7. King, D. W., McDonnell, P. M., *Evaluation of the Class 167 Combined Coordinate Index Conventional Classification System.* Bethesda, Md., Westat Research, Inc., June 1967. PB 175-744.

8. Lancaster, F. W., *Evaluation of the MEDLARS Demand Search Service.* Bethesda, Md., National Library of Medicine, January 1968.
9. Lancaster, F. W., *Information Retrieval Systems: Characteristics, Testing, and Evaluation.* New York, Wiley & Sons, 1968.
10. Salton, G., "A Comparison Between Manual and Automatic Indexing Methods." *American Documentation*, Vol. 20, No. 1 (January 1969), pp. 61-71.
11. Swanson, D. R., "On Indexing Depth and Retrieval Effectiveness." *In: Information System Sciences. Proceedings of the Second Congress on the Information Sciences, Hot Springs, Va., November 1964.* Washington, D. C., Spartan, 1966, pp. 311-319.
12. Tell, B. V., "Document Representation and Indexer Consistency: A Study of Indexing from Titles, Abstracts and Full Text Using UDC and Keywords." *In: Proceedings of the American Society for Information Science Annual Meeting, San Francisco, 1-4 October 1969.* Vol. 6: Cooperating Information Societies. Westport, Conn.; London, Greenwood Publishing Corp., 1969, pp. 285-292.

Chapter Six
Evaluation of Document Screening Processes

6.1 Introduction

In one sense most of the activities related to search for documents result in document screening. That is, the searching process is a filtering process in which, hopefully, the output becomes more refined as it is reduced in size. It is presumed, of course, that some of the desired output may be lost in the filtering process.

Document screening has come to have one of two special meanings. The first of these assumes an intermediary between the system and the user. This intermediary screens the output of the system and passes to the user a smaller set of documents out of which he has presumably screened those which are "obviously" not pertinent to the request.

The second meaning associated with screening is that the user himself may use some device other than the complete document to decide whether the document is of interest to him. That is, he may use bibliographic citations, abstracts, titles, index terms, the first and last paragraphs, and other items. These are commonly called surrogates for the document, or document representations. Having screened through the document representations, the user decides on a subset which he feels will be of interest to him and asks for the full text of these documents.

No difference exists in principle between an intermediary making a decision for the user or the user himself making such a decision from a representation of the document. The economics of the two situations may differ, but the same evaluative techniques may be used for both.

There are, of course, many variations of the above screening procedures. For example, one could have an intermediary look at titles to screen out those he considers inappropriate. The user then could use titles to screen out additional items and use abstracts to do a further refinement before requesting full-text documents. The methodology presented in the following sections will apply to such cases as long as one considers the entire screening process, no matter how complicated, to be a single procedure.

6.2 Measurement of screening effectiveness

There is a tendency to judge a screener (the intermediary between the system and the user) in terms of his ability to select the documents that might be of interest to the user. However, as we have seen previously, it is generally inappropriate to consider the user as part of the system. Therefore, if a screener, being part of the system, is judged on the basis of his ability to match his judgments against those of the user when the user's requirements may not have been fed into the system, such a procedure will tend to fault the system when it may be the user himself who is at fault. For this reason, it is recommended that an independent judge decide whether the screener is able to select documents in accordance with the verbalized request. This provides a way of judging the effectiveness of that component of the system.

One cannot ignore the relationship between the user's requirements and the ability of a screener to select documents. However, such a test should be made independently of the attempt to measure the effectiveness of the searching system.

6.3 Effectiveness of screening against the verbalized request

For convenience in discussion, we will use the word *screen* to refer to any procedure, including the personnel and document representations involved in it, which selects from the total output before presenting full-text documents to the user. Thus, a screen can include an intermediary, various document representations, and combinations of intermediaries and document representations. It can also include viewing hardware such as cathode ray tubes and microfilm readers.

In Chapter 4, a model was presented which required estimates of the probability of output by the system and selection by the screen, given relevance to the verbalized request $P(S_r, R_r | V_r)$, and the same probability, given nonrelevance to the verbalized request, $P(S_r, R_r | V_{\bar{r}})$. We will now consider how a test procedure can be organized to obtain these probabilities.

We consider the same basic structure as discussed in Chapter 3. That is, we assume that a selection of documents relevant to the verbalized request has been merged with a sample of documents not relevant to the verbalized request. Whether or not they are relevant to the user's requirement is immaterial at this stage. We assume that the system has separated the relevant and nonrelevant documents into classes according to its judgment of relevance. We also assume that the additional system output (beyond the initial test set) has been judged relevant or not relevant by a judge. The resulting output is the following 2 × 2 table:

User relevance judgment	System relevance response	
	Not relevant	Relevant
Relevant	$N(V_r, R_{\bar{r}})$	$N(V_r, R_r)$
Not relevant	$N(V_{\bar{r}}, R_{\bar{r}})$	$N(V_{\bar{r}}, R_r)$

where the entries in the cells represent numbers of documents.

Only the documents identified by the second column will actually be screened, since the others are not part of the system output. The screen sorts $N(V_r, R_r)$ and $N(V_{\bar{r}}, R_r)$ each into two categories: (1) those that pass the screen and (2) those that do not. We can represent these categories as follows:

System assignment	Screen assignment	
	Not relevant	Relevant
Retrieved, relevant	$N(S_{\bar{r}}, V_r, R_r)$	$N(S_r, V_r, R_r)$
Retrieved, not relevant	$N(S_{\bar{r}}, V_{\bar{r}}, R_r)$	$N(S_r, V_{\bar{r}}, R_r)$

Some estimated probabilities indicating how well this screening is done are then:

$$\widetilde{P}(S_r | R_r, V_r) = \frac{N(S_r, V_r, R_r)}{N(V_r, R_r)} \tag{1}$$

$$\widetilde{P}(S_r|R_r, V_{\bar{r}}) = \frac{N(S_r, V_{\bar{r}}, R_r)}{N(V_{\bar{r}}, R_r)} \qquad (2)$$

Note that these are *not* the probabilities called for in the model of Chapter 4. There we made the assumption that one should be interested in how well a screen could select among all documents with respect to the verbalized request, not just those documents which are output by the system. Under this philosophy we wish to form estimates from the following array:

Relevance to verbalized request	Screen assignment: Not relevant	Screen assignment: Relevant
Relevant	$N(S_{\bar{r}}, V_r)$	$N(S_r, V_r)$
Not relevant	$N(S_{\bar{r}}, V_{\bar{r}})$	$N(S_r, V_{\bar{r}})$

Then,

$$\widetilde{P}(S_r|V_r) = \frac{N(S_r, V_r)}{N(V_r)} \qquad (3)$$

$$\widetilde{P}(S_r|V_{\bar{r}}) = \frac{N(S_r, V_r)}{N(V_{\bar{r}})} \qquad (4)$$

The estimated probabilities of Figure 4.2 are then found as:

$$\widetilde{P}(S_r, R_r|V_r) = \widetilde{P}(R_r|V_r)\,\widetilde{P}(S_r|V_r) \qquad (5)$$

$$\widetilde{P}(S_r, R_r|V_{\bar{r}}) = \widetilde{P}(R_r|V_{\bar{r}})\,\widetilde{P}(S_r|V_{\bar{r}}) \qquad (6)$$

where $\widetilde{P}(R_r|V_r)$ and $\widetilde{P}(R_r|V_{\bar{r}})$ are the cumulative probabilities of Figure 4.2.

Test methodology is related to ways of obtaining the numbers, $N(S_{\bar{r}}, V_r)$, $N(S_r, V_r)$, $N(S_{\bar{r}}, V_{\bar{r}})$, and $N(S_r, V_{\bar{r}})$. The sequence of processing operations is as follows:

(a) Judge (1) selects the test set of documents identified as relevant or not relevant to the verbalized request.

(b) Request is processed in the usual way to obtain the system output.

(c) Documents in the system output not previously judged relevant or not relevant are so classified by Judge (1). A sample may be classified if the output is too large.

(d) The total output of the system is presented to the screen, e.g., full texts to an intermediary, document representations to an intermediary, document representations to Judge (2), and so on. Judge (2) must be knowledgeable in the subject matter, but he should not be the requester. He, rather than an intermediary, is to be used when one wishes to determine the effectiveness of the document representation as a screening device.

(e) The resulting data are substituted into equations (3) and (4) to arrive at the required estimates.

6.4 Effectiveness of screening against the user's requirements

When effectiveness of the system is measured by satisfaction of the user's requirements, there is always uncertainty as to whether the fault lies with the system or with the user. One extreme point of view is that the system must respond to the user's requirements, even though poorly articulated, and if failure to verbalize his requirements is a principal source of error, then it is the responsibility of the system to improve this interface. In any case, one frequently needs to know how well the system performs as judged by responsiveness to the user's requirements rather than by responsiveness to a verbalized request.

With respect to screening, one is interested in determining how well the screen serves as a filter for the requirements of the user. For this purpose, one need work only with the output of the system (or a sample of it in case the examination of the full output creates excessive work). The output must be put into classes by the user, usually two, but more than two can be accommodated by the methods of Chapter 4. For illustration, we consider just two classes – relevant to the user's requirements (U_r) and not relevant to the user's requirements ($U_{\bar{r}}$).

At this point we must distinguish between test of a procedure which involves an intermediary and one which does not. For a test involving an intermediary (with or without use of document representations), we need only have him screen the system output independently of the user. Then, we can construct the following table:

Relevance to user's requirements	Screen assignment	
	Not relevant	Relevant
Relevant	$N(S_{\bar{r}}, U_r)$	$N(S_r, U_r)$
Not relevant	$N(S_{\bar{r}}, U_{\bar{r}})$	$N(S_r, U_{\bar{r}})$

Then, conditional probabilities of interest are:

$$\tilde{P}(S_r | U_r) = \frac{N(S_r, U_r)}{N(U_r)} \tag{7}$$

$$\tilde{P}(S_r | U_{\bar{r}}) = \frac{N(S_r, U_{\bar{r}})}{N(U_{\bar{r}})} \tag{8}$$

A test of the effectiveness of various document representations where the judgment is made by the user rather than by an intermediary requires more careful statistical design. The reason is that the user cannot screen using both the full text and a document representation without one of these experiences affecting the other.

A test requires a high degree of cooperation from the user and the ability to interact with him. One effective test is to have the user screen the output, using the document representations which are under test. On the basis of this screening, he presumably will select a subset (S_f) for which he will request full texts. This subset will be divided into two sets: those relevant to his requirements (S_{fr}) and those not relevant ($S_{f\bar{r}}$). The user is then asked to examine the full texts of documents not selected through use of the document representations. If the output is large, he can examine only a random sample of such documents – a sample approximately equal in size to the number of representations selected.

Letting $S_{\bar{f}}$ represent the set of documents rejected by the screen (i.e., not selected for full-text examination), one can construct the following 2 × 2 table:

Screen selection	User's final judgment	
	Not relevant	Relevant
Selected	$N(S_{f\bar{r}})$	$N(S_{fr})$
Not selected	$N(S_{\bar{f}\bar{r}})$	$N(S_{\bar{f}r})$

where N stands for "number of documents in the set." From this table one can readily observe the degree of coincidence between judgments based upon full-text and document representations, and can compute the conditional probabilities of interest.

6.5 Economic evaluation of screening

If there is any economic advantage to using a human intermediary in the document screening process, the source of the advantage must lie in either a saving of manpower costs, service costs, or both. Savings in manpower costs can be effected through a differential in the pay scales of the user and the screener or in the speed with which screening decisions can be made. Savings in service costs can be accomplished if the amount of photocopying, postage, and other communications costs can be reduced by supplying the user with only a subset of the system output.

All of the costs mentioned above are direct costs, that is, directly chargeable to some budget. The cost against which one would like to offset these costs is the cost of lost documents which are improperly screened out. This is clearly an indirect cost and one to which it is difficult to assign a value. Following common practice in such cases, a measure of effectiveness can be used in lieu of indirect cost assessments. One might, for example, use as a measure of effectiveness the percent of relevant output lost due to screening. Then, one can construct the graph of Figure 6.1. The shape of the curve is speculative. Observations can be obtained by varying the intensity of screening and collecting the data of the previous section. A scatter of points will result through which a curve can be drawn.

A second way in which screening might be considered is to overcome false drops due to indexing language, indexing accuracy, or search accuracy. Thus, we might be faced with the trade-off between inexpensive input offset by expensive screening of the search output. It is in these situations that investigation by the stochastic model described in Chapter 4 becomes extremely powerful.

One must allocate screener costs (salaries and overhead) over the searches on some rational basis, perhaps the number of items perused in the screening process. Also, some measure of the user time savings must be obtained. A high degree of user cooperation is required if diaries are to be kept, but this procedure may be feasible in some cases. It is also possible to do time allocation studies by the methods discussed in Chapter 3. User time must then be priced out, with over-

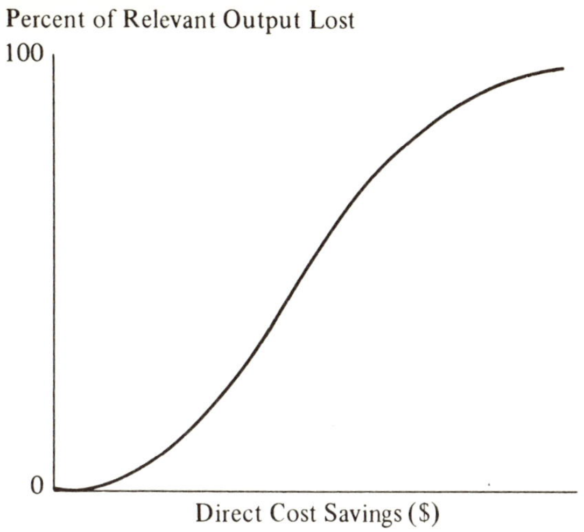

Figure 6.1 Loss in relevant output due to screening compared to cost savings.

head, and savings imputed from the resulting figures, after accounting for savings in service costs discussed above.

Economic evaluation of the use of document representations as screening devices is a more difficult problem. The reason is that there is substantial cost in preparing the representations, and only part of this cost is properly chargeable to screening. The representations are most frequently used for preparation of indexes, publication of abstracts, and other purposes which are not related to screening requirements. When the representations are required by the constraints imposed on the system, whether or not they are used for screening, it is proper to charge to screeening only the marginal costs of maintaining and using the screening file. When this is not the case, then some cost allocation must be accomplished.

After the problem of what to do with costs of document representations is resolved, the economic analysis proceeds much as outlined above. By varying the intensity of screening, one can obtain a set of points through which to plot a curve, as in Figure 6.1.

6.6 Examples of measuring screening accuracy

Two examples are given below for experiments to establish screening accuracy (*1*, *2*). The first experiment involves tight screening processes that tend to cull out most of the nonrelevant materials at the sacrifice of screening out many of the relevant documents as well. The second experiment involves much looser screening processes. Both experiments involve screening on more than one document representation.

In the first experiment, there were five different document representations, including title only, titles with abstracts, and indexes from three different sources. In addition, four intermediaries were used to screen on results from questions posed by actual searches. The final user relevance judgment was made by two persons who served as proxies on behalf of the user and who evaluated relevance based on the full text of the documents that were screened. Document representations for 25 documents were evaluated. Two measures of screening accuracy were made. The first was $P(S_r | V_r)$, and the second was $P(S_r | V_{\bar{r}})$, corresponding to equations (3) and (4) in Section 6.3.

Results are given in Table 6.1. Clearly, the title with abstract represents the best system with regard to $P(S_r | V_r)$. However, the proportion of nonrelevance chosen in $P(S_r | V_{\bar{r}})$ is about the same for the

Table 6.1 Estimated Effectiveness Probabilities [$P(S_r | V_r)$ and $P(S_r | V_{\bar{r}})$] for Screening Processes with Four Intermediaries, Five Document Representations, and Two User Judgments

	Effectiveness probabilities	
	$P(S_r \| V_r)$	$P(S_r \| V_{\bar{r}})$
Intermediary		
A	0.4700	0.0180
B	0.2905	0.0019
C	0.1676	0.0085
D	0.2585	0.0010
Document representation		
Title only	0.1676	0.0049
Title and abstract	0.5405	0.0051
Index 1	0.2265	0.0015
Index 2	0.2310	0.0031
Index 3	0.3035	0.0038
User		
I	0.3702	0.0029
II	0.2215	0.0044

title only (0.0049) and title with abstract (0.0051). One must incorporate results from both screening processes into the entire stochastic model and also establish costs to be able to decide whether screening is worthwhile and, if so, which document representation yields the best method for screening. More is said about cost/effectiveness later on in this section.

It is noted that a considerable difference exists among intermediaries concerning their accuracy of screening. This means that, when an experiment is conducted, several intermediaries probably should be used in the experiment so that intermediaries with unsatisfactory results (determined from the stochastic model) can either be trained or eliminated from the system. Also, screening accuracy differs substantially depending on a particular user's judgment. It is not too surprising that users vary in their judgment of relevance, but this means that their differences should be taken into account in an experiment of this kind.

The second experiment was conducted in a different and operational environment. In this experiment, the screening processes tended to be looser, with $P(S_r|V_r)$ about the same for titles (0.875) and abstracts (0.863) and $P(S_r|V_{\bar{r}})$ slightly better for abstracts (0.476) than for titles (0.555). The overall result is that fewer nonrelevant documents are culled out than the system above, but the number of relevant documents screened out is also substantially less.

The four screening processes (tight and loose screening on titles and abstracts) are examined further by means of the stochastic model and by cost. In this example, we assume effectiveness measures found by Lancaster (*3*) for letter search requests and searching with $P(R_r|C_r)$ equal to 0.40, 0.60, 0.80, and 1.00. Searching and input effectiveness are combined in this example. Costs and other information are given in Table 6.2. It is noted that abstracts are always sent to the users. Effectiveness measures and costs are given in Table 6.3.

There are a number of interesting results given in Table 6.3. If we look at the cost/search over the four levels of search recall (0.40, 0.60, 0.80, and 1.00), the cost/search increases moderately for all screening alternatives when search recall increases from 0.40 to 0.60 and from 0.60 to 0.80 (e.g., no screening increases from about \$66 to \$71 and from \$71 to \$80 at these levels). However, the cost/search differential becomes substantial when increasing from 0.80 to 1.00 search recall (e.g., no screening increases from about \$80 to \$117 at these levels). The reason for this is that the number of documents retrieved (X_3) necessary to achieve 1.00 recall nearly triples from 0.80 recall (126.5

Table 6.2 Alternative Retrospective Searching Processes: Effectiveness Probabilities and Costs

Alternatives	Effectiveness probabilities		Fixed costs	Variable costs
Intermediary interpretation				
By letter	$P(C_r \mid V_r)$ = 0.95	$P(C_r \mid V_{\bar{r}})$ = 0.0000034	C_4 = \$500	C_9 = \$11.25/search
Searching				
Level 1	$P(R_r \mid C_r)$ = 0.40	$P(R_r \mid C_{\bar{r}})$ = 0.0001247	C_1 = \$131,000	$C_{10} + C_{11}$ = \$0.058/item retrieved
Level 2	= 0.60	= 0.0003524		
Level 3	= 0.80	= 0.0008824		
Level 4	= 1.00	= 0.0032895		
Input			C_3 = \$5,500	$C_6 + C_7X_5$ = \$0.6125/item input
Screening				
Mail			C_5 = \$250	C_8 = \$0.20/search (titles)
				C_{13} = \$0.002/item sent (titles)
				= \$0.10/item sent (abstracts)
No screen	$P(S_r \mid V_r)$ = 1.00	$P(S_r \mid V_{\bar{r}})$ = 1.00	C_2 = \$0	C_{12} = \$0
Tight -				
on titles	= 0.168	= 0.0049	= \$0	= \$0.04/item retrieved
on abstracts	= 0.541	= 0.0051	= \$32,000	= \$0.125/item retrieved
Loose -				
on titles	= 0.875	= 0.555	= \$0	= \$0.04/item retrieved
on abstracts	= 0.863	= 0.476	= \$32,000	= \$0.125/item retrieved

X_1 = 100,000 items over a 4-year period.
X_2 = 10,000 searches per year.
X_5 = 1,000 terms on authority list.

Table 6.3 Alternative Screening Processes: Effectiveness Measures and Costs

Recall level	Screening alternative	$P(S_r \mid V_r)$	$P(S_r \mid V_{\bar{r}})$	Recall	No. rel. retr.	No. retr. (X_3)	No. sent (X_4)	Total system cost	Cost/ search	Cost/ rel. retr.
0.40	No screening	1.00	1.00	0.38	19.0	31.6	31.6	$263,400	$ 65.85	$ 3.47
	Tight - on titles	0.168	0.0049	0.06	3.2	31.6	3.2	258,720	64.68	20.21
	Tight - on abstracts	0.541	0.0051	0.21	10.3	31.6	10.3	302,600	75.65	7.34
	Loose - on titles	0.875	0.555	0.33	16.6	31.6	23.5	257,560	64.39	3.88
	Loose - on abstracts	0.863	0.476	0.33	16.4	31.6	22.3	307,400	76.85	4.69
0.60	No screening	1.00	1.00	0.57	28.5	63.9	63.9	282,200	70.55	2.48
	Tight - on titles	0.168	0.0049	0.10	4.8	63.9	5.0	271,440	67.86	14.14
	Tight - on abstracts	0.541	0.0051	0.31	15.4	63.9	15.6	327,000	81.75	5.31
	Loose - on titles	0.875	0.555	0.50	24.9	63.9	44.5	269,760	67.44	2.71
	Loose - on abstracts	0.863	0.476	0.49	24.6	63.9	41.4	337,000	84.25	3.42
0.80	No screening	1.00	1.00	0.76	38.0	126.5	126.5	319,000	79.75	2.10
	Tight - on titles	0.168	0.0049	0.13	6.4	126.5	6.8	296,160	74.04	11.57
	Tight - on abstracts	0.541	0.0051	0.41	20.5	126.5	21.0	373,000	93.25	4.55
	Loose - on titles	0.875	0.555	0.67	33.3	126.5	82.3	294,040	73.51	2.21
	Loose - on abstracts	0.863	0.476	0.66	32.8	126.5	84.9	394,600	98.65	3.01
1.00	No screening	1.00	1.00	0.95	47.5	376.3	376.3	469,000	117.25	2.47
	Tight - on titles	0.168	0.0049	0.16	8.0	376.3	8.6	394,920	98.73	12.34
	Tight - on abstracts	0.541	0.0051	0.51	25.7	376.3	26.4	553,800	138.45	5.39
	Loose - on titles	0.875	0.555	0.83	41.6	376.3	224.0	393,200	98.30	2.36
	Loose - on abstracts	0.863	0.476	0.82	41.0	376.3	197.5	621,800	155.45	3.79

to 376.3). If, on the other hand, cost/relevant document retrieved is considered, we find in all screening alternatives that costs decrease at increased recall levels up to 0.80 recall. This cost then increases for 1.00 recall.

If we look at cost/search, it would appear that both tight and loose screening on titles are the best systems at all levels of search recall. However, when considering cost per relevant document retrieved, no screening yields less cost per relevant document retrieved at low levels of search recall, and loose screening on titles appears to be about the same at 0.80 search recall and the best at 1.00 search recall. Clearly, screening by abstract under the two systems used in this example is not feasible from a cost/effectiveness standpoint. If users (and their expenses) are not considered, no screening may be best. However, loose screening on titles does cut down irrelevant materials by about one-third (126.5 to 82.3 at 0.80 recall and 376.3 to 224.0 at 1.00 recall). This culling-out process reduces the number of relevant documents retrieved by 4.7 at 0.80 recall and 5.9 relevant documents at 1.00 recall. Thus, a decision between these two systems depends largely on the users' expenses and their attitude toward the two results. The users' consideration is expanded upon in the next chapter – *Evaluation of the User-System Interface.*

References

1. Atherton, P., Unpublished research report on evaluation of document representations.
2. Dym, E. D., "Relevance Predictability. I: Investigation Background and Procedures." *In*: Kent, A., Taulbee, O. E., Belzer, J., Goldstein, G. D., eds. *Electronic Handling of Information: Testing and Evaluation.* Washington, D.C., John I. Thompson & Co.; London, Academic Press, 1967, pp. 175-185.
3. Lancaster, F. W. *Evaluation of the MEDLARS Demand Search Service.* Bethesda, Md., National Library of Medicine, January 1968.

Chapter Seven
Evaluation of the User-System Interface

7.1 Introduction

In previous chapters it has been assumed that the activities of the user can be isolated from those of the system, which operates upon stimulation by the user's request. It should be emphasized that this view of the system is taken only for diagnostic convenience. Actually, participation by the user is encouraged in most systems, and it is believed generally that retrieval effectiveness is fostered by interaction between the user and the system.[1] We will now examine some ways of evaluating the effectiveness of the user-system interface.

7.2 The interface in retrospective searching

Previously, we have shown that one can determine how closely the written request matches the intention of the requester by using the conditional probabilities $P(U_r | V_r)$ and $P(U_r | V_{\bar{r}})$. These probabilities are estimated from the frequencies with which the relevance assessments of users and independent subject-matter judges coincide, where the judges look at the verbalized request and do not consult with the users. Wide variation in these assessments might indicate a need either for training of users or a program whereby search assistants could work with users to help them refine their requests.

It is also possible to compare the coder's interpretation with the

[1] However, Lancaster (*6*) found that the "best" requests were prepared by users in their own natural language without discussion with librarians or search analysts.

user's assessment by estimating $P(U_r|C_r)$ and $P(U_r|C_{\bar{r}})$, where the assessments of the coders are based upon the verbalized request. One can test the effectiveness of interactive procedures by estimating the above probabilities with and without application of the test procedures. Such interactive procedures might take several forms, such as face-to-face discussion or telephone calls for clarification.

For example, suppose the normal system operation is to encode the verbalized request without any contact between encoder and user. Under these conditions, suppose it has been established that $\tilde{P}(U_r|C_r) = 0.60$ with a standard error of 0.03 and that $\tilde{P}(U_r|C_{\bar{r}}) = 0.05$ with a standard error of 0.02. A procedure is established through which the encoder telephones the requester to discuss every request prior to encoding. A test of this procedure reveals that $\tilde{P}(U_r|C_r) = 0.80$ with a standard error of 0.05 and that $\tilde{P}(U_r|C_{\bar{r}}) = 0.04$ with a standard error of 0.04. The estimated improvement in $P(U_r|C_r)$ is 0.20 with a standard error of $\sqrt{(0.03)^2 + (0.05)^2} = 0.06$ (see Chapter 11). Evidently, there has been a significant increase in coincidence. The nature of the improvement (whether due to improved verbalized request or to coincidence of point of view) can be tested by $\tilde{P}(U_r|V_{\bar{r}})$. These estimates will measure the ability of the user to verbalize his requirements.

Frequently, retrospective searches are not single attempts but a sequence of attempts to retrieve documents which satisfy the user. How to handle the series of trials poses special problems.

Sometimes the sequence is prespecified. That is, on the basis of a verbalized request, it is decided that a given set of terms should be coordinated and the output generated, that a specified term should be removed or replaced by a more general term and another output generated, and so on, to the end of the sequence. After all output is generated, a decision is made concerning which of the outputs to screen. When this kind of sequencing is done, it seems reasonable to consider that only one search has been done, and to consider the output which was screened to be the output from the search. For diagnostic purposes, however, all outputs may be screened in detail. Also, note that an organized practice of broadening the search has the effect of generating a curve on one of the graphs shown in Chapter 2. In general, it is appropriate to consider as one search all of the activities which relate to the processing of a given verbalized request. These activities include refinements of the verbalized request by interaction between the requester and the search analyst or coder. However, if a new request is submitted, it is appropriate to consider it to be a new search, even though the request may be the result of rethinking and rephrasing a previously submitted request which was at least partly unsuccessful. The number of resubmitted requests should be recorded by the system.

7.3 The interface in interactive systems

In recent years, emphasis has been placed on systems which are loosely described as "interactive." Four features seem to distinguish an interactive system: (1) the speed with which it can respond to requests, (2) its ability to respond to requests for system parameters (such as number of documents with a given indexing), (3) the ability to search on the basis of natural-language processing, and (4) the frequent absence of intermediaries in the search process.

A search in an interactive system is almost always iterative. That is, the user formulates a requirement and views documents that the system presents to satisfy this requirement. He may then modify his query and continue this iterative process until he is satisfied with the output or terminates the search for some other reason. Most of this can be done "on-line," so that modification of the query is an integral part of the search process. Intermediate response of the system is generally used to determine whether the direction of the search should be altered, and it may be that the full text of documents is provided only at the last stage. Variations on the basic system are almost endless.

The variability which exists among interactive systems, and the proliferation of new features which can be expected as such systems become more common, make it difficult to specify in any detail an evaluation procedure to be followed. Certain measures appear useful, however.

Because of the way in which user activities and system functions overlap in interactive systems, evaluation of the effectiveness of such systems must involve the user, even for diagnostic purposes. It is of little significance to defend an interactive system on the grounds that it could have performed well if only the user had used it correctly. A system which is not adaptable to the limits of users' abilities is simply not a good system for that set of users. Within certain limits, the performance of interactive systems can be increased by training the users, and the implementation and effectiveness of such training programs are clearly a part of the system being evaluated.

What one must try to achieve in the evaluation of interactive systems is a measure of how well the system satisfies the user's needs. A place to start is to ask the user, in a well-structured questionnaire (see Chapter 10), how much he uses the system, what proportion of his searching needs are met by the system, what he likes about it, what he dislikes about it, and how it might be improved. Much of this evaluation is qualitative (except for the trivial sense in which one can record numbers of persons with given responses). However, if there is any person whose opinions should be considered, it is obviously the user of the interactive system.

Some intensive interviews should also be conducted, either individually or in groups, to probe for sources of dissatisfaction and to find out whether a user's literature perspective is changed through use of the system. How much time is spent browsing, how much time in searching for specific requirements, and how much time in searching against ill-defined requirements?

Since most interactive systems provide consoles or other points of interaction, one can, by random sampling over time, obtain estimates of total use, and distributions by kinds of use. These data can be compared against system objectives and costs to provide management with broad data which can influence decisions to expand the service, to restrict it, or to provide more or fewer consoles.

Two summary statistics which should prove useful in evaluation are (1) the number of useful references retrieved and (2) the amount of user-console time required to obtain them. Thus, an adaptation of Figure 2.9 can be used, in which the horizontal scale refers to minutes spent searching rather than total documents retrieved.

Not much more can be said in general about the evaluation of effectiveness of interactive systems. Each evaluation must be designed on an *ad hoc* basis, depending upon the characteristics of the system and the objectives it is presumed to meet. A specific example is given in section 7.6 for an on-line system having both full-text input and humanly assigned index terms.

7.4 The interface in selective dissemination

A system which disseminates documents selectively to users is pursuing an active rather than a passive documentation role. However, the problem of matching user requirements and document characteristics is the same as that encountered in retrospective searching.

Two general classes of systems prevail. The first is a formal system in which index terms are assigned to incoming documents (humanly or by machine) and the "user profile" is also expressed in the same index terms. Documents which pass a threshold of match are then disseminated. The second class encompasses informal systems in which dissemination is based upon notes concerning subject matter of interest to specified users. Feedback is important in all selective dissemination systems, so that the user profile can be considered dynamic rather than static. It is well known that a researcher working in a relatively narrow field will be interested in widely different documents, depending upon his specific research projects. This is particularly true of researchers who work in overlapping scientific disciplines. Selective dissemination programs thus must have built into them a feedback mechanism which automatically provides a certain amount of evaluation.

The formal selective dissemination program can be evaluated by the same kind of conditional probabilities employed in the evaluation of retrospective searching. Let D_r and $D_{\bar{r}}$ denote relevance and non-relevance according to the dissemination decision. Then, one can estimate by the usual means, $\widetilde{P}(U_r|D_r)$ and $\widetilde{P}(U_r|D_{\bar{r}})$. By varying the degree of match, one can generate a curve such as that of Figure 2.6.

Some selective dissemination systems employ several levels of document surrogates. For example, the initial dissemination may consist of bibliographic entries. The user may specify those in which he is interested and receive abstracts of them. Finally, he may request full-text copies of a selection of these. Each of these stages in dissemination can be evaluated by the above means. The informal system can be evaluated in the same manner, where the judgment of the subject-matter analyst replaces the indexing score of the formal system.

In all selective dissemination systems, it is important to obtain some measures of usefulness to the user. This can be done by a user survey. Also, in systems where the initial dissemination is, in effect, an announcement (such as a list of bibliographic entries), one can use a copy of the announcement as an order form for documents or other surrogates, thus providing an automatic means for recording use.

One view of retrospective searches is that they occur only when the system has not anticipated the user's needs by selective dissemination. While this view of the role of selective dissemination is too global, there may be some validity to the hypothesis that with a good dissemination system the need for retrospective searches is reduced.

Therefore, from an evaluative standpoint, it may be useful to record over time the number of retrospective searches conducted by each user and to match this information against his response to the user survey and his recorded use of the selective dissemination program.

7.5 The interface in full-text systems

Full-text systems have enough peculiar properties to merit separate discussion. If all of a document is put into machine-readable form and is then indexed automatically, so that the computer-prepared indexing is used as a search tool, then the evaluation of the system can be handled as though the indexing had been done by hand. No special problems are encountered.

However, if the full text is entered into the system and made available for searching by the user without indexing, then some special procedures may be required.[2] Such a system is similar in some respects to an interactive system. The total burden for access to documents is placed on the user. His search strategy will consist of words and/or phrases, and he may specify the location of these (e.g., in the same paragraph or in the same sentence). For our purposes we do not distinguish between full-text systems for the entire document and full-text systems for abstracts.

The evaluation of full-text retrieval systems is not as difficult as the diagnostics. One can easily arrive at estimates of $P(U_r|R_r)$ and $P(U_r|R_{\bar{r}})$, but departures from perfection represent errors in searching strategy as well as fundamental limitations of the system. To distinguish the two may require an approximation to the best possible retrieval which can be generated by many iterations of the search by experts. Presumably, then, this will yield an estimate of system limitations, so that other departures can be attributed to the search strategies of the users.

As in the evaluation of interactive systems, the number of useful documents retrieved, plotted against a measure of search effort (time or number of documents examined), may be as good a summarization of the effectiveness of the system as one can achieve. Also, gross measures of use, the percentage of user references supplied by the system, as well as data generated by a user survey, are useful indicators of effectiveness.

[2] LITE is such a system.

7.6 Evaluation of an on-line system having manual and full-text input

An example is given to describe a comparative evaluation of the retrieval effectiveness of two indexing and search techniques. The two systems to be compared are:

(1) A manual indexing system based on humanly assigned index terms selected from a controlled thesaurus. The search file thus created can be searched on-line or off-line using Boolean-type search equations.

(2) A full-text searching system using the natural language of the complete input document or of a portion of it (e.g., an abstract).

Boolean logic can be used in searching for word combinations occurring in these texts in on-line or off-line modes. However, the on-line mode is assumed since user-system interaction is of prime concern in this chapter. Assume that word roots (stem-suffix cutoff) can also be searched, as can consecutive strings of characters wherever they appear in the text. Word proximity (e.g., co-occurrence in a paragraph or sentence) can be used as a syntactic substitute to improve the precision capabilities of searching.

The great attraction of system (2) lies in the possibility of reducing the costs of indexing. Manual indexing using a controlled vocabulary is an expensive operation; it creates its own problems (e.g., maintenance of consistency) and depends upon skilled and trained personnel who are difficult to recruit and retain. Maintenance of a dynamic, frequently updated, controlled vocabulary for such an indexing operation is a further expense. Free-language searching may offer certain economies in input operations, particularly for documents that can be obtained in machine-readable form as a by-product of another operation (e.g., wire messages or by-product paper tapes of other keyboarding procedures). However, it is important to show that the free-language search system can attain or exceed the performance capabilities of the manual system. Moreover, this performance level should be attainable without a disproportionate increase in output (searching) costs.

We can construct a stochastic model similar to the one described in Chapter 6 to evaluate an on-line interactive system. However, the processes and sources of error are somewhat different and must be redefined. The principal components of the model are as follows:

(1) *Intermediary relevance judgment*, if an intermediary is used to conduct the on-line search.

(2) *Query/system relevance response*, which is the system's response to a series of queries.

(3) *Screened system relevance response*, which corresponds to an intermediary's judgment (if an intermediary is used) and to the use of a document representation such as an abstract.

Values of $P(C_r|V_r)$ and $P(C_r|V_{\bar{r}})$ for (1) above and $P(S_r,R_r|V_r)$ and $P(S_r,R_r|V_{\bar{r}})$ for (3) above can be applied in the manner described previously. However, the query/system relevance response must be handled somewhat differently. It is possible to compensate for input inaccuracy more easily with on-line searching by sequentially broadening searches until a satisfactory number of relevant documents is retrieved. This is somewhat difficult and costly when off-line searching is performed. Thus, this has the effect of confounding search accuracy and input accuracy.

In evaluation of on-line searching, we also depart from single 2×2 measures of accuracy and apply these measures over a range of values. That is, we observe $P(R_r|C_r)$ and $P(R_r|C_{\bar{r}})$ over a broad range of values determined by a sequence of broadened searches. An example of this is given below.

In this example, we assume that an intermediary participates at three points in the overall search process. He first interprets the user's request submitted in written form, formulates search queries, and screens out documents that he considers irrelevant from inspection of document titles. We will first examine two on-line systems (one with index input and the other with abstract input) using an intermediary as stated above. These systems will be looked at with and without considering users and their costs. We will then examine the two systems as though the users actually conducted the searches at computer terminals without benefit of intermediaries.

As in Section 4.4, each alternative carries with it certain effectiveness probabilities as well as an associated set of cost figures that can be incorporated in the cost model described in Section 4.4. Table 7.1 displays the effectiveness probabilities and cost elements associated with searching abstracts and indexes on-line. In order to make direct comparisons of the two systems, experimental results of two systems reported by Salton (*8*) are given by establishing fallout $[P(R_r|C_{\bar{r}})]$. Thus, values of $P(R_r|C_{\bar{r}})$ are given for $P(R_r|C_r)$ at 0.40, 0.60, 0.80, and 1.00. The differences at each of these levels then will be the number

Table 7.1 Alternative On-line Retrospective Searching Processes: Effectiveness Probabilities and Costs

Alternatives	Effectiveness probabilites		Fixed costs	Variable costs
Intermediary interpretation				
By letter	$P(C_r \mid V_r)$ = 0.95	$P(C_r \mid V_{\bar{r}})$ = 0.0000034	C_4 = \$500	C_9 = \$11.25/search
Searching				
On-line index				
Level 1	$P(R_r \mid C_r)$ = 0.40	$P(R_r \mid C_{\bar{r}})$ = 0.000079	C_1 = \$68,200	$C_{10} + C_{11}$ = \$0.4415/item retrieved
Level 2	= 0.60	= 0.000227		= \$0.3194/item retrieved
Level 3	= 0.80	= 0.000626		= \$0.2494/item retrieved
Level 4	= 1.00	= 0.001656		= \$0.2218/item retrieved
Index input			C_3 = \$6,925	$C_6 + C_7X_5$ = \$0.6755/item input
Searching				
On-line abstract				
Level 1	$P(R_r \mid C_r)$ = 0.40	$P(R_r \mid C_{\bar{r}})$ = 0.000061	C_1 = \$191,750	$C_{10} + C_{11}$ = \$0.6768/item retrieved
Level 2	= 0.60	= 0.000132		= \$0.4029/item retrieved
Level 3	= 0.80	= 0.000417		= \$0.3756/item retrieved
Level 4	= 1.00	= 0.001280		= \$0.3235/item retrieved
Abstract input			C_3 = \$7,350	$C_6 + C_7X_5$ = \$1.6825/item input
Screening				
Mail			C_5 = \$2,500	C_8 = \$0.20/search C_{13} = \$0.002/item sent
No screen	$P(S_r \mid V_r)$ = 1.00	$P(S_r \mid V_{\bar{r}})$ = 1.00	C_2 = \$0	C_{12} = \$0
Loose – on titles	= 0.875	= 0.555	= \$0	= \$0.04/item retrieved

X_1 = 100,000 items over a 4-year period. X_2 = 4,000 searches per year. X_5 = 1,000 terms on authority list.

Table 7.2 Summary Retrieval and Cost Figures Associated with Combinations of Alternative Searching Processes

Recall level	Alternative search system	Recall	No. rel. retr.	No. retr. (X_3)	No. sent (X_4)	Total system cost	System cost/ search	System cost/ rel. retr.	User cost/ search	User cost/ rel. retr.
0.40	On-line index/ no screen	0.38	19.0	27.0	27.0	$188,708	$ 47.18	$2.48	$ 38.50	$2.53
	On-line abstract/ no screen	0.38	19.0	25.3	25.3	358,642	89.66	4.72	37.73	2.48
	On-line index/ screen on titles	0.33	16.6	27.0	21.1	192,984	48.24	2.91	37.55	2.82
	On-line abstract/ screen on titles	0.33	16.6	25.3	20.1	362,662	90.67	5.46	35.70	2.68
0.60	On-line index/ no screen	0.57	28.5	51.4	51.4	206,891	51.72	1.81	57.49	2.52
	On-line abstract/ no screen	0.57	28.5	41.9	41.9	354,649	88.66	3.11	53.42	2.34
	On-line index/ screen on titles	0.50	24.9	51.4	37.6	214,992	53.75	2.16	54.94	2.76
	On-line abstract/ screen on titles	0.50	24.9	41.9	31.5	364,444	91.11	3.66	50.42	2.53

0.80	On-line index/ no screen	0.76	38.0	100.9	100.9	242,277	60.57	1.59	89.29	2.94
	On-line abstract/ no screen	0.76	38.0	79.9	79.9	410,643	102.66	2.70	79.31	2.61
	On-line index/ screen on titles	0.67	33.3	100.9	68.1	258,159	64.54	1.94	85.34	3.21
	On-line abstract/ screen on titles	0.67	33.3	79.9	56.5	423,879	105.97	3.18	75.37	2.83
1.00	On-line index/ no screen	0.95	47.5	213.3	213.3	331,758	82.94	1.75	150.51	3.96
	On-line abstract/ no screen	0.95	47.5	175.4	175.4	518,333	129.58	2.73	136.07	3.58
	On-line index/ screen on titles	0.83	41.6	213.3	133.5	365,248	91.31	2.20	145.68	4.37
	On-line abstract/ screen on titles	0.83	41.6	175.4	112.6	545,895	136.47	2.96	127.67	3.83

of documents retrieved necessary to achieve each level and corresponding costs.

Comparisons can be made by applying the effectiveness probabilities and cost elements given in Table 7.1 to the stochastic model and cost model given in Chapter 4. Results are given in Table 7.2. Results suggest that the on-line index system is better than the on-line abstract system at all levels of search recall, considering cost/search and cost/relevant document retrieved. It is noted that, when considering cost/relevant document retrieved, screening on-line index searches costs more at recall of 0.40 and 0.60 but less at 0.80 and 1.00. On the other hand, no screening is best with the on-line abstract system at all levels of recall.

If the systems are judged by the number of documents sent to the users at each recall level, the on-line abstract system is clearly superior, particularly at high levels of recall. The number of documents sent to the users has clear implications for users' costs and satisfaction. Assume that users must also inspect the list of document titles to decide which documents to order. This process implies some level of screening accuracy depicted by $P(U_r|V_r)$ and $P(U_r|V_{\bar{r}})$, which we will assume to be 0.80 and 0.25, respectively. Assume that the users' costs are \$10/search; \$0.10/item examined; and \$1.50/item ordered. Results for user cost/search and user cost/relevant document retrieved are given in Table 7.2. If user costs alone are considered, the on-line abstract system is superior, and screening under this criterion would appear to be worthwhile. Also, it is noted that cost/relevant document retrieved begins to increase at 0.80 recall over 0.60 recall, so that the users' costs do play some role in deciding among alternate systems. When system costs are added to user costs, as when users are part of the proprietary system, the differences between the on-line index and on-line abstract systems become much less at high levels of recall, and the final decision might be made on other grounds.

If the role of intermediaries is eliminated by having the users participate directly with the search processes, accuracy should be increased, but costs may also increase since the users require individual training and a terminal source for searching. Furthermore, their base salaries may be higher than the salary of an intermediary. Improved accuracy can be simulated by eliminating interpretation and screening errors from the stochastic model. However, to be realistic, it must be recognized that an ordinary user cannot search as accurately as an experienced intermediary. Some experiments could be conducted to determine the relative search accuracy and costs.

7.7 Methodology

Ideally, in an evaluation of this type, we would like to be as realistic as possible. That is, we would like to conduct the comparative evaluation using real requests representing real information needs of real users. Moreover, we would like to select the requests in such a way that they would be representative of the various types of users of the system.

The requests should be so stratified that we would take a number of requests over a recent period from a certain type of requester, and a number of requests from a second type, and so on. For each of the test requests, the following is done:

(1) Collect from the user, on a special form, a list of documents already known to be relevant to a request.

(2) Translate the request into a search strategy and process the search against the file. The search analyst who conducts the test search should not know which are the "known relevant" documents. Only the evaluation staff will know this. Then observe, for each system, when 0.40, 0.60, . . . , 1.00 of the relevant documents are retrieved.

(3) Have the requester examine the documents retrieved by the search and assess each one for "relevance," using a special form to record his decisions and to give reasons why certain documents are not relevant. If the search retrieves a large number of documents, ask the requester, for test purposes, merely to examine a random sample.

(4) Derive values of $P(C_r|V_r)$ and $P(C_r|V_{\bar{r}})$ on the basis of the requester's relevance assessments and observed nonrelevant retrieved.

$P(R_r|C_r)$ is found by the proportion observed (0.40, . . . , 1.00). Total relevant at each level is found by dividing the number of relevant retrieved by 0.40, 0.60, . . . , 1.00, respectively. Total nonrelevant is found by subtracting the total number in the file by the total relevant, and $P(R_r|C_{\bar{r}})$ can then be estimated at each level. The above procedures will yield values which can then be incorporated into the stochastic model at each level of search. We also must observe time and total retrieval in order to obtain corresponding cost figures.

7.8 Synthetic requests

The above procedures make the assumptions that most requesters will already know some relevant documents at the time they make their requests to the system and that these documents can therefore be used as a recall base. This is the methodology used successfully by Lancaster in his large-scale evaluation of MEDLARS (*6*). Over 60 percent of the requesters in this study were able to name relevant documents in advance. In some systems, however, we cannot rely exclusively upon this technique because fewer of the requesters will be able to identify relevant documents within the data base to be evaluated.

Other methods that may be used are as follows:

(1) *Parallel search in another system* – Assuming that one can find one or more other systems (these could be manual indexes, machine indexes, or printed indexes) that partly overlap the file of interest, a parallel search is conducted in the other systems for each of the test requests in order to locate documents that appear to be relevant.

(2) *Source document test* – If no other systems are found that substantially overlap the coverage of the system, the above procedure for estimating recall cannot be used. Under these circumstances, one will have to use a more artificial or synthetic procedure. The method involves the use of source documents. It works as follows. Extract at random from the data base a set of documents, say 100. For each of these documents a subject specialist should make up a request for which the source document would be a major value relevant response. These requests are then translated into search strategies and processed against the system. The retrieved citations are assessed for relevance. Recall is either 100 or zero depending on whether or not the source document was retrieved. At the single search level, the recall estimate is pretty meaningless, but if over 100 searches we find that we have hit the source document 90 times, then our overall recall estimate is 90 percent. This procedure for estimating recall is really a "quick and dirty" procedure which is much less satisfactory than using real requests. However, it does give a recall estimate that is valid for comparing two retrieval modes and one may have to rely on it if all else fails. We would always want to use some real-life requests in conjunction with the source document searches, deriving our estimates from the former.

7.9 Failure analysis

In the evaluation of document transfer systems, it may not be enough merely to derive performance figures. An analysis may be needed to determine causes of system failures. This type of failure analysis has been conducted extensively by Lancaster in the evaluation of MEDLARS (*6*) and the Bureau of Ships SHARP system and by King (*1, 5*). Without a failure analysis to tell why certain things occur, reasonable decisions as to the best course of action cannot be made. For example, one may find that full-text searching is clearly inferior to manual indexing. However, this may have nothing directly to do with the full text as a document surrogate. Perhaps the search strategies used were inadequate and a much higher accuracy is potentially achievable with improved strategies.

Having derived performance figures, one can subject each search to a detailed analysis to determine causes of failures in the controlled-vocabulary searching and causes of failures in the full-text searching. These failures can be expected to break down into the following broad groups:

(1) *Indexing failures.* These are failures of policy and practice. They would include such causes as indexing errors, indexing omissions, and failures due to the policy as to the number of terms assigned in indexing. In the full-text searching they would mostly relate to the inadequacy of the full-text surrogate as a content-indicator.

(2) *Vocabulary failures.* There will be two main types in any system:

(a) Failures due to lack of specificity.

(b) Failures due to ambiguous or spurious relations between terms.

(3) *Search strategy failures.* These include errors of strategy, searching policy failures, and failures to cover all retrieval approaches.

(4) *Interaction failures.* These are failures due to the fact that a stated request does not always accurately reflect a person's information need.

Failure analysis involves an examination of the document, indexing records, requests, search strategies, and relevance assessment forms. The completed failure analysis, in conjunction with the performance figures, will allow assessment of the true capability of full-text searching and balancing of this capability against cost considerations.

References

1. Atherton, P., King, D. W., Freeman, R. R., *Evaluation of the Retrieval of Nuclear Science Document References Using the Universal Decimal Classification as the Indexing Language for a Computer-based System.* New York, American Institute of Physics UDC Project, May 1, 1968.
2. Flood, B., "Analysis of Questions Addressed to a Medical Reference Retrieval System: Comparison of Question and System Terminologies." *American Documentation,* Vol. 18 (October 1967), pp. 216-227.
3. Keen, E. M., *Search Strategy Evaluation in Manual and Automated Systems.* Presented at ASLIB Annual Conference, Harrogate, England, 9-12 October 1967.
4. Keen, E. M., "User-controlled Search Strategies." *In*: Tonik, A. B., ed. *Information Retrieval: The User's Viewpoint, An Aid to Design.* Philadelphia, International Information, Inc., 1967, pp. 141-154.
5. King, D. W., McDonnell, P. M., "Evaluation of Coordinate Index Systems During File Development, Part II: An Application." *Journal of Chemical Documentation,* Vol. 6, No. 4 (November 1966), pp. 235-240.
6. Lancaster, F. W., *Evaluation of the MEDLARS Demand Search Service.* Bethesda, Md., National Library of Medicine, January 1968.
7. Salton, G., *Automatic Information Organization and Retrieval.* New York, McGraw-Hill, 1968.
8. Salton, G., "A Comparison Between Manual and Automatic Indexing Methods." *American Documentation,* Vol. 20, No. 1 (January 1969), pp. 61-71.
9. Salton, G., *Evaluation Problems in Interactive Information Retrieval.* Ithaca, N. Y., Cornell University, August 1969.

Chapter Eight

Evaluation of Composition, Reproduction, Acquisition, Storage, and Presentation Systems

8.1 Introduction

In Chapter 1, we indicated that complete transfer of documents from author to user normally involves six basic functions – composition, reproduction, acquisition and storage, identification and location, presentation, and assimilation. Chapters 2 through 7 dealt with evaluation of identification systems and several processes related to these systems. One reason why so much attention has been given to identification is that this function is performed at both the central and local levels. Furthermore, considerable attention has been paid to the development of mechanized search systems as a result of the wider availability of computer facilities. Thus, much interest has been aroused in experimentation and evaluation of both passive and active identification systems.

Interest in the other functions – composition, reproduction, acquisition, storage, and presentation – has been somewhat less widespread.[1] Nevertheless, a proprietary system engaged in these activities

[1] Almost no attention has been paid in the literature to the assimilation function, i.e., the user's perception of the document. We feel that this function may take on more importance in the future as far as evaluation is concerned. It is possible that documents may be reformatted to facilitate reading at different levels or that the printing style may change to accommodate rapid reading as that becomes more popular. Such changes will warrant evaluation and assessment.

must consider them all in evaluating the overall system. Examples of such proprietary systems are: (1) the National Technical Information Service (formerly CFSTI) and ERIC, both of which perform virtually all of the functions necessary to transfer government-sponsored scientific and technical reports, and (2) professional societies, such as the American Institute of Physics, the American Chemical Society, and the American Psychological Association, that are involved in primary publication programs. These organizations must consider all of the functions and their interrelationships when evaluating and designing their overall systems.

This chapter discusses the evaluation of acquisition and storage systems that apply to both central and local information systems, and presents an example of an evaluation of a central system incorporating composition, reproduction, storage, and presentation functions.

8.2 Evaluation of document acquisition and storage systems

A view held consistently throughout this book is that the overall objective of a document transfer system is to facilitate the user's access to literature of interest. This objective does not imply that every document the user wants must be stored in the local collection. Since all systems that provide published information to users operate under some kind of budgetary limitation, the operational problem becomes one of maximizing service within whatever monetary, space, political, and other constraints are imposed by the environment within which the system operates.

Viewed in this light, funds spent for maintaining and adding to the collection cannot be spent on such activities as current awareness programs, selective dissemination, development of special indexes and bibliographies, and other activities which foster access to documents. The acquisition problem clearly involves every phase of a document transfer system, and in that respect is no different from the problem of evaluating any other major function of the system.

To date, the literature has not contained any generalized global solutions to system problems, and we assume that this condition will persist in the foreseeable future. Thus, in our evaluation of acquisition as well as other functions, we will direct our attention first to the evaluation of effectiveness and then conclude with some remarks on economic models.

8.3 Measuring the effectiveness of acquisition programs

Some methods were proposed in Chapter 3 for determining the extent to which potential users obtain their references through the system being tested. Those methods will also yield some gross measures of the adequacy of the file. The results obtained in Chapter 3 will, of course, reflect a wider spectrum of reasons for use (or nonuse) of the system than just availability of references.

In this section we are interested primarily in answering the question, "How effective are the procedures for locating, acquiring, and making available to users references that are of interest to them?" This question is much broader than just evaluating the file, and is more difficult.

The acquisition program must be evaluated in terms of the objectives that the system is designed to achieve. Such objectives usually involve some assumption about the speed with which users must receive information. These requirements can be quite different from one system to another. An information system on poisons for the use of doctors, for example, can be expected to require a faster response time than one dealing with animal nutrition for use in animal husbandry research.

Assumptions about requirements can be verified by a user study (see Chapter 10). Such a study can also reveal the need for maintaining a browsing collection, foreign language collections, indexes, translations, and so on. The results of the user study may then be used to refine the statement of objectives. However, any modification of objectives must be undertaken by system management – not by the evaluator. It is appropriate for him to *recommend* a modification in objectives, but not to assume such a modification as a background against which to evaluate.

The evaluation can be done in two stages. First, one can determine how adequately the collection serves the needs of users. Second, one can examine the procedures for selecting materials and making them available.

The first stage can be initiated with the same kind of sample of potential users (potential in the sense of matching system objectives) that was described in Chapter 3. In that chapter, two samples of documents were identified – one of recently used references and one of documents which the researcher would like to have at that moment. Although some bias is created by knowledge of documents that are readily accessible, it seems wisest here to use only the sample of recently used references. We want to know where they came from. Further, since an important consideration in acquisition systems is how quickly new literature is put into the system, we want them classified by publication date (or whatever other date represents the earliest time at which they might have been available to the system). A summary table, such as Table 8.1, can be used to display the results.

No standards exist for what is "good" and what is "bad." However, the numbers in the cells of Table 8.1 should permit subjective evaluation of performance in the light of objectives to provide a specified proportion of literature needs locally and to provide browsing and current awareness service.

Table 8.1 Summary of Sources of Recently Used Documents

	Age since publication				
Item	Less than 1 month	1 to 3 months	3 months to 1 year	Over 1 year	Total
Source of document					
(1) From researcher's own personal collection	____	____	____	____	____
(2) From system collection under evaluation:	____	____	____	____	____
(a) Normal processing	____	____	____	____	____
(b) Special order	____	____	____	____	____
(c) Accelerated special order	____	____	____	____	____
(3) From outside sources	____	____	____	____	____
Totals	____	____	____	____	____
(4) Number of documents known to be in the file	____	____	____	____	____
Source of awareness					
(5) Current awareness or selective dissemination system	____	____	____	____	____
(6) Searching proprietary file	____	____	____	____	____
(7) Searching other files	____	____	____	____	____
(8) Browsing proprietary file	____	____	____	____	____
(9) Browsing other files	____	____	____	____	____
(10) Reference in published paper	____	____	____	____	____
(11) Other researchers	____	____	____	____	____
(12) Other sources					
Totals	____	____	____	____	____

In the user survey, or in the process of obtaining a sample of test references, one can also obtain measures of user satisfaction with respect to acquisition procedures. Judgments might be obtained on the following matters:

(1) Proportion of the user's reference needs which are provided by items in the collection.

A background would have to be developed to define needs and to set a period of common reference. The results could be checked against actual data of Table 8.1.

(2) User's opinion with respect to weaknesses in the collection.

Subject matter areas which need augmentation, as well as specific journals, indexes, abstracting services, and other sources, should be identified.

(3) User's opinion with respect to responsiveness to requests for acquisition.

Data should be obtained on adequacy of principal support, assistance in locating materials, initiation of queries concerning interest, time delays, and so on. One would probably not do a separate user study to obtain data, but questions concerning them could easily be combined with other questions that might be required as a part of the total evaluation.

The data to be obtained in the second stage of the evaluation are produced by a survey of budgets, procedures, and policies. Answers should be provided to the following questions:

(1) What is the annual budget for acquisitions? What is its proportion of the total operating budget? How much of the budget is for new materials and how much for continuing subscriptions?

There are no satisfactory standards against which these figures can be checked. However, it should be reasonably easy to determine whether the budget matches the user's requirements determined above.

(2) What activities are undertaken to locate documents of possible interest? How are these activities tied in with current awareness? Is the system such that frequently requested serials will automatically be brought to the attention of the Acquisitions Department?

(3) What is the average elapsed time between receipt of a purchase request and mailing the order for the item requested?

The required information usually can be obtained by matching purchase orders against dated request slips. One should watch particularly for backlogs in checking requests against the files and in actual placement of orders.

(4) What is the average delay from receipt of the item to making it available to users in general and requesters in particular?

The data can usually be obtained by matching items placed in the collection with shipping notices, invoices, receiving forms, or whatever other documentation that shows date of receipt. One should check, in particular, the size of the indexing or cataloging backlog if such a step is a prerequisite to making materials available. One should also find out whether requested items must go through this step before use by the requester.

The above data can be classified into:

(1) Measure of the collection.
(2) Measure of opinions of users.
(3) Measure of acquisition performance.

Since there are no standards, the use of these measures in establishing policy must be subjective.

Typically, a retrieval system will maintain a collection that satisfies part of the needs of users and will rely on borrowing from outside sources to satisfy the remainder of users' needs. In the following section we consider the allocation of resources between acquisition (and maintenance) of a collection and borrowing as needed from outside sources.

8.4 Economic evaluation of acquisition programs

The spectrum of document transfer systems considered in this book is broad enough to include systems in which no full-text documents are stored in the system. A system which collects and distributes abstracts is an illustration. In such cases, an abstract can be considered to be a document with no loss in generality of the methods presented here.

A system which is even less collection-oriented is one in which bibliographic data concerning documents are classified in various ways to serve as a switching device to direct researchers to the literature of interest to them. Such a system would be exemplified by a catalog with no immediately supporting book collection (as in a regional union catalog) or by the files and indexes of a referral center.

ELEMENTS OF COST IN ACQUISITION AND BORROWING

When one considers costs, it is important to define the entity to which the costs are chargeable. For example, the establishment of a national library in a specific field may enable a local library to "save" costs by borrowing from the national library, but the total cost to society may be greater. When we refer to costs in this section, we will mean costs to the proprietary system under the control of the local funding entity and not those to the universal system of which the proprietary system is a part.

In addition, except as otherwise specified, we will identify costs with expenditures, thereby ignoring the difficulties inherent in quantifying items which have come to be known as "intangible costs."

Broad categories of costs associated with acquiring and owning documents are as follows:

(1) *Acquisition costs,* including selection, bibliographic checking, ordering, receiving, and bookkeeping.

(2) *Indexing costs,* including preparation of cards, if any, analysis and coding of subject categories, marking for storage, and entry to mechanized systems.

(3) *Subscription or purchase and binding costs* (where applicable).

(4) *Searching costs,* the costs of processing the file, which increase as the size of the file increases.

(5) *Circulation costs,* including recordkeeping, replacement of lost items, repair, and so on.

(6) *Maintenance costs*, including shelf straightening, storage, and repair.

Costs for acquisition, indexing, and binding are a function of the number of items acquired, where "item" may be interpreted to be a journal, a book, or a scientific paper. Searching costs are a function of file size, but do not apply to collections in which the identity of the item is prespecified. Circulation costs are a function of the number of items loaned, while maintenance costs are a function of total file size.

Cost of borrowing an item can be classified as:

(1) *Personnel costs* of locating the item, ordering it, circulating it when received, and so on.

(2) *Out-of-pocket costs* to pay for postage, photocopying (if applicable), and fees.

(3) *Intangible costs*, such as delay costs and the costs of not having the item available in the browsing collection.

Cost comparisons are never as simple as those implied by the above listings. For example, having an item in the proprietary collection is no guarantee that it will be available when requested. It is often on loan, being indexed, being bound, misplaced, or lost. It is therefore unfair to compare owning with borrowing on the assumption that access is *always* fostered by owning. But one can assume that, on the average, holding the item in the proprietary collection reduces access time.

A study prepared for the National Science Foundation by the Center for Research Libraries (*10*) showed that relatively few serial titles account for a major portion of requests for serials. The degree of concentration, of course, will depend upon the system collection and environment, but the evidence is indisputable that the uses per document per year drop off sharply as the document collection increases in size. Since all systems operate with limited funds, the management of every system must choose between using funds for acquisitions or for other service improvements, such as preparation of special indexes and bibliographies, or increases in the number or level of personnel.

One deterrent to heavy investment in documents is the observed decline in their use as they become older. It has been found (*10*) that, in research libraries, the use of serials declines about 7 percent per year, on the average, as time progresses away from date of issue. The relationship is inexact in the first few years of the issue, but serves well as a planning figure.

A PRELIMINARY ECONOMIC MODEL

It has become customary to compare costs on a "present value" basis. That is, we determine a planning period of, say, 20 years, and then we determine the amount of money required to be set aside today to meet the stream of costs to be incurred during the succeeding 20 years. Use of a nonzero interest rate causes the present value to be smaller than the expenditure required in the future by the amount of the compounded interest on the present value. The higher the interest rate, the smaller the present value.

It has also become customary to adjust expenditures by an assumed inflation rate. The higher the inflation rate, the more money must be set aside to meet future expenditures.

In general, let c_t denote costs in the year t with a T-year planning period. Assume costs are incurred at the beginning of each year, and let j be the annual rate of inflation and i be the annual rate of interest, compounded annually. Then, the present value can be written:

$$c = \sum_{t=0}^{T-1} c_t \left(\frac{1+j}{1+i}\right)^t \qquad (1)$$

The costs in time period t are a sum of the following costs: (1) acquisition, (2) indexing, (3) subscription and binding, (4) searching, (5) circulation, (6) maintenance, and (7) borrowing costs. One adds whichever costs apply to the given case, applies equation (1), and adds overall years of the planning period.

Some methodology for obtaining cost estimates, as well as sample costs for research libraries, is given in Williams (*10*). That report also provides some rough guidelines concerning levels of use that make owning less costly than borrowing for research libraries. It is shown, for example, that if a serial title (with 10 years of back issues) is used less than about five times per year, on a strictly economic basis its acquisition must be justified on other than out-of-pocket costs – perhaps on the basis of user time or browsing availability. The results should not be considered widely generalizable, however. It is necessary to do cost studies in systems in which economic evaluation must be performed. Some suggestions on methodology were given in Chapter 3.

EXAMPLE WITH HYPOTHETICAL COSTS

Consider a 10-year planning period with the assumption that a document held for the entire 10 years will have zero salvage value. (Otherwise, the discounted salvage value must be subtracted from the present value of costs.) Assume also a 5-percent interest rate and a 3-percent inflation rate. Thus, $(1+j)/(1+i) = 1.03/1.05 = 0.981$. This is approximately the equivalent of a 2-percent interest rate, ignoring inflation.

Consider the purchase of a research monograph for \$12.50. It is anticipated that initial demand might amount to about five requests per year, and that demand will decline by 10 percent per year. Assume that estimated costs are as follows:

(1) *Acquisition costs*: \$20, found by dividing total labor costs

involved in acquisitions activities (plus an overhead charge) by the total number of acquisitions in a year.

(2) *Indexing costs*: $15, found by dividing total materials and labor costs in indexing, plus overhead, by number of items indexed.

(3) *Purchase cost*: $12.50.

(4) *Searching costs*: $1, found by dividing total machine costs plus labor and overhead in screening and other search-related activities, by number of documents in the file.

(5) *Circulation costs*: $2.50, found by dividing total labor and overhead costs identifiable with circulation by number of items loaned.

(6) *Maintenance costs*: $0.25, found by dividing the total of amortized building and equipment costs, shelf maintenance, repairs, and building maintenance by number of items stored.

(7) *Borrowing costs*: $6, found by adding postage and borrowing fees to the quotient of total personnel and overhead costs in the borrowing activity and the number of items borrowed.

An example of the required computations is shown in Table 8.2. Column (8) shows the present value of owning costs, that is, projected total costs multiplied by the present value adjustment. The total of this column is a numerical evaluation of equation (1) for the owning alternative. Column (9) gives the comparable present values of the borrowing alternative, that is, $6 times column (1) times column (2). For the hypothetical data shown, owning is the lower cost alternative.

For periodical subscriptions, the computations are slightly more complex. Column (2) must take into account:

- Increased demand as the file of back issues accumulates, and
- Decline in demand with age.

For example, suppose a journal is expected to have five requests during the first year of acquisition and that demand is expected to decline 10 percent per year with increasing age. Then, five requests are expected during the first year, 5 + 4.5 = 9.5 during the second year, 9.5 + 4.1 = 13.6 during the third year, and so on.

A second required adjustment is that searching and maintenance costs, column (5), will increase linearly with the number of volumes in storage. Finally, column (4) must include annual subscription costs and check-in, claiming, marking, and other recurring annual costs. A model that includes all of these adjustments, as well as others, is given in the Appendix in Williams (*10*).

Table 8.2 Illustration of Computing Present Values of Costs of Owning and Borrowing – Hypothetical Data

			Costs of owning					
Year (1)	Estimated demand (2)	Present value adjustment (3)	Initial costs (4)	Searching & maintenance (5)	Circulation costs (6)	Total (7)	Present value (8)	Present value of borrowing costs (9)
1	5.0	1.000	$47.50	$1.25	$12.50	$61.25	$ 61.25	$ 30.00
2	4.5	0.981	0	1.25	11.25	12.50	12.26	26.46
3	4.1	0.962	0	1.25	10.25	11.50	11.06	23.64
4	3.7	0.944	0	1.25	9.25	10.50	9.91	20.94
5	3.3	0.926	0	1.25	8.25	9.50	8.80	18.36
6	3.0	0.908	0	1.25	7.50	8.75	7.95	16.44
7	2.7	0.891	0	1.25	6.75	8.00	7.13	14.46
8	2.4	0.874	0	1.25	6.00	7.25	6.34	12.60
9	2.2	0.857	0	1.25	5.50	6.75	5.78	11.34
10	1.9	0.841	0	1.25	4.75	6.00	5.05	9.60
Totals	32.8						$135.53	$183.84

The determination of costs is critical in the economic evaluation of acquisition policies and procedures. The methodology presented in Chapter 3 may be useful in cost determination.

8.5 Evaluation of storage processes

A substantial amount of work has been performed at Purdue University concerning storage models (*4, 5, 6, 7*). These models were developed to establish storage arrangements that would minimize wasted space. The general approach to minimizing the wasted space is to measure the dimensions of books in a given collection and divide the collection once at each possible point, measure the gain in space at each point, and choose the point that is best. This procedure is then repeated for all possible pairs of subdivision points, with the net gain measured and the best pair noted. This process is continued until there are as many subclasses as there are book sizes. A whole set of possible shelving patterns is generated with their related spatial cost, and the best cutting points may be noted for any number of subdivisions.

Table 8.3 gives the results for a representative sample of the Purdue collection at optional shelf heights. Following the initial large gains for the first three classes, the capacity gain decreased rapidly as the number of size classes increased. Thus, it was felt that no more than three or four classes would be justified in order to reduce wasted space sufficiently.

Table 8.3 Efficiency of Storage by Size Class

	Potential capacity increase	
Number of size classes	Storage by height (%)	Storage by width (%)
1	0	27
2	38	94
3	47	111
4	51	116
5	53	121
10	58	128

8.6 An example of evaluating a composition, reproduction, storage, and presentation system

An example is given here to describe evaluation of a proposed composition, reproduction, storage, and presentation system (*3*). The American Psychological Association (APA) has developed the basic concepts for a National Information System for Psychology (NISP), which is designed to enhance communication and information transfer among psychologists (*1*). The object of NISP is to develop information services and products that can best serve the needs of these scientists through better information control and by distribution methods that permit more highly discriminating user/manuscript matching and by faster document transfer in a feasible cost/effectiveness manner. NISP incorporates both formal and informal information transfer processes. However, the heart of the system involves information transfer of unit communications in the form of print-on-paper. A distinction is made in the system between unit communication and conventional printed journal articles and other common documents because of the forms the units may take and because of the unique ways in which these units are processed from author to user.

Information transfer has several advantages by means of the journal mode:

(1) High-quality manuscripts, both editorially and technically, due to the reviewing process.

(2) High-quality printing.

(3) Convenient storage of journals in office or "local" libraries.

(4) Author prestige or social value.

The disadvantages of journal communications include the following:

(1) There is a time delay from manuscript submission to availability, which averages 11 months in manuscript processing.

(2) Since the screening process is so fine (approximately 70 percent of the manuscripts are rejected), many useful articles may be denied the users due to stringent review criteria.

(3) Many potential manuscripts may not be submitted to the sponsoring agency, since authors may not wish to adhere to stringent reviewing rules and time delay.

(4) The selective dissemination characteristics of journal "pack-

aging" of articles may not be sufficiently discriminating, since over eight articles are sent to the subscriber for each one read.

During the sixties, the APA felt that the cost/effectiveness of their journal system could be improved. In 1963, it was estimated that the average initial readership of APA journal publications was approximately 520 readings per article (*2*). Extrapolating this number to current membership, it was estimated that this figure was approximately 690 readings per article in 1969, which means, roughly, that APA members "read" an average of 57.6 APA journal articles per year. The users were exposed (by journal subscription) to approximately 480 journal articles on the average, so that they were sent many articles that went unread. With a cost of $1,316,000 for the primary journal, the cost per article read was approximately $0.80. Considering the cost of reviewing articles prior to publication, this cost was estimated to be a total of approximately $1 per article read.

APA proposed a unit communication system which would at least partially overcome the disadvantages of the journal system and retain its advantages. In the proposed unit communication system, manuscripts submitted to APA were to take one of the following forms: unedited printed manuscripts, edited journal articles, or edited annals. The particular form that each manuscript took depended on two selection criteria: (1) likelihood of relevance (or usefulness), and (2) quality of the article in the standard review sense. Highly relevant articles, articles of superior quality, and classics in the field were to end up in the annals. However, all manuscripts were to be made available to users upon receipt at APA, with the duration from receipt to availability substantially reduced. Some manuscripts were to be selected and sent automatically to users who subscribed to certain categories. Thus, a user could receive certain manuscripts automatically or he could choose to order manuscripts individually. Presumably, inherently bad manuscripts would be available, but would not be distributed except on request. All materials would be available so that good articles would not be denied due to stringent review and authors would feel greater freedom to submit their materials. Thus, all of the disadvantages of the journal mode were, at least conceptually, eliminated by the unit communication approach. Furthermore, the annals would retain the advantages of the journal system for those articles warranting special treatment and withstanding the test of time.

The model for the unit communication system incorporating APA-originated manuscripts involves four basic functions: composition, reproduction, storage, and presentation. These functions are broken down into the following general processes:

(1) Composition – review (for journal articles and annals only).
(2) Reproduction – input processing and reproduction.
(3) Storage – full-text storage for appropriate manuscripts.
(4) Presentation – selective distribution and request processing.

Reproduction is considered first.

The following alternative printing processes were considered from a cost/effectiveness viewpoint: (1) typing by the author, (2) copier process, (3) offset printing using one form of reproduction masters, (4) offset printing u·ing another form of reproduction masters, and (5) present journal printing.

The approximate costs of these printing processes are shown in Figure 8.1 (for a 10-page manuscript), by number of copies produced. Figure 8.2 shows the cost for (3) above and for the present journal publications.

One can clearly see that:

(1) If no (0) copies are desired, one should merely keep the original typed copies in the archives.

(2) If 1-5 copies are desired, one should use the copier process.

(3) If 5-10,000 copies are desired, one should use the proposed offset process.

(4) If over 10,000 copies are desired, one should use the present journal printing.

The problem, of course, is that the number of copies to be distributed per given manuscript is not known ahead of time. As mentioned previously, when a new manuscript enters the system some copies may be sent to subscribers immediately while others may be distributed upon request. Thus, the demand for each manuscript may vary from zero to several thousand. Some of the printing processes listed above are not cost-feasible unless one prints more than 10 copies. Thus, some methodology must be developed concerning the number of copies to print (and store) in anticipation of future demand.

The cost/effectiveness analysis assumes that the primary objective of the APA system was to facilitate the transfer of relevant (used) articles from authors to users. There is substantial evidence (*2, 9*) that articles (and other information materials) vary considerably by fre-

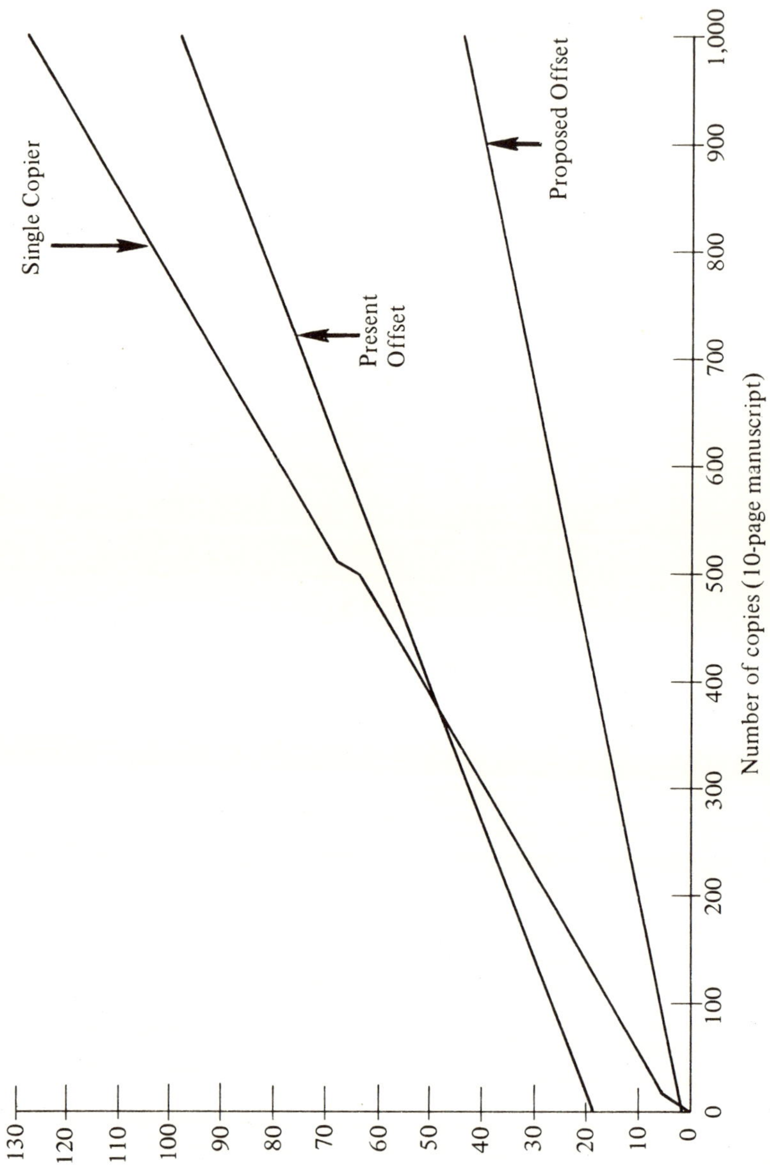

Figure 8.1 Cost of printing 0-1,000 copies by single copies, present offset, and proposed offset.

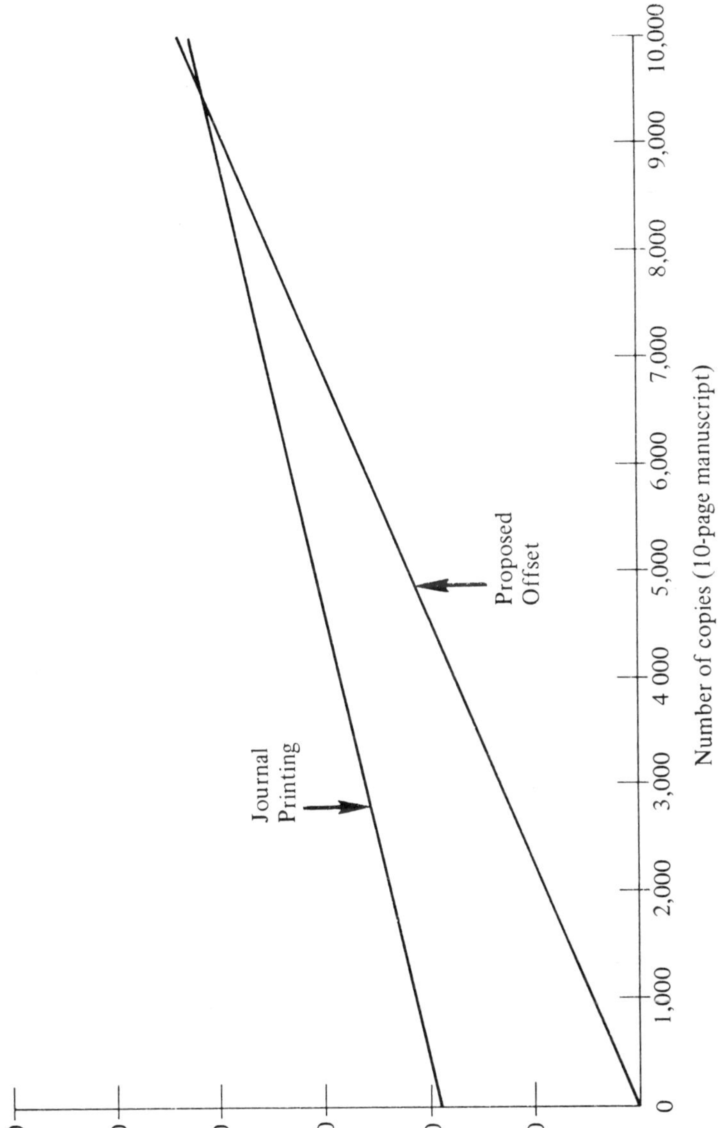

Figure 8.2 Cost of printing 0-10,000 copies by journal printing and proposed offset.

quency of use. That is, a few articles are read with high frequency and a large number are read infrequently or used by other than the authors or their sponsors.

As mentioned previously, APA journal articles may be read approximately 690 times on the average. However, some articles are read much more (10 percent are read more than 1,000 times) and some, much less (roughly 20 percent are read less than 10 times). A rough estimate is given below in Table 8.4 for the entire distribution of number of readings per manuscript.

Table 8.4 Readership Distribution

Readership	Proportion of manuscripts	Cumulative proportion of manuscripts
0	0.10	0.10
1-10	0.08	0.18
11-50	0.15	0.33
51-100	0.10	0.43
101-200	0.12	0.55
201-500	0.20	0.75
501-1,000	0.16	0.91
1,001-2,000	0.08	0.99
> 2,001	0.01	1.00

The optimal (least cost) number of copies printed may be estimated with the readership distribution shown above. The ideal situation is to print the exact number of copies necessary to satisfy demand for each manuscript, but this is not possible. Assume, for example, that the average number of pages per manuscript is 10 and that 100, 150, 200, 250, and 500 copies are 5 candidates for the number of copies printed. Each print quantity results in some overstocking and in some reprinting. The amount of overstocking and reprinting, which greatly affects cost, depends on the readership distribution. If printing is done in lots of 100 copies, demand for 43 percent of the manuscripts is satisfied by the 100 copies (although some of these are substantially overstocked) and the remaining 57 percent require additional printing. A second printing of 100 takes care of an additional 12 percent of the manuscripts and 45 percent still require additional stock, and so on.

The total number of printing lots of 100 is computed as follows in Table 8.5.

Table 8.5 Computation of Lots of 100

Readership	Manuscripts X	Proportion of mss. X	No. of lots of 100	=	Total lots
<100	5,000	0.43	1		2,150
200	5,000	0.12	2		1,200
300	5,000	0.067	3		1,005
400	5,000	0.067	4		1,340
500	5,000	0.067	5		1,675
600	5,000	0.032	6		960
700	5,000	0.032	7		1,120
800	5,000	0.032	8		1,280
900	5,000	0.032	9		1,440
1,000	5,000	0.032	10		1,600
1,100	5,000	0.008	11		440
1,200	5,000	0.008	12		480
1,300	5,000	0.008	13		520
1,400	5,000	0.008	14		560
1,500	5,000	0.008	15		600
1,600	5,000	0.008	16		640
1,700	5,000	0.008	17		680
1,800	5,000	0.008	18		720
1,900	5,000	0.008	19		760
2,000	5,000	0.008	20		800
2,100	5,000	0.003	21		315
2,200	5,000	0.003	22		330
2,300	5,000	0.003	23		345
Total					20,960

Similarly, the total number of printing lots of 500 is computed as follows in Table 8.6.

Table 8.6 Computation of Lots of 500

Readership	Manuscripts X	Proportion of mss. X	No. of lots of 500	=	Total lots
<500	5,000	0.75	1		3,750
1,000	5,000	0.16	2		1,600
1,500	5,000	0.04	3		600
2,000	5,000	0.04	4		800
2,500	5,000	0.01	5		250
Total					7,000

Table 8.10 gives a detailed breakdown of reproduction costs. These costs are summarized below in Table 8.7.

Table 8.7 Printing Costs

Item	Cost per unit ($)
Master	0.1838 per master per page
Binding	0.0200 per copy
Duplication	0.0044 per impression
Set-up for duplication	1.000 per lot
Collating	0.100 per lot per page
	0.005 per page

For printing in lots of 100 copies of 10 pages, we have the following costs in Table 8.8.

Table 8.8 Printing Costs for 100 Copies of 10 Pages

Item	Manuscripts X	Copies X	Pages X	Lots X	Cost ($) =	Total cost ($)
Master	5,000		10		0.1838	9,190
Binding		100		20,960	0.0200	41,920
Duplication		100	10	20,960	0.0044	92,224
Set-up for duplication				20,960	1.0000	20,960
			10	20,960	0.1000	20,960
Collating				20,960	0.0500	1,048
			10	20,960	0.0050	1,048
Total						187,350

The remaining costs can be derived from Table 8.11. The total printing and binding costs for this distribution are approximately $187,350 (cost is broken down subsequently). Corresponding costs for other printing quantities are as given below in Table 8.9.

Table 8.9 Total Printing & Binding Costs for 100, 150, 200, 250 and 500 Copies

Printing quantity (copies)	100	150	200	250	500
Total printing & binding costs	$187,350	$187,000	$185,000	$197,400	$247,900

Clearly, if no effort is made to discriminate highly used from infrequently used manuscripts, the optimum number of copies to print is roughly 200.

A series of reproduction decision models has been developed (*9*) that can be applied to unit communication reproduction processes in order to decide whether or not to disseminate copies selectively and to determine how many copies to print and store in anticipation of demand. The models are of two kinds. The first model is used to predict future demand based on a subject analyst's assessment, characteristics of manuscripts (e.g., subject, author), characteristics of users (i.e., subject interests), and observed demand when available. The second model determines the printing quantity that minimizes costs, based on the estimated future demand and the probability distribution about the estimate.

Another question to be answered concerns whether the optimum print quantity above holds for manuscripts having fewer or more than 10 pages. If the same analysis were performed for manuscripts having 2 pages and 20 pages, the printing quantity for each would be a minimum of 200.

The following cost analysis for the unit communication system assumes that the system is fully operational at a level of 5,000 manuscripts per year and that there are 1,000 members per subject category.

Table 8.10 gives acquisition, reproduction, storage, and presentation costs per unit. Table 8.11 presents a further breakdown of printing costs by number of copies and number of pages.

The total cost of the unit communication system can be estimated from the unit costs given in Tables 8.10 and 8.11. A large range of printing and distribution options might be considered. For example, it may be better to (1) selectively distribute the full text of all manuscripts, (2) satisfy all readership requests on demand, or (3) selectively distribute the full text of a portion of the highly read manuscripts and satisfy remaining needs by request. Examples of cost

Table 8.10 Acquisition, Reproduction, Storage, and Presentation Costs

Acquisition function	Cost
Input processing:	*Per manuscript*
Screening	$1.00
Evaluation & subject analysis	1.60
Accessioning	0.25
Input descriptive catalog	1.00
Total	$3.85
Reproduction function	
Printing:	*Per master per page*
Machine rental	$0.1000
Duplication	0.0400
Paper	0.0038
Labor	0.0400
Total	$0.1838
Printing:	*Per impression*
Machine rental	$0.0010
Duplication	0.0005
Paper	0.0019
Labor	0.0010
Total	$0.0044
Binding:	*Per copy*
Binding	$0.0100
Labor	0.0100
Total	$0.0200
Printing:	*Per lot*
Labor set-up	$1.00
Printing:	*Per lot per page*
Labor	$0.10
Collating:	*Per lot*
Labor set-up	$0.05
Collating:	*Per page*
Machine & labor	$0.005

Table 8.10 Acquisition, Reproduction, Storage, and Presentation Costs (Continued)

Storage function	
	Per copy
Storage	$0.02

Presentation function	
Initial:	*Per copy*
Identification	$0.11
Shipping and handling	0.09
Total	$0.20
Request processing:	*On demand*
Mail room	$0.06
Accounting	0.08
Identification and verification	0.10
Files and audit	0.08
Shipping and handling	0.20
Total	$0.52

analysis are given in the following tabulation for (1) and (2), and two examples are given for (3). (Total costs for these four examples are given in Tables 8.12, 8.13, 8.14, and 8.15.) For combinations of selective distribution and on-demand distribution, it is assumed that readership above 1,000 is satisfied by selective distribution of one example and above 200 for the second example. The analyses also assume (1) the readership distribution given above, (2) over-printing of 30 percent using the reproduction decision models, and (3) an average of 10 pages per manuscript. Results are summarized in Table 8.16.

The least expensive procedure appears to be selective distribution of manuscripts with readership of over 200. It is noted that all of the unit communication procedures have few manuscripts distributed per manuscript read and all of these are considerably less than the journal mode (8.0). The number of manuscripts distributed per manuscript read is 1.3 for selective distribution of readership over 200.

Another requirement of the unit communication system is that it has the capability to treat highly regarded or classic articles that

Table 8.11 Printing Costs by Pages and Copies

Number of copies	2 pages	10 pages	20 pages	Multiple[a] X
100 copies				
Master	0.368	1.838	3.676	5,000
Binding	2.000	2.000	2.000	20,960
Dupl.	0.009	0.044	0.088	2,096,000
Set-up (Dupl.)	1.200	2.000	3.000	20,960
Collating	0.060	0.100	0.150	20,960
150 copies				
Master	0.368	1.838	3.676	5,000
Binding	3.000	3.000	3.000	15,200
Dupl.	0.009	0.044	0.088	2,280,000
Set-up (Dupl.)	1.200	2.000	3.000	15,200
Collating	0.060	0.100	0.150	15,200
200 copies				
Master	0.368	1.838	3.676	5,000
Binding	4.000	4.000	4.000	11,800
Dupl.	0.009	0.044	0.088	2,360,000
Set-up (Dupl.)	1.200	2.000	3.000	11,800
Collating	0.060	0.100	0.150	11,800
250 copies				
Master	0.368	1.838	3.676	5,000
Binding	5.000	5.000	5.000	10,400
Dupl.	0.009	0.044	0.088	2,600,000
Set-up (Dupl.)	1.200	2.000	3.000	10,400
Collating	0.060	0.100	0.150	10,400
500 copies				
Master	0.368	1.838	3.676	5,000
Binding	10.000	10.000	10.000	7,000
Dupl.	0.009	0.044	0.088	3,500,000
Set-up (Dupl.)	1.200	2.000	3.000	7,000
Collating	0.060	0.100	0.150	7,000

[a]The total cost is found by multiplying the table entry by the corresponding multiple.

Table 8.12 Total Acquisition, Reproduction, Storage, and Presentation Costs for the Unit Communication System at Full Operation with All Manuscripts Selectively Distributed

Readership	Prop. of mss.	No. of mss.	Total readership	No. of copies distributed	No. of copies printed	Acquisition costs	Reproduction costs	Storage costs	Presentation costs	Total costs
0	0.10	500	0	500,000	500,000	$ 1,925	$ 32,900	$ 100	$ 100,000	$ 134,925
1-10	0.08	400	2,200	400,000	400,000	1,540	26,300	80	80,000	107,920
11-50	0.15	750	22,900	750,000	750,000	2,888	49,400	150	150,000	202,438
51-100	0.10	500	37,800	500,000	500,000	1,925	32,900	100	100,000	134,925
101-200	0.12	600	90,300	600,000	600,000	2,310	39,500	120	120,000	161,930
201-500	0.20	1,000	350,500	1,000,000	1,000,000	3,850	65,800	200	200,000	269,850
501-1,000	0.16	800	600,400	800,000	800,000	3,080	52,700	160	160,000	215,940
1,001-2,000	0.08	400	600,200	800,000	800,000	1,540	51,900	80	160,000	213,520
> 2,001	0.01	50	110,000	150,000	150,000	193	9,700	10	30,000	39,903
Total	1.00	5,000	1,814,300	5,500,000	5,500,000	$19,251	$361,100	$1,000	$1,100,000	$1,481,351

Table 8.13 Total Acquisition, Reproduction, Storage, and Presentation Costs for the Unit Communication System at Full Operation with All Requests Satisfied on Demand

Readership	Prop. of mss.	No. of mss.	Total readership	No. of copies distributed	No. of copies printed	Acquisition costs	Reproduction costs	Storage costs	Presentation costs	Total costs
0	0.10	500	0	0	0	$ 1,925	$ 0	$ 10	$ 0	$ 1,935
1-10	0.08	400	2,200	2,200	2,900	1,540	1,500	60	1,100	4,200
11-50	0.15	750	22,900	22,900	29,800	2,888	6,400	630	11,500	21,418
51-100	0.10	500	37,800	37,800	49,100	1,925	5,100	1,000	18,900	26,925
101-200	0.12	600	90,300	90,300	117,400	2,310	7,800	2,300	45,200	57,610
201-500	0.20	1,000	350,500	350,500	455,700	3,850	32,900	9,100	175,300	221,150
501-1,000	0.16	800	600,400	600,400	780,500	3,080	53,100	15,600	300,200	371,980
1,001-2,000	0.08	400	600,200	600,200	780,300	1,540	53,100	15,600	300,100	370,340
> 2,001	0.01	50	110,000	110,000	143,000	193	10,700	4,200	55,000	70,093
Total	1.00	5,000	1,814,300	1,814,300	2,358,700	$19,251	$170,600	$48,500	$907,300	$1,145,651

Table 8.14 Total Acquisition, Reproduction, Storage, and Presentation Costs for the Unit Communication System at Full Operation with Selective Distribution for Manuscripts with Over 1,000 Readership

Readership	Prop. of mss.	No. of mss.	Total readership	No. of copies distributed	No. of copies printed	Acquisition costs	Reproduction costs	Storage costs	Presentation costs	Total costs
0	0.10	500	0	0	0	$ 1,925	$ 0	$ 10	$ 0	$ 1,935
1-10	0.08	400	2,200	2,200	2,900	1,540	1,500	60	1,100	4,200
11-50	0.15	750	22,900	22,900	29,800	2,888	6,400	630	11,500	21,418
51-100	0.10	500	37,800	37,800	49,100	1,925	5,100	1,000	18,900	26,925
101-200	0.12	600	90,300	90,300	117,400	2,310	7,800	2,300	45,200	57,610
201-500	0.20	1,000	350,500	350,500	455,700	3,850	32,900	9,100	175,300	221,150
501-1,000	0.16	800	600,400	600,400	780,500	3,080	53,100	15,600	300,200	371,980
1,001-2,000	0.08	400	600,200	800,000	800,000	1,540	51,900	80	160,000	213,520
> 2,001	0.01	50	110,000	150,000	150,000	193	9,700	10	30,000	39,903
Total	1.00	5,000	1,814,300	2,054,100	2,385,400	$19,251	$168,400	$28,790	$742,200	$958,641

Table 8.15 Total Acquisition, Reproduction, Storage, and Presentation Costs for the Unit Communication System at Full Operation with Selective Distribution for Manuscripts with Over 200 Readership

Readership	Prop. of mss.	No. of mss.	Total readership	No. of copies distributed	No. of copies printed	Acquisition costs	Reproduction costs	Storage costs	Presentation costs	Total costs
0	0.10	500	0	0	0	$ 1,925	$ 0	$ 10	$ 0	$ 1,935
1-10	0.08	400	2,200	2,200	2,900	1,540	1,500	60	1,100	4,200
11-50	0.15	750	22,900	22,900	29,800	2,888	6,400	630	11,500	21,418
51-100	0.10	500	37,800	37,800	49,100	1,925	5,100	1,000	18,900	26,925
101-200	0.12	600	90,300	90,300	117,400	2,310	7,800	2,300	45,200	57,610
201-500	0.20	1,000	350,500	1,000,000	1,000,000	3,850	65,800	200	200,000	269,850
501-1,000	0.16	800	600,400	800,000	800,000	3,080	52,700	160	160,000	215,940
1,001-2,000	0.08	400	600,200	800,000	800,000	1,540	51,900	80	160,000	213,520
> 2,001	0.01	50	110,000	150,000	150,000	193	9,700	10	30,000	39,903
Total	1.00	5,000	1,814,300	2,903,200	2,949,200	$19,251	$200,900	$4,450	$626,700	$851,301

Table 8.16 Total Cost, Cost per Mss. Read, and Mss. Distributed per Mss. Read for Several Selection Processes

Printing & distribution procedure	Journal mode	All mss. selectively distributed	All requests satisfied on demand	Selective distribution over 1,000	Selective distribution over 200
Total cost	$1,316,000	$1,481,351	$1,145,651	$960,641	$851,301
Cost per mss. read	$0.80	$0.82	$0.63	$0.53	$0.47
Mss. distr./ mss. read	8.0	3.0	1.0	1.1	1.3

should be preserved in libraries and offices for future reference. These manuscripts will probably be printed in the annals and will be sold primarily to institutional members. Furthermore, since fewer copies are sent directly to users (through journal subscription), there needs to be an effective current awareness capability and reference search system.

An additional major decision problem concerns pricing. One strategy is to charge one price for manuscripts sent selectively and another for manuscripts ordered on demand. For the APA system, it was felt desirable to maintain a positive net income. An analysis was performed on the procedure in which manuscripts with over 200 readership were selectively distributed to determine whether cost per unit was dependent on total readership. The relationships below in Table 8.17 were found.

Table 8.17 Total Readership and Cost

Total readership	Cost per selectively distributed mss.	Cost per mss. distributed on demand
900,000	$1.18	$0.43
1,800,000	$0.75	$0.33
3,600,000	$0.80	$0.51

These figures could be considered rough estimates for establishing price. It was also noted that income from demand was determined from demand times price, but that demand also varied with price. The price-demand relationship was not known.

References

1. American Psychological Association, Office of Communication Management and Development, *Program Plan for a National Information System for Psychology.* Washington, D. C., December 1969.
2. American Psychological Association, *Reports of the American Psychological Association's Project on Scientific Information Exchange in Psychology,* Vol. I. Washington, D. C., December 1963.
3. King, D. W., *Cost/Benefits Analysis.* A Study Conducted for the American Psychological Association. Bethesda, Md., Westat Research, Inc., November 1969.
4. Leimkuhler, F. F., "The Bradford Distribution." *Journal of Documentation,* Vol. 23, No. 3 (September 1967), pp. 197-207.
5. Leimkuhler, F. F., *A Literature Search and File Organization Model.* Presented at the 31st National Meeting of the Operations Research Society, New York, June 1967.
6. Leimkuhler, F. F., "A Literature Search Model" (Abstract). *Bulletin of the Operations Research Society of America,* Vol. 15, Supplement 1 (Spring 1967), pp. B56-57.
7. Leimkuhler, F. F., *Mathematical Models for Library Systems Analysis.* Prepared for a Conference at the Drexel Institute of Technology, Philadelphia, September 17-20, 1967. (NSF Grant N-2394.)
8. Maier, J. M., "Analyzing Acquisitions and Cataloging Costs." *Library Resources and Technical Services,* Vol. 13, No. 1 (Winter 1969), pp. 127-136.
9. Wiederkehr, R. R. V., King, D. W., *The Determination of Optimum Document Reproduction Procedures at the Clearinghouse for Federal Scientific and Technical Information.* Bethesda, Md., Westat Research, Inc., August 1967.
10. Williams, B., *Library Cost Models: Owning Versus Borrowing Serial Publications.* Chicago, Center for Research Libraries, 1968.

Chapter Nine

A Net Benefit Model for Evaluating Document Transfer Systems[1]

9.1 Introduction

Most efforts to evaluate document transfer systems have dealt with systems in the research and development stage, and have been concerned primarily with demonstrating the technical feasibility of certain subsystems, such as indexing. As mentioned in Chapter 2, these evaluations have emphasized such measures as the recall ratio and the precision ratio, and often have not taken into account factors of cost and benefits. In the research and development stage of a system, where the primary objective is to demonstrate technical feasibility, this approach appears appropriate. However, when management considers the operational feasibility, the primary objective should shift toward demonstrating economic feasibility, and performance measures should reflect both cost and benefits. In Chapter 2, we showed how performance measures can be related to cost and benefits. The purpose of this chapter is to develop a framework for quantitative economic analysis of document transfer systems involving a single measure of the difference between cost and benefits stated in monetary units. This single measure is *net benefit*.

[1] A major portion of this chapter was conceived and prepared by R. R. V. Wiederkehr (5).

9.2 A rationale for the economic evaluation of document transfer systems

The evaluation of a system in general and a document transfer system (or subsystem) in particular may be considered to be a problem of economic choice which, according to Hitch and McKean (*3*), has the following five elements:

(1) *An objective or objectives.* What aims are we trying to accomplish with the equipment and personnel that the analysis is designed to compare?

(2) *Alternatives.* By what alternative equipment, procedures, and/or personnel may the general objectives be accomplished? The alternatives are frequently referred to as *systems.*

(3) *Costs or resources used.* Each alternative system requires certain costs or the using up of certain resources.

(4) *A model or models.* Models are abstract representations of reality. They may assume the form of a complex set of mathematical relationships, or the form of small-scale representations of reality. For evaluation purposes, the essential relationships that should be represented by models are those between system inputs and system outputs.

(5) *A criterion.* A criterion is a decision rule or test by which one chooses one alternative system rather than another. Therefore, one can conduct a comparative evaluation by applying the criterion to each of the various alternative systems.

Whereas Hitch and McKean considered these five elements in connection with evaluating military systems, we shall review them again in connection with evaluating document transfer systems.

(1) *Objectives*

The objectives of a document transfer system may be viewed from a number of levels. A higher-level objective is to provide informational support in meeting organizational goals; a lower-level objective is to satisfy users' informational needs, requests, or wants. Regardless of the level, however, document transfer systems play a support role and are of value only insofar as they assist organizations or individuals in meeting their goals.

(2) *Alternatives or systems*

As mentioned in Chapter 1, a document transfer system may be defined to be a combination of equipment, personnel, and procedures for performing the following functions: composition, reproduction, acquisition and storage, identification and location, presentation, and assimilation. Any number of alternative processes may be used to accomplish these functions.

(3) *Costs or resources used*

As mentioned in Chapter 3, in arriving at estimates of document transfer system costs, it is necessary to consider two categories: fixed or investment costs, and operating costs. The fixed costs are the one-time costs of developing, constructing, and implementing the system, while the operating costs are the recurring costs of running and maintaining the system year after year. The operating costs may also be subdivided into fixed costs and costs that vary by frequency of use and level of use.

An acceptable cost analysis should involve: (1) selecting a planning period and an interest rate, (2) estimating the fixed costs, the operating costs for each year of the planning period, and the residual value of the system at the end of the planning period, and (3) on the basis of (1) and (2), computing the overall cost – either by the present value method or the average annual cost method. A complete description of a cost analysis is beyond the scope of this book; however, more detailed analysis is available in Grant and Ireson (*2*).

(4) *Models*

For a document transfer system, the main outputs are wanted information and the value derived from this information. The main inputs are the system cost and the user's search effort required to retrieve the wanted documents. Models are derived in this chapter for cost, benefit, and net benefit.

(5) *Criterion*

When both benefits and costs can be expressed in the same units, a generally acceptable criterion is to select the alternative which maximizes the net benefit, i.e., the benefit minus the cost. This choice is equivalent to maximizing the profit.

Although it is not generally possible to express the benefits objectively in the same units as the cost, it is instructive to assume that appropriate factors can be selected which will convert the benefits from nonmonetary to monetary units. In this chapter, therefore, it will be assumed that benefits and costs can be expressed in the same units, and that the net benefit is a suitable measure for evaluating alternatives.

A second measure which is often employed is the benefit-to-cost ratio. For example, Murdock and Liston (*4*) have proposed using the benefit-to-cost ratio as a suitable measure for evaluating document transfer systems. It is therefore of interest to determine the relationships between the net benefit and the benefit-to-cost ratio. Such relationships are developed in the following section.

9.3 Relationships between cost-benefit measures

For a document transfer system operating at a given performance level, let C and B denote the costs and the benefits, respectively. As the performance level varies, C and B also vary and can be conveniently described by a curve of B versus C. The bold lines on Figure 9.1 illustrate how B and C might vary for two alternate document transfer systems, I and II.

Two measures which are readily derived from B and C are the net benefit or profit, P, and the benefit-to-cost ratio, R. These measures may be computed as follows:

$$P = B - C \tag{1}$$

$$R = B|C \tag{2}$$

From equation (1), it follows that the lines of constant P on Figure 9.1 are lines with a slope of unity and an intercept of P. From equation (2), it follows that the lines of constant R on Figure 9.1 pass through the origin and have a slope of R. Consequently, Figure 9.1 can be used to study how the benefit, the net benefit, and the benefit-to-cost ratio simultaneously vary with cost (and therefore with performance level).

For a situation where adequate resources are available for the selection of one of several alternative systems, the generally accepted measure of relative economic worth is the net benefit; i.e., the benefit

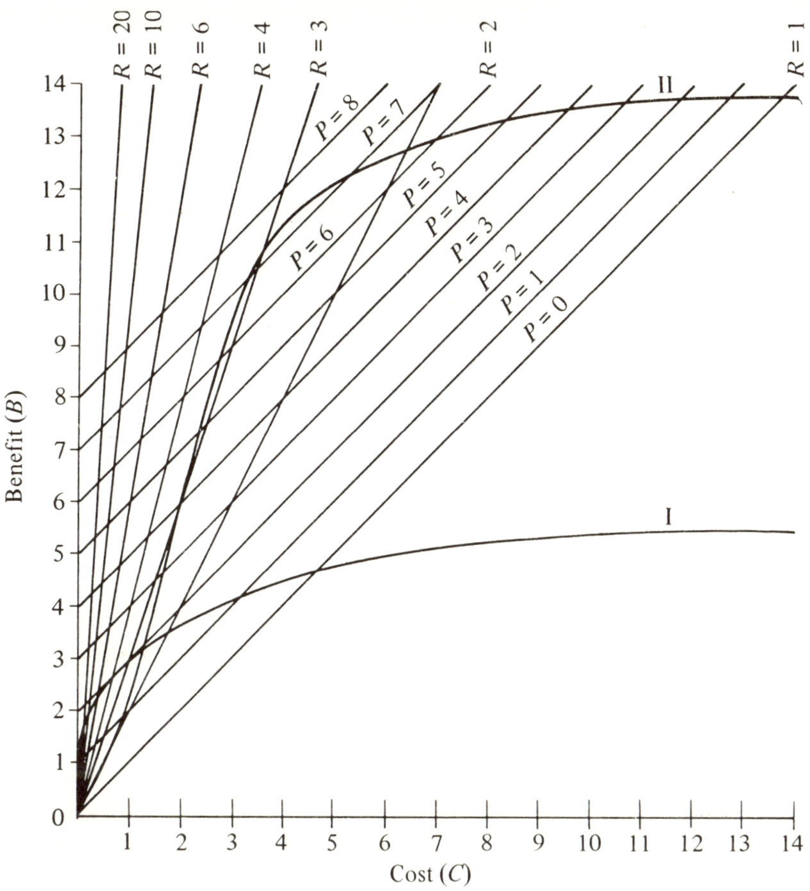

Figure 9.1 Benefit-cost relationships for two alternate document transfer systems (I & II).

minus the cost. The optimum choice in this case consists of selecting the alternative system, which maximizes the net benefit, *P*.

For the two document transfer systems represented in Figure 9.1, one can see that for System I the maximum net benefit is 2 and occurs at a cost of 0.8, while for System II the maximum net benefit is over 7 and occurs at a cost of 5. Hence, if only one of these systems were to be selected, System II would be preferable to System I.

In general, maximizing the benefit-to-cost ratio does not yield the optimum choice. However, one instance where this choice would be optimum is the following: A number of Type I or Type II systems are to be purchased for a fixed budget and the total benefit equals the benefit per system times the number of systems. Here the total net benefit is maximized by selecting the number of Type I systems which just consume the fixed budget.

9.4 Models for evaluating the performance of search identification systems

For the purpose of this chapter, we intend to concentrate on models that describe the net benefit of a system in which document transfer is accomplished by documents identified by searching.

A search system for identification may be used for a number of different purposes, in a number of different subject areas, and by a number of different types of users. For example, a search system may be used for any of the following purposes:

(1) To identify a specific document whose author and title are known.

(2) To identify a specific document known to exist but whose author and/or title are unknown.

(3) To identify some documents containing information on a given subject.

(4) To identify *all* documents within the physical file containing information on a given subject (internal bibliographic search).

(5) To identify *all* documents both within and without a physical file containing information on a given subject (internal and external bibliographic searches).

(6) To identify a sampling of recent documents containing information on one or more subjects to become aware of current developments.

(7) To browse.

Use may also be classified according to subject matter, user characteristics, and so on.

A search system for identification may perform well for some types of use and poorly for others. In addition, the value of the output may be great for some types of searches and low for other types. A well-designed search system should perform well for those types of searches that have a high value. Therefore, in evaluating an overall document transfer system, it is important to distinguish between the various types of use.

In this chapter, attention is focused on a number of searches, all of which are restricted to a particular elementary type of use. For example, if the above categorization of use were considered appropriate, then the collection of all internal bibliographic searches, i.e., (4) above, would constitute an elementary class of search. Corresponding to the other six categories would be six more elementary classes of searches.

The simplest type of identification system is one which performs searches belonging to only one elementary class of search. Investigators who make no distinctions between various types of use, in effect, are assuming that they have an elementary document transfer system.

Four types of models for elementary identification systems are considered:

(1) *The search characteristic curve.* A model that relates the search return to search effort for various levels of identification system performance.

(2) *The acquisition characteristic curve.* A model that relates the return to the file size and file composition.

(3) *The user benefit curve.* A model that relates user benefit to identification.

(4) *The net benefit model.* A model that relates net benefit to the level of system performance.

These models are discussed in Sections 9.5 through 9.8.

9.5 Search characteristic curve

Each use of a document transfer system by a user may be considered to be a search. For a given class of elementary search, it will be assumed that the output of the system consists of a number of items that are examined at least in part by the user, so that he judges each item with respect to its relevance to his search desires. In general, there will be k different levels of relevance, ranging from not relevant to extremely relevant. A common approach is to assume that k is equal to 2, and that the two levels of relevancy of items are "relevant" and "not relevant." For the moment, it will be assumed that $k = 2$.

Search results were described in Chapter 2 by the following 2 × 2 table:

User relevance judgment (V)

System relevance response (R)		Not relevant ($V_{\bar{r}}$)	Relevant (V_r)	Total
		D_U		
Relevant (R_r)	D_S	a	b	$a + b$
Not relevant ($R_{\bar{r}}$)		c	d	$c + d$
Total		$a + c$	$b + d$	$a + b + c + d$

The total number of items examined by the user is a measure of the user's search effort. As a result of this effort, the user will gain certain rewards; a measure of these rewards is the number of relevant documents found among those examined. The relationship between the search return, expressed by the number of relevant documents examined, and the search effort, expressed by the number of documents examined, is called the *search characteristic curve.*

Properties of the search characteristic curve have been studied; the following useful normalized form for a search characteristic curve was derived by Wiederkehr (5):

$$r_F = 1 - (1 - f^{1/k})^j \tag{3}$$

where

- r_F = $b/b + d$, the fraction of relevant documents in the file examined (or recall),
- f = $a + b/a + b + c + d$, the fraction of the file examined,
- N_F = $a + b + c + d$, the total number of documents in the file,
- M_F = $a + c$, the number of relevant documents in the file,
- n = $a + b$, the total number of documents examined,
- m = b, the number of relevant documents examined when the number of documents examined is n, and
- k,j = the search performance parameters, i.e., parameters which describe the performance of a search system. The larger the value of these parameters the better the performance of the search system.

The equivalent unnormalized form of the search characteristic curve is:

$$m = Mr_F = M_F \left\{ 1 - [1 - (\frac{n}{N_F})^{1/k}]^j \right\} \tag{4}$$

Equation (4) permits computation of the expected number of relevant documents that will be retrieved for a given elementary class of search as a function of the number of documents examined, n, the number of relevant documents in the file, M_F, the size of the file, N_F, and the search performance parameters. Thus, measures described in Chapters 2, 3, and 4 yield inputs to the models described in this section.

9.6 Acquisition characteristic curve

Search characteristic curves relate the returns resulting from a given search policy to the number of documents examined. A similar relationship exists between the returns resulting from a given acquisition policy and the number of documents acquired, indexed, and filed. This latter relationship is called the *acquisition characteristic curve.* Just as the search characteristic curve describes the effectiveness of a search policy, the acquisition characteristic curve describes the effectiveness of the acquisition and storage policy.

For a given body of knowledge to be covered by a given document transfer system for a given body of users, let N be the total number of documents, and let M be the number of documents wanted by the body of users. The total number of documents, N, can be subdivided into the M, wanted documents, and the remaining N-M, unwanted documents. For example, documents written in a foreign language which cannot be translated feasibly would constitute a part of the unwanted documents.

If the acquisition policy is such that all N documents are acquired, then all of the M wanted documents will be a part of the file of the document transfer system. Although such a policy provides perfect coverage of wanted documents, it can be exceedingly costly, especially when N is very large; therefore, that policy is rarely adopted.

A more feasible acquisition policy involves acquiring only a subset of the N documents. Let N_F be the number of documents in such a subset, i.e., the number of documents that are acquired, indexed, and placed in the file. If N_F is less than N, there is, of course, a chance that not all of the M wanted documents will be a part of the file, i.e., the number of wanted documents in the file is less than M. Let M_F be the number of wanted documents which are part of the file. Note that M_F is a measure of the return resulting from certain acquisition.

The relationship between M_F and N_F for a family of acquisition policies will be defined to be the acquisition characteristic curve, and is represented graphically in Figure 9.2. The normalized version of the acquisition characteristic curve, also shown in Figure 9.2, is obtained by dividing the abscissa by N and the ordinate by M. The resulting ratios may be defined to be the coverage, C, and the fraction of wanted documents contained in the file, W, and are given by the following equations:

$$C = \frac{N_F}{N} \tag{5}$$

$$W = \frac{M_F}{M} \tag{6}$$

Applying the same rationale used to obtain analytical expressions for the search characteristic curves, it can be shown that the acquisition curves of Figure 9.2 can be represented by the following equation:

$$W = 1 - (1 - C^{1/h})^i \tag{7}$$

Values to be incorporated into equation (7) may be derived from the methodology given in Chapter 4.

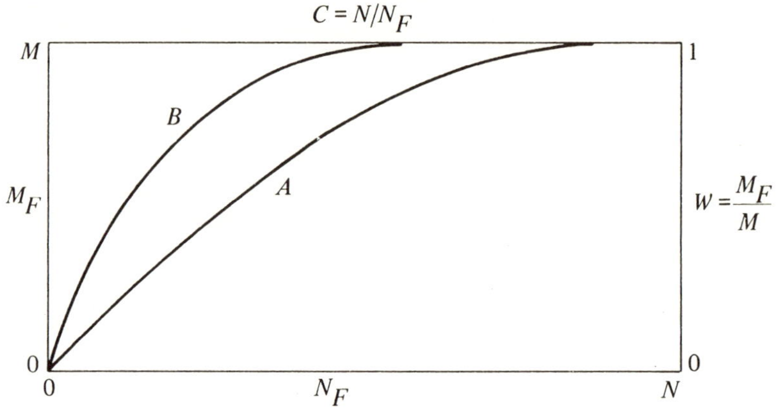

Figure 9.2 Acquisition characteristic curve.

9.7 User benefit curve

Each search generates a number of relevant documents from which the user derives a certain amount of benefit (see Chapter 1). If the user obtains all the relevant documents as a result of a search, the user benefit derived from the search is maximum. On the other hand, if the user obtains only a fraction of the relevant documents as a result of a search, the user benefit derived from the search is a fraction of the maximum benefit. Among the typical reasons given in Chapter 4 for a search producing only a fraction of the maximum number of relevant documents are the following:

(1) The file against which the search was processed contained only a fraction of the relevant documents, i.e., the file coverage was not 100 percent.

(2) Errors were made either in indexing the document or in preparing the query.

(3) The depth of search was not sufficiently great to identify all relevant documents in the file.

Consider how the user benefit derived from a search varies as the fraction of relevant documents identified varies from zero to unity. If none of the relevant documents is identified, we may assume that the user benefit is zero. As more and more of the relevant documents are identified, the user benefits rise continuously. When all of the relevant documents are retrieved, the user benefits will certainly achieve their maximum value.

Because it is difficult and perhaps unreasonable for the user to determine the maximum value of the benefit derived from a search that gives him all the relevant documents, it is not convenient for the user to think in terms of the fraction of maximum user benefit. The fraction of maximum user benefit ν, will increase steadily from zero to unity as the fraction of relevant documents examined, r, varies from zero to unity. A method for arriving at a relationship between ν and r is to ask the user to estimate subjectively values of ν for each of a series of values for r. But first it is helpful to relate r, the fraction of the universe of relevant documents, to r_F, the fraction of relevant documents in the file, and W, the file coverage. By definition, it follows that

$$r \equiv \frac{m}{M} = \frac{m}{M_F} \cdot \frac{M_F}{M} \equiv r_F \cdot W \tag{8}$$

Since subjective estimates may be expected to lack precision, it appears appropriate to express the relationship between v and r by the following equation:

$$v = 1 - (1 - r)^u \qquad (9)$$

where u is a parameter that describes the rate of increase of v with respect to r. For small values of r, u is approximately *equal* to the rate of increase of v with respect to r. The relationship between v and r is called the *fractional user benefit curve.*

A few examples will clarify the meaning of fractional benefit curves and the parameter u. As a first example, consider a user interested in finding one, or at most two, relevant documents on a given subject. Additional relevant documents will be of very little additional benefit for his search needs. Furthermore, suppose that the total number of documents relevant to his search request is 50. Since the user is interested in obtaining, at most, 2 of 50 relevant documents, he is interested in a recall, r, of only 2/50 or 0.04, a sufficiently small value of r for equation (9) to be applicable, i.e.,

$$u \cong \frac{v}{r} = \frac{1}{0.04} = 25 \qquad (10)$$

As a second example, consider a user who is interested in conducting an exhaustive bibliographic search on a given subject. Each additional relevant document, on the average, will add equally to his benefit, and only when he obtains all of the relevant documents will his benefit reach its maximum. In this case the fractional user benefit is equal to the fraction of relevant documents retrieved, i.e., $v = r$. This is equivalent to using a value of u equal to unity in equation (10).

9.8 Net benefit model

The net benefit is defined as the benefit minus the costs. For this subtraction to be meaningful, the benefit and cost should be commensurable, i.e., they should have the same units. To convert the fractional user benefit to the user benefit expressed in dollars, a dollar value should be assigned to the maximum user benefit, and the fractional user benefit should be multiplied by this dollar value.

And what should this dollar value be? Assuming that the objective of the document transfer system is to provide informational support in meeting organizational goals, this dollar value should be the price that management is willing to pay for the service provided by the particular type of search for the particular type of user.

Usually, there are other means of obtaining similar services for which the price *can* be readily established, and this can be used by the managing body as a frame of reference for arriving at an appropriate price. For example, additional research assistants can be hired to conduct searches using services that would be available in the absence of the document transfer system. High-caliber research assistants who provide high quality probably could be attracted by high salaries, and it should be possible to match approximately the quality of search (except for response time) of the system with an appropriate-caliber research assistant. From the salary and time requirements of such a research assistant and any additional expenses to be incurred in executing a search, the cost of a search can be readily computed.

If the response time of the search conducted by the research assistant and of that conducted by the system were the same, the cost of the search conducted by the research assistant would be a reasonable price to use. However, if the system's response time for a search were substantially less than that of the research assistant, it might be desirable to pay a premium for more rapid service, the amount of the premium depending on the urgency of the search results. In any event, management could establish an appropriate price to pay for the maximum user benefit derived from a particular type of search by a particular type of user. Let this price be denoted by B. Then for a search that yields a fractional user benefit of v, the user benefit per search expressed in dollars is $B \cdot v$. For s searches, therefore, the total benefit, B_T, is simply:

$$B_T = B \cdot v \cdot s \tag{11}$$

Although equation (11) appears to be a simple expression, it should be remembered that v requires a string of relationships, *viz.*, equations (3), (7), (8), and (9), to be evaluated. This point will be brought out subsequently in an example.

9.9 A comprehensive cost model

Cost for a simple document search system will be considered in this section.[2] The average annual cost of a simple document search system consists of two components: a fixed cost and a variable cost. How the cost is resolved into these components depends on what management policies are adopted.

It is assumed here that costs vary with respect to three factors: (1) number of documents in the file, N_F, (2) number of searches per year, s, and (3) number of documents examined per search, n. All other costs are assumed to be fixed. More specifically, it is assumed that the total annual cost, C_T, may be expressed as follows:

$$C_T = C_0 + C_1 \cdot N_F + (C_2 + C_3 \cdot n) \cdot s \tag{12}$$

where

- C_0 = fixed cost,
- C_1 = the marginal cost of increasing the size of the file by one document,
- C_2 = the contribution to the cost per search, which does not vary with the number of documents examined, and
- C_3 = the marginal cost per search of increasing by one the number of documents examined in a search.

The annual net benefit, P_T, is defined to be the difference between B_T and C_T, i.e.,

$$P_T = B_T - C_T \tag{13}$$

Substituting equations (11) and (12) into (13) yields the following expression for the net benefit:

$$P_T = (B \cdot v - C_2 - C_3 \cdot n) \cdot s - C_1 \cdot N_F - C_0 \tag{14}$$

One application of equation (14) is to compare the relative merits of alternative document transfer systems. If all of the cost and benefit parameters required to compute P_T are available for one or more

[2] The costing approach given below is somewhat different from that given in Chapters 3 through 7 in order to develop net benefit of a search.

simple document transfer systems, the value of P_T can be estimated for each system using equation (14).

For several simple document transfer systems designed to fulfill the same objectives, the system with the largest value of P_T is preferred. However, since P_T may be viewed as a random variable, the uncertainty in the P_T values of the various alternative systems should also be considered before one system is claimed to be better than all the others – for there may be no statistically significant difference between the values.

Another use of equation (14) is to predict improvements in the operation of a given document transfer system by estimating the increase in net benefit associated with changes in various system parameters and decision variables. For small changes in these quantities the rate of increase in net benefit with respect to the quantity can be obtained by taking derivatives of P_T given by equation (14).

These two applications of equation (14) are illustrated by a hypothetical example in the following section.

9.10 Hypothetical example

Assume that the performance of a simple document transfer system is characterized by the following relationships and data:

Search characteristic curve

$$r_F = 1 - (1 - f^{1/2})^{10} \tag{15}$$

Acquisition characteristic curve

$$W = 1 - (1 - C)^5 \tag{16}$$

File size

$$N_F = 100{,}000 \text{ documents}$$

Total number of documents

$$N = 200{,}000 \text{ documents}$$

User benefit curve

$$r = W \cdot r_F \tag{17}$$

$$\nu = 1 - (1 - r)^2 \tag{18}$$

Estimated benefit per search, B

lower estimate – \$10.00
upper estimate – \$20.00

Costs

overall fixed costs, C_0 = \$25,000
cost per document, C_1 = \$0.25
fixed cost per search, C_2 = \$2.00
cost per search per document, C_3 = \$0.03

Number of searches per year

$$s = 10{,}000$$

Typically, the number of documents examined, n, is 500. The above parameters and data are summarized in Table 9.1.

Since f is 500/100,000, r_F is 0.52 from equation (15). Since C is 0.5, W is 0.969 from equation (16), and r is 0.50 from equation (17). For r equal to 0.50, ν equals 0.753 by equation (18). According to equation (11), therefore, B_T should be between:

$$B_T{}^l = \$20 \cdot (0.753)(10{,}000) = \$150.6\text{K} \qquad \text{low estimate}$$

and

$$B_T{}^h = \$40 \cdot (0.753)(10{,}000) = \$301.4\text{K} \qquad \text{high estimate}$$

The costs computed according to equation (12) are:

$$\begin{aligned} C_T &= \$25\text{K} + \$0.25 \times 100\text{K} + \$(2 + .03 \times 500)10\text{K} \\ &= \$220\text{K} \end{aligned}$$

Table 9.1 Summary of Hypothetical Parameters and Data

Search	k	=	1/2
	j	=	60
	n	=	500
Acquisition	h	=	1
	i	=	5
	N_F	=	100,000
	N	=	200,000
Benefits	B	=	\$20 to \$40
	u	=	5
Costs	C_0	=	\$25,000
	C_1	=	\$0.25
	C_2	=	\$2.00
	C_3	=	\$0.03
Demand	s	=	10,000

Hence, the net benefit lies between

$$P_R{}^l = \$199.6\text{K} - \$220\text{K} = -\$69.3\text{K} \qquad \text{low benefit}$$

and

$$P_T{}^h = \$399.3\text{K} - \$220\text{K} = \$81.4\text{K} \qquad \text{high benefit}$$

Thus, one can see that, under the conditions specified above, the system is questionable and not clearly justified from a net benefit analysis standpoint. Suppose, however, that the system is modified to yield the same recall (0.52), with total retrieval of 500 documents reduced to 100 documents. Also, assume that this improvement increases the number of searches per year to 20,000, increases fixed costs to \$50,000, and increases fixed cost per search to \$4.

$$C_T = \$50\text{K} + 0.25 \times 100\text{K} + \$(4 + 0.03 \times 100)10\text{K} = \$215\text{K}$$

$$B_T{}^l = \$20(0.753)(20{,}000) = \$301.4\text{K} \qquad \text{low estimate}$$

$B_T{}^h$ = \$40(0.753)(20,000) = \$602.7K high estimate

$P_T{}^l$ = \$301.4K - \$215K = \$86.4K low benefit

$P_T{}^h$ = \$602.7K - \$215K = \$387.8K high benefit

Thus, the system modification would appear to be entirely justified from the standpoint of net benefit.

As indicated in the first example, the uncertainty in benefits per search may be crucial in estimating the net benefit. However, when comparing one system with another, this uncertainty is not nearly so important, for one would expect that the same relative ranking of systems according to net benefit would be preserved regardless of whether the high or low estimate were employed.

To continue with the first example, assume that the benefit per search is equal to the break-even value (\$220K), i.e., the value for which P_T is zero. This valuc is readily found to be approximately B = \$29.00. For this value of B, questions such as the following may be asked:

(1) What benefit could be gained by enlarging the size of the file, and maintaining the same policy?

(2) Should users, in general, examine more than 500 documents, the typical number, or less?

(3) If the search policy can be improved to the extent that (2) is increased by one unit, how much would the net benefit increase?

(4) If the acquisition policy can be improved to the extent that a value is increased by one unit, how much would the net benefit increase?

Answers to questions such as these should be particularly useful in deciding which direction of development appears to be most fruitful.

Questions (1) and (2) are now considered in terms of the above hypothetical document transfer system.

(1) *Effect of file size*

The effect of file size on the net benefit can be obtained by differentiating P_T with respect to N_F while holding the other parameters in Table 9.1 fixed. From equations (14) and (12), it follows that:

$$\frac{\partial P_T}{\partial N_F} = B \cdot S \cdot \frac{\partial v}{\partial N_F} - c \qquad (19)$$

From equations (3) through (9) and for $k = 1/2$, $h = 1$, it can be shown that:

$$\frac{\partial v}{\partial N_F} = -u(1-r)^{u-1}\left[w \cdot b \cdot (1-f^k)^{j-1} \cdot \frac{n}{N_F{}^2} \cdot kf^{k-1} r_F\, a(1-c)^{i-1} \cdot \frac{1}{N}\right]$$

Using values from Table 9.1 for these parameters yields:

$$\frac{\partial v}{\partial N_F} = -2(1-r)\left[w \cdot 10(1-f^{1/2})^9 \cdot 1/2 f^{-1/2} \cdot \frac{n}{N_f^2} - r_f \cdot \frac{5 \cdot (1-c)^4}{N}\right]$$

and in view of equation (19):

$$\frac{\partial P_T}{\partial N_F} = (29)(10{,}000)(.00032) - (0.25)$$

$$= \$93.40$$

Therefore, at the operational conditions shown in Table 9.1, increasing the file size by one document will increase the net benefit by \$93.40.

(2) *Effect of examining more documents*

From equation (14) it follows that:

$$\frac{\partial P_T}{\partial n} = B \cdot s \cdot \frac{\partial v}{\partial N} - c_3 \cdot s \qquad (20)$$

From equations (9), (8), and (3) for $R = h = 1$, it can be shown that:

$$\frac{\partial v}{\partial n} = u\,\frac{(1-r)^{u-1}(1-f)^{j-1}}{N_f}\, j \cdot w$$

And in view of equation (20):

$$\frac{\partial P_T}{\partial n} = (29)(10{,}000)(-0.000092) - (0.03) \cdot (10{,}000)$$

$$= -\$326.80$$

Therefore, at the state of operation shown in Table 9.1, if each user examines one more document, the net benefit will change by -\$326.80.

Similarly, by differentiating P_T with respect to other parameters one can predict how much the net benefit should increase per unit increase in these parameters. For example, $\partial P_T/\partial j$ is an estimate of the increase in net benefit per unit increase in b, a parameter that characterizes the effectiveness of the search policy; $\partial P_T/\partial i$ is an estimate of the increase in net benefit per unit increase in a, a parameter that characterizes the effectiveness of the acquisition policy; $-\partial P_T/\partial C_i$ for $i = 0,1,2,3$ are estimates of how much the net benefit will decrease per unit increase in the cost C_i; and $\partial P_T/\partial s$ is an estimate of how much the net benefit will increase if the number of searches per year can be increased by one.

Knowledge of these estimates suggests which areas of research and development should yield the greatest payoff measured in terms of net benefit. For example, improving the acquisition policy to the extent that parameter i increases by one unit may yield a much greater increase in net benefit than the same increase in j. This would suggest that it should be more fruitful to devote more research and development to improving the acquisition policy than to improving the search policy.

References

1. Arthur Andersen & Co., *Research Study of Criteria and Procedures for Evaluating Scientific Information Retrieval Systems.* Washington, D.C., March 1962.
2. Grant, E. L., Ireson, W. G., *Principles of Engineering Economy.* 4th Edition. New York, Ronald Press, 1964.
3. Hitch, C. J., McKean, R., *The Economics of Defense in the Nuclear Age.* Cambridge, Mass., Harvard University Press, 1960.
4. Murdock, J.W., Liston, D. M., Jr., "A General Model of Information Transfer." *American Documentation,* Vol. 18, No. 4 (October 1967), pp. 197-208.
5. Weiderkehr, R. R. V., "A Net Benefit Model for Evaluating Elementary Document Retrieval Systems." *In: Evaluation of Document Retrieval Systems: Literature Perspective, Measurement, Technical Papers,* Chapter 3.5. Bethesda, Md., Westat Research, Inc., December 31, 1968.

Chapter Ten
User Surveys and Marketing Research

10.1 Introduction

A user survey is a valuable tool for providing information about the following facets of document transfer systems:

(1) Characteristics of planned systems that are required to meet the needs of a definable user population.

(2) Characteristics of users of an ongoing system, classified by level of use (including potential users who do not now use the system).

(3) Characteristics of the documents wanted by users, including such characteristics as age, subject matter, and source.

(4) Sources of dissatisfaction with the system.

(5) Need for system awareness activities.

(6) Need for user education activities.

10.2 Structure of the user survey

A user survey obviously requires input from the user or potential user. The process can be characterized by the degree of interaction between the data source (the user) and the researcher (evaluator). The following modes of communication may have varying degrees of utility, depending upon objectives and time and cost restraints.

Depth interviews perhaps provide the maximum degree of interaction. A trained interviewer, knowledgeable in the arts of document retrieval, sits down with a user and discusses with him his information needs, behavior patterns, biases, and attitudes. He may actually follow the user through his process of interacting with his information environment. The interview is loosely structured, in the sense that only a few formal questions are required. Questions evoke responses which lead to the formulation of other questions.

This technique requires that the interviewer exercise great skill in probing for attitudes that are not expressed overtly. Cost of interviewing is high because of this skill requirement and the amount of time that must be spent with each interviewee. Although some bias is always present because of the active role of the interviewer, it can be partly controlled by dividing the interviews among several interviewers and by careful training.

What one gains from such interviews is impressions of attitudes rather than quantifications, although, of course, quantification can be readily achieved on a zero-one basis, subject to sampling error and a certain amount of bias.

Group interviews capitalize upon interactions among users, with a moderate amount of stimulus from the interviewer. A small group of users (8 to 10 is common) is brought together in an informal atmosphere and participants are stimulated to discuss their information needs. The moderator (interviewer) stimulates the discussion of appropriate facets of the problem and guides the discussion away from irrelevancies, but his primary role is to listen.

Group interviews have unique advantages. They are:

(1) The environment of the group and the permissive atmosphere created by the moderator evoke the expression of ideas and feelings in a spontaneous manner not obtainable to the same degree in individual interviews. Aided by other participants and the moderator, group members are assisted in the verbal expression of their ideas, concepts, attitudes, and experiences. Through the process of interaction, these expressions are frequently challenged and more fully developed.

(2) The group provides a climate of emotional support that permits expression with complete candor.

(3) Group interviews provide direct observation of the respondent by reason of the presence of research professionals. By planning a series of group interviews, a number of hypotheses can be formulated and modified in accordance with responses. Because the data are collected by an experienced psychologist, areas of relevance can be

recognized and pursued more effectively than in the ordinary type of interview conducted by interviewers.

(4) Group interviews permit the use of techniques and special displays that are not practical for interviews in the working environment. Also, experimental tests can be introduced if the occasion requires information best obtained in this manner.

Structured interviews provide a way of obtaining information from users when it is possible to communicate with them directly. Since the interviewer asks specific questions and records the answers, the interview environment is more formal than that of the group or depth interview. The role of the interviewer is passive in order to reduce biases, although it is virtually impossible to eliminate all bias.

Structuring of the questions makes quantification easy, but opinions may be recorded inaccurately by this procedure. This is particularly true if the respondent is required to express a viewpoint which he has developed inadequately in his own mind.

Frequently, the design of the questionnaire (the survey instrument) can be fostered by group interviews which tend to crystallize the issues and to reveal the kinds of questions which can or cannot be answered.

Questionnaires[1] are forms which are completed by the respondent, not in the presence of any interviewer. While this mode of obtaining information tends to be inexpensive, it is subject to hazards. Nonresponse error is particularly troublesome. Those who voluntarily complete a questionnaire frequently have different characteristics than those who do not. Misinterpretation of questions or instructions, leading to response error, is also a problem. In general, questionnaires should not be used unless the questions are simple and unless a high response rate can be anticipated. The response rate can be increased by telephone follow-up at increased cost.

It is usually necessary to interview a sample of nonrespondents to obtain an estimate of nonresponse bias, an activity which may be so costly as to destroy the cost advantage of using questionnaires rather than interviews. It is almost always best to reduce the overall sample size and insure higher response rates by follow-up.

Observation of user behavior is sometimes a productive way of obtaining information. For example, a recording of retrospective

[1]For our purposes, we will classify diaries kept by users as questionnaires, since the degree of interaction with the respondents is essentially the same.

searches submitted to a system may provide information on interests, ability to structure searches, and gross use. In order to make observational systems work effectively, provision must be made for regular and routine recording, with various checks on completeness and clerical accuracy. Generally, such systems can be made more effective by requiring the user to input some feedback data reflecting his satisfaction with the service.

10.3 Decision framework for user surveys

Answers to the following questions set the stage for the user survey:

(1) What information is needed?
(2) What can be obtained?
(3) How can it be obtained?
(4) What will alternative ways cost?
(5) What are the restrictions on cost, time, personnel, and other factors?

Information needed is dependent upon the objectives of the evaluation. There is no single set of objectives for user studies that will cover all situations. What is important is that objectives be stated concisely and that they relate to the decisions which must be made.

Two situations must be distinguished. In the first, the purpose of the study is to add to the store of knowledge concerning user behavior, man-machine interfaces, information flows, and so on. Such studies have very general objectives which are motivated by a desire for scientific inquiry. As a result, needed information is loosely specified and often the structure of the study develops only after the investigation is under way.[2]

A second evaluation situation arises when facts are needed about users of specific or contemplated systems. Information needs can be specified in advance of the user contacts (although there is always the possibility that the study can progress in stages, the structure of each

[2] A number of such studies appear in the literature, and it is recommended that the investigator examine them carefully before launching a study which may duplicate findings (or mistakes) already documented in the literature. In particular, one should check the appropriate chapters of recent volumes of the *Annual Review of Information Science and Technology* of the American Society for Information Science, for a fairly complete listing of evaluation studies.

stage being dependent on findings at an earlier stage). The sharpness of focus on specific questions distinguishes this class of studies from the first class discussed above.

Evaluation objectives vary from study to study, but most often the evaluator is concerned with measuring extent of use and determining sources of dissatisfaction and potentials for improving the system. Thus, answers to questions such as the following tend to provide the basis for decision:

(1) Who uses the system and how much do they use it?

(2) What other systems do they use, and how much do they use them?

(3) How large is the potential user population and how large is the potential use?

(4) Why do certain members of the population fail to use the system?

(5) What are the differences in characteristics between users and nonusers?

(6) How satisfied are users?

(7) What modifications are needed to improve the system and how much would use be increased by such improvements?

Information attainable may not coincide with information needed; typically, it will not. We consider each of the questions posed above with respect to attainable information.

The answer to who uses the system, and how much, requires, first of all, a definition of "use." It seems wisest to identify services rendered and to define use in terms of accepting the offer of such service. The following are suggested as use measures for the specified services within a definable time period.

(1) Retrospective searches – number of searches conducted. Include on-call bibliographies. Define a search to include all submissions in iterative searching as a single use. (Data obtainable by recordkeeping.)

(2) Special indexes (card files, organized listings, etc.) – number of times referred to. Estimators obtainable by survey.

(3) Search assistance – number of requests submitted. Obtainable by recordkeeping.

(4) Announcement services – number of announcements and distribution lists. Obtainable by recordkeeping. Persons perusing them

cognitively and number of items ordered from the announcement lists are estimated by survey of recipients.

(5) Selective dissemination (abstracts or full texts) – number of recipients. Obtainable by recordkeeping. Proportion found "useful" can be estimated by survey. Typical questions: "Have you previously seen this item?" "If 'yes,' was it worth your while seeing it?"

One attractive measure of the extent of use for researchers whose effort is reflected in written reports is the number of items listed as references and the proportion which are "in the system," that is, in full text, abstract, index, or bibliographic form. If, in addition, we determine by survey the items which the user obtains from the system and those he thinks are in the system, we have a measure of the effective utilization of the system.

Use of other systems can be determined only by survey. One possibility is to inquire about which information services were used during a recent period, listing specifically indexes, bibliographies, card catalogs, abstracting publications, information centers (and their specific services), and so on. (For measures of "how much," see the above paragraph.)

Potential users are hard to identify; hence, any enumeration of them is subject to substantial error. What can be done is to have knowledgeable persons identify the scientific disciplines whose reference needs seem to match, at least partially, the subject matter of the system. Membership lists, organized geographically, may provide an inexpensive yet satisfactory measure of the size of the potential user population. Their literature orientation and use patterns, however, can be determined only by sample survey. Rosters of personnel or membership directories probably provide the best source for drawing samples.

Nonusers can provide some of the potentially most useful data to the system evaluator, but they are difficult to identify. Every user is to some degree a nonuser, so it seems advisable to draw a sample from the potential user population. Having identified a potential user, one must determine: (1) how many references he uses, (2) where he obtains them, (3) how many are in the system being evaluated, (4) whether the user knows of the system and how it works, and (5) his statement as to why he does not use the system. Some probing may be required to determine the real motivation for the user's behavior.

Differences in characteristics of users and nonusers may reveal reasons for nonuse. In particular, one should look for lack of system awareness on the part of persons in certain disciplines, cost and convenience considerations, and the proportion of needs which could be satisfied by the system.

User satisfaction has been partly discussed above, but it is worth noting that the opinions of nonusers may be more important than those of users.

System modifications suggested by users should reflect their experience. While the designer is responsible for devising a system which is responsive to users' needs, the user is the only one who can say whether those needs are being met. In interviewing to obtain this information, "open-ended" questions are best. Such questions are asked after rapport has been established. The user is invited to comment on the services he would like to have, on time delays which seem excessive, on gaps in the collection which are troublesome to him, on the form of materials submitted to him, and on any other features of the system which, in his opinion, need improvement. The interviewer must not be an advocate, but a recorder, in this activity. Indeed, this is true of all of the information requirements listed above. For this reason it is advisable that interviewing be done by persons other than the information system staff.

As discussed above, some information can be obtained by recording, some by questionnaire, and some by personal interview, either structured or in depth.

Costs of obtaining user information vary widely, depending upon the technique used and the size of the sample. (Some considerations in sample design are given in Chapter 12.) Several order-of-magnitude estimates of costs (as of 1968) are given below. These can be expected to vary by a factor of two or more, depending upon circumstances.

Depth interviews can be expected to take around one-half day each, and almost an equal length of time to organize and analyze. Considering the skill of the interviewer, and allowing for 100 percent overhead, these interviews may cost about $100 each, but the cost per interview may be expected to decrease as the number of interviews increases; about $50 is likely to be a minimum.

Group interviews require more organization and more time to analyze from tape transcripts; they are likely to cost in excess of $600 each.

Structured interviews are likely to take from ½ hour to 2 hours each. Figuring 1 hour each, with some time for travel and waiting, perhaps five interviews can be completed in a day at a cost (with 100 percent overhead) of $10 per interview. To this must be added costs of study design, tabulation, and data analysis. A total cost of $25 to $40 per interview is common in the field of commercial surveys for a total sample size of about 500 interviews.

Questionnaires are inexpensive to send out, but one must be willing to live with nonresponse and other biases, or to supplement questionnaires by personal interviews, with a sample also of nonrespondents. Design, tabulating, and analysis costs are comparable to those of the personal interview, so that one, in effect, saves only the $10 interviewing cost. A somewhat higher interviewing cost must be added for subsampling nonrespondents.

Observation of user behavior is inexpensive if tied into the record-keeping of services used (e.g., retrospective searches conducted). It can be extremely expensive if one must actually observe the researcher in his information environment. No order-of-magnitude estimate of cost seems appropriate.

Constraints on the user survey rather than considerations of effectiveness may actually determine its nature. A small budget may rule out a personal interview survey; a short time for completion may prevent recording observations on behavior; and unavailability of skilled personnel may prevent the use of group interviews. Obviously, one must live within the constraints or try to modify them.

10.4 Marketing research

Traditional marketing research techniques can be applied in the evaluation of new information products or services. Many factors are involved in marketing new information products and services; these factors are illustrated in the conceptual model of Figure 10.1.

Generally, we are interested in the final cost/benefits trade-off of new information products and services. Costs which must be considered include fixed costs, such as costs of inputting material to the data base and product research, and variable costs. Variable costs will be affected by decisions related to product alternatives found from product research, including scope, packaging, organization, and format. As shown in Figure 10.1, variable costs also depend on sales and distribution alternatives (e.g., frequency of distribution, distribution directly to the scientist versus through a librarian, etc.), and on advertising and promotion alternatives (e.g., through media such as primary journals, professional meetings, and promotion flyers). Other variable

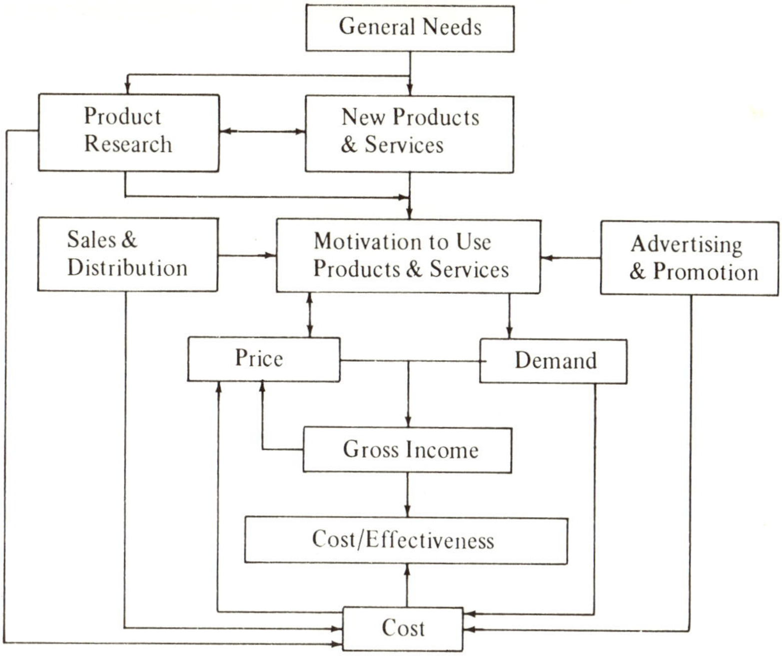

Figure 10.1 Conceptual model for marketing information products and services.

costs, including production and distribution, are dependent on demand.

Income, on the other hand, depends on price and demand, where demand is created from user motivation to use the products and services. As shown in Figure 10.1, this motivation is generated by providing information products and services that satisfy user needs, the price the user is willing to pay for the products and services, sales and distribution procedures, and, finally, by appropriate advertising and promotion. All of these factors are important considerations in the development and marketing of new information products and services; accordingly, they are considered thoroughly in the marketing research study described below.

This example of a marketing research study is directed toward several of these factors as they relate to a proposed current awareness publication. In particular, the example is intended to establish demand, user preferences, price, and related information for the publication.

The following *new product factors* and their alternatives must be examined in relation to the proposed publication:

(1) *Scope.* The literature which is to be included initially in the publication. This decision will allow estimation of volume and cost.

(2) *Packaging.* The units in which the publication is to be presented. Alternatives are: (a) a single announcement journal covering the whole of the field; (b) separate journals devoted to, say, three or four broad subject areas; or (c) a large number of separate announcement sheets covering highly specific subject areas.

(3) *Organization.* How the individual entries will be organized in the publication. This is partly dependent on how the publication is packaged. A number of alternatives are possible, including: (a) broad subject categories based upon a classification scheme; (b) a strict, closely classified order based on the scheme; or (c) a keyword arrangement based on assigned natural-language descriptors.

(4) *Contents of the unit entry.* The minimum would be full bibliographic citation. Other items, such as classification numbers and natural-language descriptors, may also be included.

(5) *Format.* Size, layout and type which may be decided upon.

The following *distribution factors* should also be examined in relation to the current awareness publication:

(1) *Frequency.* How often should the journal be published? This decision is partially based on the desires of the users and the scope of material to be covered.

(2) *Channels.* Should the publication be directed to ultimate users or should it be directed to librarians or other information transfer intermediaries? Both of these questions may be quite important.

Advertising and promotion may be investigated with regard to:

(1) *Media.* Such media as primary journals, promotion flyers, and professional meetings could be considered with regard to probable exposure and to costs.

(2) *Appeals.* A number of possible advertising appeals, such as timeliness, time saving, price, convenience, and breadth of coverage, could also be considered.

The final consideration concerning motivation to use the new current awareness journal is *price*. Price may involve a number of optional strategies that should be considered in a market research study.

The market research study must also involve the *cost* associated with alternative new product factors, distribution factors, and advertising and promotion factors, as well as the probable effect of these factors and price on *demand*. A general research procedure requires that the acceptability of various product alternatives be determined. A second step involves estimating costs for each of the alternatives over a range of likely demand for the publication. A third step is to estimate demand related to product factors and price, and to establish the best distribution, advertising, and promotion strategies needed to maximize demand at a reasonable cost. From this procedure, new product factors, advertising strategies, distribution, and price can be determined on the basis of the cost/benefits trade-off as depicted in Figure 10.1.

The following steps might be taken in a market research study:

(1) Alternative methods of packaging the citations are considered and accurate estimates made of the costs involved in producing a publication in various ways over a range of possible demand. Certain hypotheses relating to distribution and advertising will also have to be made in order to establish tentative price estimates.

(2) Similar preliminary decisions can be made on the contents of the unit entry, and format and organization of the individual issue.

(3) A sample issue of the journal (mock-up), or a portion of an issue, can then be produced for demonstration in user studies.

(4) Group interviews can be held with selected users who are given a copy of the sample issue and are asked questions relating to their preferences on packaging, format, contents, and arrangement, and on the price they would be willing to pay for such a publication. The group should be encouraged to discuss the publication freely, so that all comments, recommendations, and criticisms can be collected. This interview should be recorded for further analysis.

The group interview is conducted primarily to test certain hypotheses about use of the publication, to assist in the formulation of further hypotheses, and to aid in the design of questionnaires. The group interview should also be addressed to questions relating to possible modes of advertising and distribution.

(5) A questionnaire can then be designed to accompany the sample issue in a mailed user study. Questionnaire design can be expected

to benefit greatly from the results of the group interview process. The questionnaire should address itself to the following points:

(a) Given certain alternative ways of packaging the citations, would the recipient be willing to subscribe to one type of package and, if so, how much would he be willing to pay for an annual subscription?

(b) How frequently should the publication appear for maximum utility?

(c) For what purposes would the publication be used?

(d) What are the user preferences for method of organization, format, and contents of the unit entry?

(e) What other types of materials should be included in the publication to make it most useful?

(f) What other types of information services or products are needed by the user?

Additional data should also be collected on personal characteristics of the respondent, including categorization of principal fields of interest, type of work in which engaged, present current awareness activities, and major journals read. These data may be of value for a number of purposes, including determination of optimum methods of packaging and decisions on methods of advertising.

(6) The questionnaire should be pretested on a small sample of, say, 20 users, and modified on the basis of the pretest results.

(7) The mock-up and questionnaire are then mailed to a sample (statistically designed) of potential users and a sample of libraries.

(8) Follow-up mailings may be necessary, and a sample of nonrespondents can be contacted by telephone for a bias check.

(9) Data from completed questionnaires are then reduced and analyzed. These data allow extrapolations to be made on probable demand for the publication. Data can also be used to ascertain user preferences concerning organization, content, and format. The price that users are willing to pay can also be found.

(10) On the basis of such a study, final decisions can be made on format, organization, packaging, and price.

Chapter Eleven
Statistics Primer

11.1 Introduction

Although statistics is an important tool of the system evaluator, it is sometimes a deterrent as well, since the use of statistical jargon tends to turn away those unsophisticated in the technology. Our objective in this chapter is not to teach evaluators to be statisticians, but to assuage the panic in the mind of the evaluator when he encounters statistical concepts. At the same time, the reader may learn a few fundamental statistical ideas.

11.2 Some preliminary concepts

Much of statistics has to do with summarizing and presenting large masses of data. This activity nearly always involves the development of figures which give perspective. Examples are the number of index terms assigned per document, number of documents retrieved per search, and maximum number of terms specified per search. Often these summary statistics are derived from samples. One knows, there fore, that they are only approximations – but to what? And how accurate are they?

The total collection of things being studied (such as documents, index terms, users, indexers) is called a *universe*. Each member of the universe has *characteristics* – a document has number of words, language in which written, index tags assigned, and so on. When these characteristics are quantitative, such as number of index tags, they are called *variables.* If the variable is the number of documents retrieved and a particular search retrieves ten, then ten is called a *variate,* i.e., a specific value for a variable. All of the variates for a specific variable in the universe taken together make up a statistical *population*. Thus a universe is made up of *things* and a population is made up of *numbers.*[1]

This seems like a roundabout way of getting to the main point that a *parameter* is any number referring to a population, e.g., the largest, the smallest, the average, or the most common value. Sample data are summarized into *statistics* (the plural of *statistic*) which are estimates of population parameters. For example, the average of a sample is presumed to be an estimate of the population average.

How accurately do such statistics estimate population parameters? It depends upon how the sample is drawn, how large the sample is, and how variable the population is.

11.3 Statistical description

Before discussing reliability, we will consider some simpler concepts. Many statistical measures are used simply as shorthand descriptions of data. The average (*arithmetic mean*) is, of course, such a measure. Another is the *median,* that is, the middle value when all of the values are put in increasing or decreasing order. The median is little influenced by extreme values; hence it is useful in representing data which are subject to infrequent but unusual values. For example, searches may typically produce less than 30 documents, but may occasionally produce 500. If one represents the data by the average, the few large observations may pull the average up to where it is representative of neither the normal search nor the extreme search. The median, on the other hand, remains quite stable under these circumstances.

The median separates the data into two equal parts by size. *Percentile points* separate the data into 100 equal parts by size (assuming enough observations so that such small subdivisions of the data are feasible). The 25th and 75th percentile points are called *quartile points* and, with the median, divide the data into four parts. The distance between the first quartile point (25th percentile) and the third quartile point (75th percentile) is a measure of the dispersion of the data.

[1]Frequently, however, they are not distinguished.

Some data are symmetric around the middle value, that is, the lowest value is about the same distance below the median as the highest value is above it. Other data are *skewed*; they are said to be *skewed to the right* if dispersion above the median is greater than dispersion below the median, and *skewed to the left* if the opposite holds. Tags assigned per document, pages per document, and retrievals per search are all variables which are skewed to the right.

Consider the simple numerical illustration taken from Lancaster (*3*) and summarized in Table 11.1. The data are obviously skewed to the right. It is also obvious that the *range* is no greater than 27. Grouping of the data by threes masks the identity of the original observations, but makes a summary picture more readily discernible.

The association of frequencies with numbers in Table 11.1 is called a *frequency distribution*; in this case it was obtained from a sample, so it is properly called a *sample distribution.*

Using the original values (in their ungrouped form), one finds that their average is 6.48 and their median is 6. As noted earlier, one expects the mean (the average) to be greater than the median in a right-skewed distribution.

The most common measure used to describe a distribution is the arithmetic mean, and this is true for all but wildly skewed populations. The most common measure of dispersion is the *standard deviation,* which is the square root of the average squared deviation from

Table 11.1 Number of Pre-identified and Independently Located Relevant Documents Used as the Base for Recall Ratios in 299 Searches

Number of documents in base	Frequency
0-2	49
3-5	92
6-8	89
9-11	32
12-14	18
15-17	10
18-20	6
21-23	0
24-27	3
Total	299

the mean. Let's do it with numbers. The computations are shown in Table 11.2 for hypothetical data representing search time. The common symbol for the mean is μ and that for the standard deviation is σ.

$$\mu = 428/8 = 53.5$$

$$\sigma = \sqrt{1086/8} = 11.6$$

In this illustration we assume that the population consists of eight observations, so that μ and σ are parameters of that population.

If the eight observations are a sample from a large population of possible searches, we denote the mean by $\bar{x}$ and the standard deviation by s. We also divide by 7 rather than by 8 in computing the standard deviation (i.e., by $n - 1$ where n is the sample size). Thus,

$$\bar{x} = 53.5 \text{ (as above)}$$

$$s = \sqrt{1086/7} = 12.5$$

This is the kind of hocus-pocus that drives nonstatisticians up the wall. One may as well take on faith the statistician's assurance that one obtains a "better" estimate of the standard deviation by dividing by $n - 1$ rather than by n.

Table 11.2 Search Time, in Minutes, for Eight Searches, with Computation of Mean and Standard Deviation

Search time (minutes) X	$X - \mu$	$(X - \mu)^2$
46	-7.5	56.25
52	-1.5	2.25
30	-23.5	552.25
48	-5.5	30.25
60	6.5	42.25
64	10.5	110.25
70	16.5	272.25
58	4.5	20.25
428	0	1,086.00

11.4 Variability and uncertainty

What does the standard deviation mean? It depends to some extent on how much we know about the population whose standard deviation we have. Let's assume we know very little. Then we can at least make the following statement:

The probability that the absolute difference between an individual observation and the population mean will exceed k standard deviations is less than $1/k^2$.

Lest we fail to grasp the significance of this startlingly clear exposition of a principle, we will do it with numbers. Suppose we know that the average search time is 35 minutes and the standard deviation is 5 minutes. What is the probability that a randomly drawn search will take longer than 50 minutes or less than 20 minutes? Twenty and 50 are three standard deviations away from the mean ($k = 3$), so the probability is less than 1/9, i.e., less than $1/k^2$. How much less? We don't know. The probability can, of course, be translated into relative frequencies. That is, in 100 searches one would expect less than one-ninth of them (about 11) to take less than 20 or more than 50 minutes.

If search time is normally distributed, we can make a much stronger probability statement. With the same data as above we can say:

The probability that the absolute difference between an individual observation and the population mean will exceed three standard deviations is equal to 0.0027.

That is, one would expect such a rare event only about 27 times in 10,000 trials. The basis for this statement will be examined subsequently. Evidently, knowing that search time is normally distributed contributes a great deal to one's ability to make probability statements.

If one draws a random sample from a normal population, he will expect the actual sample values to cluster around the population mean, with the frequency of observations becoming smaller and smaller as one gets farther away from the mean, either above it or below it. If he were to continue drawing samples, making the variable classes (see Table 11.1) narrower and narrower, he would find that, when plotted, the frequency distribution would approach the shape of Figure 11.1.

This curve has a mathematical expression, but we need not be concerned with it here. The probability of drawing a random observation with value between a and b is the area under the curve between a and b divided by the total area under the curve. The symbols μ and σ stand for the mean and standard deviation of the distribution.

Inspection of Figure 11.1 discloses a number of features of the normal distribution.

(1) μ is the median of the distribution (the middle) and the graph is symmetric around μ.

(2) σ is the distance from the center of the distribution to the "knee" of the curve.

(3) The graph extends indefinitely in both directions, without ever touching the horizontal axis.

(4) In spite of (3), the normal distribution can be a good approximation to distributions with finite ranges, because virtually all (99.73 percent) of the distribution is within three standard deviations of the mean.

In order to find normal probabilities, one would use tables rather than graphs. Fortunately, only one normal distribution needs to be tabled. The one universally found is called the standard normal distribution, whose mean is 9 and standard deviation is 1 (see Figure 11.2).

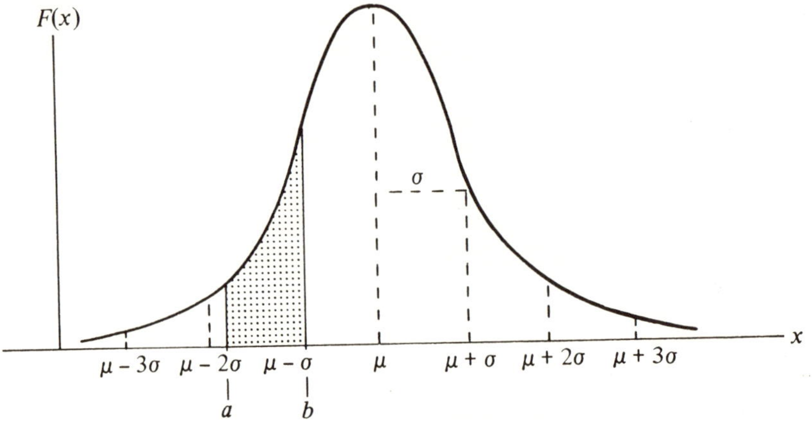

Figure 11.1 Normal curve with mean μ standard deviation σ.

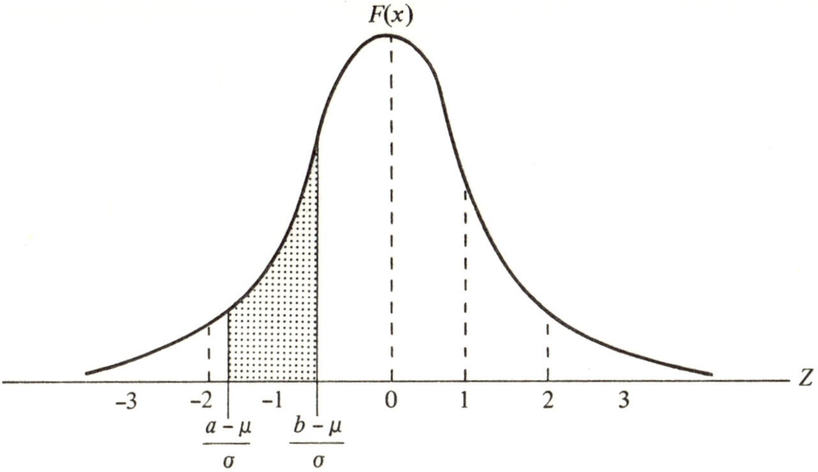

Figure 11.2 Standard normal curve.

If x is a value in a normal distribution with mean μ, standard deviation σ, then $(x - \mu)/\sigma$ is the corresponding value in the standard normal distribution.

Tables of areas (probabilities) of the standard normal curve are given in almost any textbook in statistics and will not be repeated here. However, some checkpoint data may be useful. About 68.3 percent of the area lies within one standard deviation of the mean, about 95.4 percent within two standard deviations, and about 99.8 percent within three standard deviations.

Measurements taken on physical phenomena are frequently distributed in an approximately normal fashion, but most measurements on document transfer systems are not normally distributed – they tend to be skewed to the right. One might infer, then, that the normal distribution is not very useful to us, but this is not the case. In the first place, it may be possible to transform the observations to make them approximately normal (see Section 11.6 on lognormal distribution). Secondly, most estimates of population parameters tend to be more nearly normally distributed than the observations on which they are based. We discuss this phenomenon in the following section.

11.5 Reliability of estimates

Let's say we observe 100 randomly drawn searches and find that the average total retrieval is 17.4 documents. This figure, we presume, is an estimate of the "true" average response, which is, of course, unknown. We want to know how much reliability we can place in the estimate of 17.4.

The indicator of reliability which we use is the *standard error of the mean.* It is the standard deviation divided by the square root of the number of observations in the sample, and is written

$$s_{\bar{x}} = s/\sqrt{n}$$

It is important to understand its meaning. Consider the above illustration in which 100 sample observations had a mean of 17.4. Suppose now that we drew another sample of 100 *from the same population,* recorded its mean, drew another sample and recorded its mean, drew another sample and recorded its mean, and so on, until we had a large number of sample means. The standard deviation of this distribution of sample means is what we are estimating by $s/\sqrt{n}$.

Furthermore, even though the original values are quite highly skewed (as is likely in total retrievals), *the distribution of means tends toward normality as the sample size increases.* Therefore, with modest sample sizes we can be reasonably sure of probability statements about the sample mean obtained from a normal curve probability table, even though the original observations may be far from normal.

Suppose, in the above example, that the standard deviation computed from the sample of 100 values was 8.4. Then, the standard error of the mean is estimated by

$$s_{\bar{x}} = 8.4/\sqrt{100} = 0.84$$

This formula says that (see above) the probability is approximately 0.68 that the mean (17.4) is within 1 standard error (0.84) of the true mean, 0.95 that it is within 2 standard errors (1.68), and 0.998 that it is within 3 standard errors (2.52). Thus, the standard error establishes how *reliable* the estimate 17.4 is. Note that the formula $s_{\bar{x}} = s/\sqrt{n}$ makes it possible to estimate the standard error from the standard deviation of a *single sample* of size *n.* We do not have to do repeated sampling. The repeated sampling idea was introduced only for the purpose of explaining the concept of the standard error of the mean as the standard deviation of a distribution of sample means.

Also, observe the effect of sample size (n). The square root of sample size appears in the denominator of $s_{\bar{x}}$, so in order to double precision (cut the standard error in half), one needs to take four times as large a sample. Thus, to cut the standard error from 0.84 to 0.42, one would need to increase sample size from 100 to 400. This characteristic of the standard error is important, because it shows that there are decreasing marginal returns from increasing sample sizes.

Most common statistical measures have standard errors (although not all are computed from as simple a formula as $s_{\bar{x}}$) and all can be interpreted in terms of probability by reference to the normal curve if the sample sizes are large enough. Other probability distributions must be used for small samples, but to discuss them completely in this chapter would require too much space.

11.6 The lognormal distribution

As stated above, many variables in document transfer evaluation are skewed to the right. Experience has shown, however, that if one takes the logarithms of the observed values, the values transformed in this manner are approximately normally distributed. Consider the data taken from King (*2*) which appear in Table 11.3. Some terms will appear infrequently, but no term can be used less than zero times. On the other hand, the maximum number of times a term can be used is limited only by the number of documents in the file. Therefore, one would expect the distribution of usage to be skewed to the right. This is, in fact, the case, as is shown in Table 11.2.

The last column of Table 11.3 has been plotted on log-probability paper in Figure 11.3. The straight line fit indicates a good fit of the lognormal distribution, that is, the distribution whose logarithms are normally distributed. The fact that the fit is good permits one to read off probabilities of interest directly from the graph. For example, 50 percent of the terms are used over 12 times, and 25 percent are used over 50 times (approximately).

11.7 Confidence limits

We have seen in Section 11.5 how the standard error can be used as an indicator of reliability. Frequently, however, results are expressed in terms of *confidence limits,* so it is important to understand this concept as well.

A *confidence coefficient* is a number between 0 and 1 which represents how certain one is that the population parameter of interest

Table 11.3 Number of Documents Indexed per Term in a Sample Evaluation of the Glass Technology File of the U.S. Patent Office

Number of documents	Frequency (terms)	Cumulative frequencies: Actual	Cumulative frequencies: Percent
0	22	22	5.6
1	30	52	13.1
2	25	77	19.4
3	16	93	23.5
4	15	108	27.3
5	15	123	31.1
6	20	143	36.1
7	14	157	39.6
8	9	166	41.9
9	7	173	43.7
10	14	187	47.2
11	3	190	48.0
12	11	201	50.8
13	5	206	52.0
14	2	208	52.5
15	3	211	53.3
16 - 20	19	230	58.1
21 - 25	24	254	64.1
26 - 50	49	303	76.5
51 - 75	17	320	80.8
76 - 100	22	342	86.4
101 - 150	20	362	91.4
151 - 200	12	374	94.4
201 - 300	12	386	97.5
301 - 400	10	396	100.0

is contained within a confidence interval. That is, if a 0.9 confidence interval of the mean is (20, 30), one is "90 percent confident" that the mean really lies within the interval 20 to 30. The mean, of course, is either in the interval or is not, so 0.9 cannot be interpreted as a probability in the ordinary sense. However, the *procedure* for finding the limits 20 and 30 is such that in many trials 90 percent of the intervals so computed (whatever their endpoints are) will cover the true value of the mean.

To place confidence limits on the mean for a large sample, one obtains the constant from a normal area table representing the number of standard deviations (plus and minus from the mean) which include

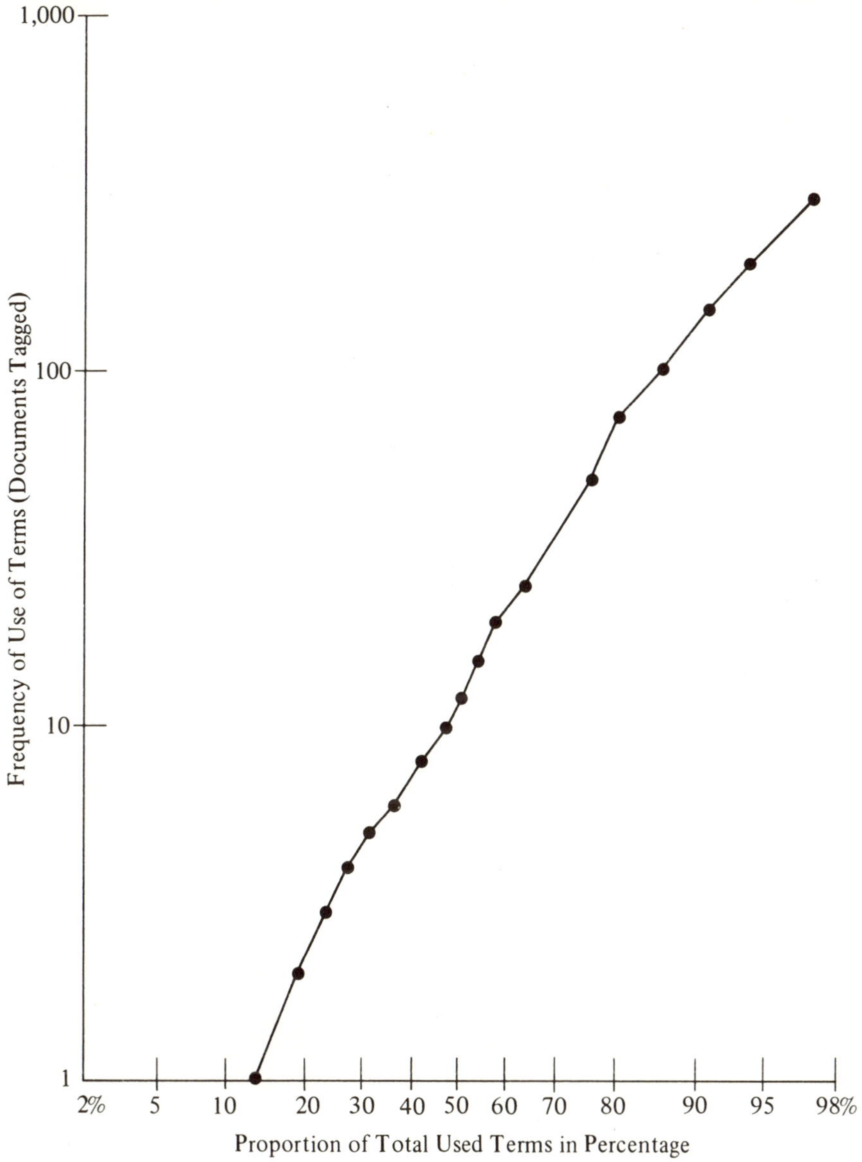

Figure 11.3 Cumulative distribution of frequency of use of index terms.

that proportion of the normal curve area designated by the confidence coefficient. This constant is multiplied by the standard error of the mean, the result added to the mean to get the upper limit, and subtracted from the mean to get the lower limit.

Consider again the example in which for 100 searches the average response was found to be 17.4 documents and the standard deviation 8.4 (standard error 0.84). Ninety percent of the area under a normal curve is contained within ±1.64 standard deviations of the mean. Therefore, one obtains:

$$\text{Upper limit} = 17.4 + 1.64\,(0.84) = 18.8$$
$$\text{Lower limit} = 17.4 - 1.64\,(0.84) = 16.0$$

One is "90 percent confident" that the true mean lies between these values, but, of course, one does not really know whether it does or does not.

11.8 Relative frequencies

A special case – that in which we observe the relative frequency with which something happens – occurs so frequently in document transfer evaluation that it merits separate attention. Some examples are: proportion of retrieved documents found relevant, proportion of relevant documents missed in searching, proportion of searches judged successful by users, and proportion of used references contained in the collection.

In all such cases one obtains a count of the number of documents, searches, and so on, having the desired characteristic and divides this number by the number examined to obtain the relative frequency of occurrence. Under some conditions the relative frequency can be identified with an estimate of probability (see Chapter 4), which we will denote by p. The standard error of $\tilde{p}$ is $\sqrt{p(1-p)/n}$. Suppose, for example, that in a sample of 160 searches 120 were judged "successful." Our estimate of the overall proportion of successful searches is

$$\tilde{p} = 120/160 = 0.75$$

and its standard error is

$$s_{\tilde{p}} = \sqrt{0.75(0.25)/160} = 0.034$$

When sample sizes are moderately large (such as 160), one can use the normal area table to interpret reliability (unless p is close to 0 or to 1, in which case specially prepared tables should be used). In our example, one can be reasonably sure (with about 0.95 confidence) that the estimate $\tilde{p} = 0.75$ is within 2 standard errors (0.068) of the true value.

Some cautions should be observed. First, although $\sqrt{\tilde{p}(1 - \tilde{p})/n}$ is not a bad estimate of the standard error for any sample size, one cannot use the normal curve for interpretation unless the product n is of substantial size for small values of p. Cochran (*1*) suggests the following restrictions:

p	n greater than
0.5	30
0.4 or 0.6	50
0.3 or 0.7	80
0.2 or 0.8	200
0.1 or 0.9	600
0.05 or 0.95	1,400

Thus, the normal approximation cannot be used at all in many document retrieval applications. Suppose, for example, that one out of four known relevant documents is retrieved. We have $\tilde{p} = 1/4 = 0.25$ and $\sqrt{\tilde{p}(1 - \tilde{p})/n} = 0.22$, but under no circumstances would one use the normal probability table in setting confidence limits.

In evaluating searches such as in the above example, it might appear that one could add the number of "successes" over several searches and divide by the combined total of "trials" to arrive at an estimate, $\tilde{p}$, and then to compute the standard error by $\sqrt{\tilde{p}(1 - \tilde{p})/n}$. This procedure is incorrect, since the unit of observation is now the *search* and not the individual document. Consider the following illustration. Assume that 20 searches yield the estimates of recall shown in Table 11.4. Each of these 20 estimates is from a small sample and one must find a way of combining results. One way is to take a ratio of the totals, i.e.,

$$\tilde{p} = 71/131 = 0.542$$

CAUTION: The standard error of this estimate is *not*

$$\sqrt{0.542(0.458)/131} = 0.043$$

The correct standard error for this estimate is found from the following impressive formula:

$$s_{\tilde{p}} = \sqrt{\frac{[\Sigma y^2 - 2(p)\,\Sigma xy + (p)^2\,\Sigma x^2]}{m(m-1)(\bar{x})^2}}$$

where m is the number of samples (20) and x and y are as defined in Table 11.4. Substituting numbers yields:

$$s_{\tilde{p}} = \sqrt{\frac{[409 - 2(0.542)\,628 + (0.542)^2\,(1{,}155)]}{20(19)(6.55)^2}} = 0.064$$

Alternatively, one may average the ratios (the last column of Table 11.4) and arrive at an estimate:

$$\tilde{p} = 0.516$$

Table 11.4 Recall Estimated from 20 Sample Searches

Search	Number retrieved (y)	Number in base (x)	Ratio $p = (y/x)$
1	1	2	0.50
2	7	7	1.00
3	1	3	0.33
4	11	16	0.69
5	2	4	0.50
6	8	14	0.57
7	4	6	0.67
8	3	5	0.60
9	3	4	0.75
10	4	14	0.29
11	5	7	0.71
12	0	1	0
13	2	6	0.33
14	3	6	0.50
15	0	8	0
16	6	7	0.86
17	2	4	0.50
18	2	4	0.50
19	1	6	0.17
20	6	7	0.86
Totals	71	131	0.54

This estimate has the standard error of

$$s_{\tilde{p}} = \sqrt{\frac{\Sigma(\tilde{p} - \bar{p})^2}{m(m-1)}} = 0.061$$

In general, the question of which of the latter two methods should be used is controversial. In a specific case it can be determined on theoretical grounds. In most of the cases actually encountered, it has been found that a simple average of ratios is the better estimate and this is the one which we generally recommend.

11.9 Tests of hypothesis

Hypothesis testing is a less useful procedure than is commonly supposed. Basically, in hypothesis testing we make an assertion about the population and, on the basis of sample observations, either accept the assertion or reject it. For example, two indexing procedures are under study – call them A and B. We may take as our hypothesis: Procedure A yields the same number of errors per document as Procedure B. In an experiment we naturally don't expect to find *exactly* the same number of errors, so we allow ourselves some leeway due to "experimental error," or "sampling variation." But how much leeway?

Although we oversimplify slightly by ignoring some experimental design concepts (see Chapter 13), we identify the following quantities:

	Procedure A	Procedure B
Number of observations	$n_A = 50$	$n_B = 100$
Means	$\bar{x}_A = 2.5$	$\bar{x}_B = 2.0$
Standard deviations	$s_A = 3.0$	$s_B = 4.0$

Let us suppose, for the design we have chosen, that the *standard error of the difference between the two means* is

$$s_{A-B} = \sqrt{s_A^2/n_A + s_B^2/n_B}$$

$$= \sqrt{0.18 + 0.16} = 0.58$$

The difference in means (0.5) is less than 1 standard error (0.58), so we must conclude that this isn't a very "rare event" in view of the hypothesis. Thus, we probably would accept the hypothesis of no difference.

Suppose, however, we have the same means and standard deviations as above, but now the sample sizes are $n_A = 500$ and $n_B = 1{,}000$. With these sample sizes, the standard error is 0.18 and the difference in means is over three times the standard error. We would have to conclude that this is an unlikely outcome in view of the hypothesis, so we would reject the hypothesis. Under such circumstances it is customary to say that the differences in the two procedures are *statistically significant.* However, we have just shown that the judgment may be more a function of sample size than of sample differences.

There is substantial justification for the point of view that any two procedures are fundamentally different (otherwise they would be indistinguishable), and therefore their differences can be found to be statistically significant (or the hypothesis of equality can be rejected) if a large enough sample is taken. If one takes this point of view, he must conclude that hypothesis testing is indeed a sterile activity. For this reason, throughout this procedural guide, estimation and standard errors have been emphasized rather than tests of significance (or tests of hypothesis).

It should also be noted that statistical significance has nothing to do with economic significance. A difference in average total retrieval of 0.1 documents might be statistically significant (if sample sizes were large enough), but it has no economic significance whatever and would have no effect upon the users' acceptance of the system.

11.10 Reporting evaluation results

Much potentially useful evaluation is wasted because it is not reported properly. Although it is difficult to set up a reporting system which will meet every possible need, it is easy to set down some principles which should govern most reporting.

The evaluation report should include:

(1) A clear statement of the objectives of the evaluation, relating it to other studies or results reported elsewhere.

(2) A description of the procedures employed.

(3) A reporting of the experimental results, including sample

sizes, experimental arrangements, and principal summarizations of the data. Detailed data may appear in an appendix, or references may be made to its location elsewhere.

(4) Analysis of the results with regard to the objectives, including the estimation of parameters and assignment of measures of reliability or significance.

(5) Conclusions with regard to the objectives and the effect of the evaluation on future studies, as well as recommendations for changes in policy as a result of the research.

There is no fixed format for the report. As a matter of clarity of presentation, it is usually desirable to put much of the detail in the appendix.

The following is presented as a checklist of things that might appear somewhere in the report, depending upon the subject matter of the research:

(1) Description of the file.
  (a) Number of documents in the file
  (b) Subject matter
  (c) Relationship of the file to other files, with partial overlap of subject matter or usage
(2) Description of the indexing system.
  (a) Term list
  (b) Coding forms
  (c) Indexing procedures
  (d) Indexing personnel
(3) Description of search procedures.
  (a) Hardware or other devices used
  (b) Definition of a search (or trial, or search sequence)
  (c) Search personnel
  (d) Source of search questions (who selected them, are they known to be in the file, and so on)
  (e) Method of determining relevance, if appropriate; otherwise whatever determination of effectiveness is used
  (f) Analysis of search failures
  (g) Search time, cost, and other measures
  (h) Some examples

It is completely appropriate to extract from the complete report for special purposes, but somewhere there should be available a complete report which includes the above detail, even though it may only be a file copy. Furthermore, the numerical data of the report should be backed up by carefully labeled, dated, and indexed worksheets, so that future studies can make full use of the work already accomplished. It is a good idea to bind up such worksheets, along with the recording forms for the experimental data, and to retain them for a period of time. Microfilm can be used when the original recording forms become too bulky.

11.11 Some extensions of statistical methodology[2]

Tests of hypotheses

A *statistical hypothesis* is an assumption about the distribution of a variable. We are concerned primarily with hypotheses that specify the value of a parameter, such as, "The mean number of terms per search is 2," although other types are possible, such as, "This distribution is normal." A *test of hypothesis* is a procedure to determine whether to accept or reject the hypothesis. The procedure invariably involves sampling; hence, the decision is not infallible. The theory of hypothesis testing is designed to reduce the probabilities of incorrect decisions.

Hypothesis testing is useful when a decision must be made regarding *two* alternative courses of action, with the preferable course depending on the (unknown) value of a parameter. For example, the decision to build a new system may depend on the amount of use that would be made of the system. A hypothesis is framed so that acceptance of it leads to one course of action, rejection to the other.

A test of a hypothesis is constructed by determining which samples support the hypothesis and which do not. In testing the hypothesis that the mean of a distribution is 2, for example, a reasonable criterion would require that samples for which $\bar{x}$ is close to 2 support the hypothesis. To be more precise, one might let values of $\bar{x}$ between 1 and 3 lead to acceptance of the hypothesis. This completely determines the test *procedure,* but a number of other considerations must be taken into account before the test can be evaluated.

Untested assumptions. In order to make probability statements concerning errors, it is often necessary to assume that a distribution is

[2]This section is intended for reference only. It need not be read or understood as a prerequisite for any of the other chapters.

of a given type, such as normal or binomial. Such an assumption forms an integral part of the test, but is not part of the hypothesis being tested. Assumptions of normality or near normality are widely used (and misused). When testing hypotheses concerning means of more than one population, one often makes the assumption that the variances are equal. These assumptions are made for convenience in computing probabilities, but there should be a rational basis for them, such as experience with similar situations or prior tests.

Two hypotheses. Although we have spoken of testing a single hypothesis, it is customary to frame two hypotheses so that rejection of either one is equivalent to acceptance of the other. It is desirable that one hypothesis name a single value of the parameter. Together with the assumptions, this single value can be used in computing probabilities. For example, if it is assumed that a distribution is normal and it is hypothesized that $\mu = 2$, then when the hypothesis is true, $(\bar{x} - 2)/(s/\sqrt{n})$ has a *t*-distribution with parameter $n - 1$. The hypothesis which specifies a single value for the parameter is called the *null hypothesis.* The other hypothesis is called the *alternate hypothesis.* When the null hypothesis is $\mu = 2$, the alternate might be $\mu > 2$, $\mu < 2$, or $\mu \neq 2$. When $\mu = 2$ is tested against $\mu > 2$, it is implied that one decision is appropriate when μ is greater than 2, and the other is appropriate if μ is 2 or less. Similar remarks are true for the other alternate hypotheses.

Consider again the proposed document transfer system. If a well-defined population of potential users is available, it might be known that the system will be a success if the potential users make an average of 2 or more requests during the year. An appropriate null hypothesis would be $\mu = 2$, and the alternative, $\mu > 2$.

Two types of error: significance. The error of rejecting the null hypothesis when it is true is called a *type I error,* and that of accepting the null when it is false is called *type II error.* In testing a specific null hypothesis, one can choose the probability with which he is willing to commit a type I error. This probability is called the level of significance of the test and is denoted by α. The choice of a 0.05 level means the tester is constructing a test that will reject the null hypothesis 5 percent of the time *when the null hypothesis is true.*

The alternate hypothesis, as a rule, allows for many possible values of the parameter. For each specific value allowed by the alternate hypothesis, there is a probability β of type II error. A graph, showing the probability β as a function of the true value of μ, might look like the following for a test of $\mu = 2$ against $\mu > 2$ with $\alpha = 0.05$:

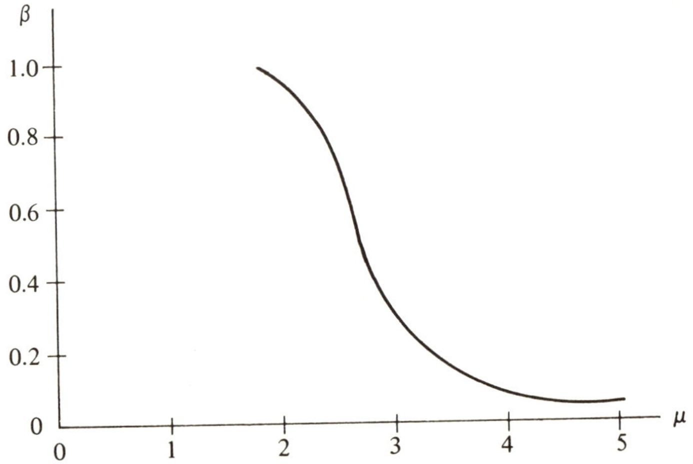

Note that the error probability is very large when μ is near 2 and decreases as μ increases. The speed with which the error decreases depends heavily on the sample size and on α.

The tester can also specify something about the error probability β. For example, he might wish to be 90 percent sure of rejecting the null hypothesis when $\mu = 3$. That is, he requires $\beta = 0.10$ when $\mu = 3$. In the situation depicted by the graph, when $\mu = 3$, $\beta = 0.25$, which does not meet the requirement. In order to decrease β, he can increase α. If this is not acceptable, he can increase the sample size.

A decrease in any one of α, β, and n can be achieved by increasing one of the others. It is desirable to keep α, β, and n small since α and β are error probabilities and n directly affects cost. In a given situation, where costs and seriousness of errors are known, good balance can be achieved, but such situations are too complex to be considered here. We choose, for convenience, $\alpha = 0.05$ and assume the sample size has been predetermined.

The test statistic. Corresponding to the two possible decisions in a test are samples of two kinds: those which support the null hypothesis and those which support the alternate hypothesis. More specifically, the procedure of a test involves computing the value of a statistic, and accepting the null or alternate hypothesis, depending on the value computed. A test requires a statistic whose distribution is known when the null hypothesis is assumed true. For example, if normality is assumed and the null hypothesis is $\mu = 2$, then the statistic $(\bar{x} - 2)/(s/\sqrt{n})$ has a t-distribution with parameter $n - 1$, as mentioned above.

The critical region of a test is comprised of those samples which lead to rejection of the null hypothesis. When a test statistic is used, the critical region can conveniently be thought of as the values of the statistic which lead to rejection. The critical region depends on the null and alternate hypotheses and on the level of significance chosen.

The null and alternate hypotheses must be considered together when selecting a critical region. Samples in the critical region should support the alternate hypothesis against the null. In the example above, with null hypothesis $\mu = 2$ and test statistic $(\bar{x} - 2)/(s/\sqrt{n})$, one would expect $\bar{x}$ to be near 2 if the null hypothesis were true, so he would expect the test statistic to be near zero. If the alternate hypothesis, $\mu > 2$, were true, then $\bar{x}$ would be expected to be greater than 2, so the statistic would be greater than zero (on the average). The critical region would then contain only large positive values of the statistic. However, if the alternate hypothesis were $\mu \neq 2$, then both large positive and large negative values of the statistic would be in the critical region.

After determining the types of values to place in the critical region, one uses the level of significance to determine the exact values. Suppose the null hypothesis is $\mu = 2$, the alternate hypothesis is $\mu > 2$, and $\alpha = 0.05$. Then large positive values of $(\bar{x} - 2)/(s/\sqrt{n})$ will be in the critical region, and the probability of obtaining a value in the critical region, when the null hypothesis is true, will be 0.05, since $(\bar{x} - 2)/(s/\sqrt{n})$ will be greater than $t_{0.95}$ when μ is equal to 2. The critical region is then determined by the inequality

$$\frac{\bar{x} - 2}{s/\sqrt{n}} > t_{0.95}$$

If, on the other hand, the alternate hypothesis is $\mu \neq 2$, then the appropriate critical region is

$$\frac{\bar{x} - 2}{s/\sqrt{n}} > t_{0.975} \text{ and } \frac{\bar{x} - 2}{s/\sqrt{n}} < t_{0.025}$$

since large positive *and* large negative values lead to rejection.

Summary. The hypothesis testing procedure always begins with a decision concerning two alternatives. Then one should:

(1) Select a null and alternate hypothesis to the two alternatives.

(2) Select a level of significance. If type II errors are important, make specifications concerning β.

(3) Find a test statistic whose distribution is known when the null hypothesis is true. If this distribution depends on other assumptions as well, verify that the assumptions are reasonable.

(4) Find the critical region, using 1, 2, and 3.

(5) Select a sample, make the computations, and accept or reject the null hypothesis as the sample data dictate.

Bivariate analysis

Correlation. When two variables in a population are of interest, it is often desirable to have a measure of the relationship between the two. For a population of searches, one might wish to investigate the relationship between search time and user satisfaction, or between false drops and number of terms used in the query. One such measure is the *covariance* of the two variables.

Assume that the given population is finite with N units, and the scores of the variables are represented by X and Y. (Each unit in the population has both an X-score and a Y-score.) Then the covariance S_{XY} of the two variables is defined to be:

$$S_{XY} = \frac{\Sigma(X - \bar{X})(Y - \bar{Y})}{N} \qquad (1)$$

If high values of one variable are associated with high values of the other, S_{XY} will be large and positive. If high values of one variable tend to occur with low values of the other, S_{XY} will be large and negative.

A disadvantage of the covariance is that it depends on the measurement scales chosen for the variables. When one of the variables is time, measurement in seconds will produce a covariance 60 times as large as would measurement in minutes. A measure related to the covariance, but independent of the scales of measurement, is the *correlation coefficient* ρ, which is defined:

$$\rho = \frac{S_{XY}}{S_X S_Y} \qquad (2)$$

The range of ρ is from -1 to 1. At either extreme a perfect straight line relationship between the two variables is indicated.

A correlation of zero implies that there is no *linear* relationship between the two variables, but does not imply that the variables are totally unrelated. If the X, Y scores fall into a circular pattern such as the one below, ρ would be 0, but the variables are strongly related.

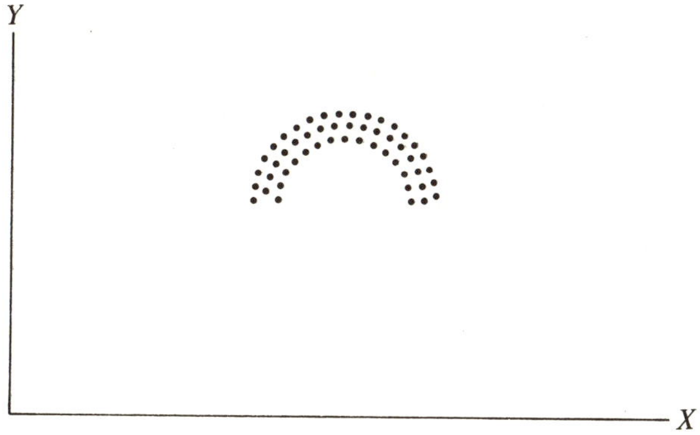

Just as the mean and variance do not completely specify a distribution, neither does the correlation coefficient completely describe the relationship between two variables.

Analogous to equations (1) and (2), the *sample covariance* s_{XY} is defined:

$$s_{XY} = \frac{\Sigma(x - \bar{x})(y - \bar{y})}{n - 1} \quad (3)$$

where x and y represent sample values of the two variables, and the *sample* correlation coefficient r is:

$$r = \frac{s_{XY}}{s_X s_Y} \quad (4)$$

If a random sample of n units is selected from a bivariate normal distribution, then the variable $1/2\ ln[(l + r)/(l - r)]$ has, approximately, a normal distribution with mean $1/2\ ln[(l + \rho)/(l - \rho)]$ and standard deviation $1/\sqrt{n - 3}$. This fact can be used to test hypotheses about ρ or set confidence intervals on it. With most books of tables, one need only compute r. Given the values of r and n, confidence limits for ρ can be read directly from the tables.

Regression. Regression analysis, like correlation analysis, is concerned with situations in which two (or more) variables are of interest. In correlation analysis the variables are treated symmetrically; neither plays a distinctive role. In regression analysis the emphasis is on prediction of the values of one variable when values of the other are known. The variable whose values are known is called the *independent variable* and is designated by X. The variable to be predicted is called the *dependent variable* and is designated by Y.

For each X-value, the set of all units in the population with that particular value form a subpopulation called an *X-array.* The mean value of the Y-variable for a given X-array is denoted by $\bar{Y}_X$. For the weight Y of a man randomly chosen from all men in the United States, a good prediction would be $\bar{Y}$, the mean weight of all such men. But if the man's height X were known, $\bar{Y}_X$, the mean weight for all men of height X would be a better prediction for the man's weight. An assumption inherent in the last statement is that $\bar{Y}_X$ is known for every value of X. This is usually not the case. Given the value of X, $\bar{Y}_X$ must usually be estimated. Regression analysis involves such estimation procedures.

To begin with, it is assumed that the relationship between $\bar{Y}_X$ and X can be expressed by a mathematical formula (a regression equation). In particular, we shall deal with *linear* regression, which entails the assumption that there is a straight-line relationship between $\bar{Y}_X$ and X. Mathematically, this assumption is expressed:

$$\bar{Y}_X = A + B(X - \bar{X}) \qquad (5)$$

Both X and $\bar{X}$ are assumed known, so the problem is reduced to specifying values for A and B. Equation (5) is a *general* equation for a straight line. It becomes the equation of a specific line when A and B are replaced by numbers. A and B are unknown and must be estimated. It might seem that no real progress has been made. The original problem was to estimate $\bar{Y}_X$ and the derived problem is to estimate A and B. However, there are as many values of $\bar{Y}_X$ as there are values of X. To estimate each one separately might involve hundreds of estimates. The objective of equation (5) is to tie together all the values of $\bar{Y}_X$ using an expression involving only two parameters, A and B. Once estimates for A and B have been found, any one of the $\bar{Y}_X$'s can be estimated. If a and b denote the estimates of A and B and Y_X denotes the estimate of $\bar{Y}_X$, then substituting these estimates into equation (5) yields the *estimated line of regression*:

$$\tilde{Y}_X = a + b\,(X - \bar{X}) \tag{6}$$

To find the estimates a and b, a sample is required. Values of X are arbitrarily selected (duplicates are allowed), and for each X-value a unit is randomly selected from the corresponding X-array. (Note the distinction between this sort of sampling and choosing a random sample from the entire population as in correlation analysis.) A sample of Y-values is thus obtained, with each sample value y corresponding to a selected X-value. Under certain assumptions, listed below, the best estimates a and b are given by the equations:

$$a = \bar{y} \text{ and } b = \frac{n\Sigma Xy - \Sigma X \Sigma y}{n\Sigma X^2 - (\Sigma X)^2} \tag{7}$$

where $\bar{y}$ is the mean of the entire sample, n is the sample size, and the X's involved in the summations are just those values which were selected.

As an illustration of equations (7), suppose the following X-values are selected and sampling yields the y-values.

X:	2	2	4	6	6	ΣX	=	20
Σy:	5	3	3	3	1	ΣX	=	15

Then an Xy and an X^2 row must be computed:

ΣXy:	10	6	12	18	6	ΣX	=	52
X^2:	4	4	16	36	36	ΣX^2	=	96

Thus

$$a = \bar{y} = \frac{\Sigma y}{n} = \frac{15}{5} = 3$$

and

$$b = \frac{n\Sigma Xy - \Sigma X \Sigma y}{n\Sigma X^2 - (\Sigma X)^2} = \frac{5(52) - 20(15)}{5(96) - (20)^2} = \frac{-40}{80} = -0.5$$

The estimated regression line is:

$$\tilde{Y}_X = 3 - 0.5\ (X - \bar{X}) \tag{8}$$

The following is a graph of the X, y data, above, with the estimated regression line:

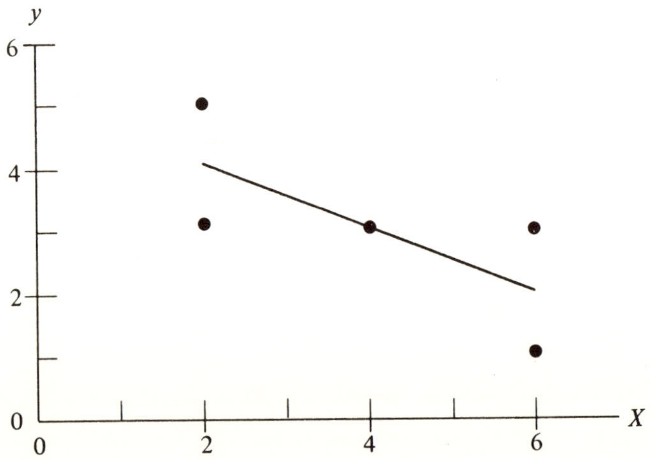

The estimate b is the slope of the estimated regression line (as B is the slope of the true line). In this illustration, $b = -0.5$, indicating that for each unit X increases, $\tilde{Y}_X$ decreases half a unit.

The assumptions under which the regression estimates (7) are derived are:

(1) Regression is linear (equation 5).
(2) The X-values are known with no (or negligible) error.
(3) The y's are independent. (The value of one does not affect the value of another.)
(4) The distributions of the Y-variable have the same variance in every X-array.

The assumption that regression is linear is often based on the data at hand. It presents no major problem if one is careful not to make predictions outside the range of the available X's. Many complex relationships are nearly linear for a narrow range of the independent variable. Thus, if it is not known that regression is linear, many different X-values should be selected to give the data a chance to exhibit any nonlinear tendencies that exist. On the other hand, if linearity is assured, a good method for choosing the X-values is to take half the values as low as possible, the other half as high as possible. This will reduce the variability of the estimates.

Estimation and reliability. Properties of the estimates, a, b, and $\tilde{Y}_X$ will be discussed in this section. In addition to the four assumptions given above, normality is assumed; that is, it is assumed that the distribution of Y is normal in each X-array. The common variance of these Y-distributions is denoted by $S^2{}_{Y \cdot X}$. The subscripts indicate that this variance is computed from the regression of Y on X, in contrast to the variance S^2 of the overall Y distribution, which is computed without reference to the auxiliary variable X. The square root $S_{Y \cdot X}$ of $S^2{}_{Y \cdot X}$ is called the *standard error of estimate.* An estimate of $S_{Y \cdot X}$ is $s_{Y \cdot X}$, where:

$$s_{Y \cdot X} = \sqrt{\frac{1}{n-2} \Sigma [y - a - b(X - \bar{X})^2]} \tag{9}$$

The quantity $[y - a - b(X - \bar{X})]$ represents the vertical deviation of a sample y from the estimated regression line.

The estimate b has a normal distribution. Its mean is B and its standard deviation is $S_{Y \cdot X} / \sqrt{\Sigma (X - \bar{X})^2}$, where the summation and $\bar{X}$ again refer to the selected X-values. The quantity $[(b - B)/s_{Y \cdot X}]$ $\sqrt{\Sigma (X - \bar{X})^2}$ has a t-distribution with parameter $n - 2$.

The estimate $\tilde{Y}_X$ also has a normal distribution. Its mean is $\bar{Y}_X = A + BX$, and its standard deviation is:

$$S_{\tilde{Y}_X} = S_{Y \cdot X} \sqrt{\frac{1}{n} + \frac{(X - \bar{X})^2}{\Sigma (X - \bar{X})^2}}$$

The ratio

$$\frac{\tilde{Y}_X - \bar{Y}_X}{s_{Y \cdot X} \sqrt{\frac{1}{n} + \frac{(X - \bar{X})^2}{\Sigma (X - \bar{X})^2}}}$$

has the t-distribution with parameter $n - 2$, and can be used to set confidence intervals on $\bar{Y}_X$.

It is important to note that the paragraph above refers to estimation of the *mean* value of Y for a given X-array. In predicting a *single* value Y_X, one uses the fact that the ratio

$$\frac{Y_X - a - b(X - \bar{X})}{s_{Y \cdot X}\sqrt{1 + \frac{1}{n} + \frac{(X - \bar{X})^2}{\Sigma(X - \bar{X})^2}}}$$

has the t-distribution with parameter $n - 2$.

To illustrate the formulas of this section, consider the problem of predicting the number of times (Y) a document will be requested in a year, given its age (X) in years. Assumptions (1) through (4) and the normality assumption will be made. Suppose the values of X selected are 0, 0, 2, 2, 4, and 4. Then a random sample of documents is selected, two each from sets of documents 0, 2, and 4 years old. The number of times (y) each document is requested for the year is recorded. Suppose the outcomes are listed in the second row of the following table. (The succeeding rows contain the necessary computations.)

1.	X :	0	0	2	2	4	4	ΣX	= 12
2.	y :	5	3	5	1	3	1	Σy	= 18
3.	X^2 :	0	0	4	4	16	16	ΣX^2	= 40
4.	X_y :	0	0	10	2	12	4	ΣX_y	= 28
5.	$\tilde{Y}_X = a + b(X - \bar{X})$:	4	4	3	3	2	2		
6.	$y - a - b(X - \bar{X})$:	1	-1	1	-1	1	-1		
7.	$[y - a - b(X - \bar{X})^2]$:	1	1	1	1	1	1		
								$\Sigma[y - a - b(X - \bar{X})^2]$	= 6
8.	$X - \bar{X}$:	-2	-2	0	0	2	2		
9.	$(X - \bar{X})^2$:	4	4	0	0	4	4		
								$\Sigma(X - \bar{X})^2$	= 16

$$a = \bar{y} = \frac{\Sigma y}{n} = \frac{18}{6} = 3 \qquad b = \frac{n\Sigma Xy - \Sigma X\Sigma y}{n\Sigma X^2 - (\Sigma X)^2} = -\frac{48}{96} = -0.5$$

$$\tilde{Y}_X = 3 - 0.5(X - \bar{X})^2$$

$$s^2_{Y \cdot X} = \frac{1}{n - 2}\Sigma[y - a - b(X - \bar{X})]^2 = \frac{6}{4} = 1.5$$

$$s_{Y \cdot X} = 1.225$$

The point estimate for B is -0.5. That is, for every year of age, the requests for a document decrease, on the average, half a request per year. A 95 percent confidence interval for B would be

$$b + \left(s_{Y \cdot X} / \sqrt{\Sigma(X - \bar{X})^2}\right) t_{0.025} < B < b + \left(s_{Y \cdot X} / \sqrt{\Sigma(X - \bar{X})^2}\right) t_{0.975}$$

or

$$-0.5 - (1.225/\sqrt{16})\, 2.776 < B < -0.5 + (1.225/\sqrt{16})\, 2.776$$

$$-1.35 < B < 0.35$$

The estimates $\tilde{Y}_X$ of $\bar{Y}_X$ are given in row 5 of the table. The estimate for $\bar{Y}_0$ is 4. A 95 percent confidence interval for $\bar{Y}_0$ is

$$4 + s_{Y \cdot X} \sqrt{\frac{1}{n} + \frac{(X - \bar{X})^2}{\Sigma(X - \bar{X})^2}}\; t_{0.025} < \bar{Y}_0 < 4 + s_{Y \cdot X} \sqrt{\frac{1}{n} + \frac{(X - \bar{X})^2}{\Sigma(X - \bar{X})^2}}\; t_{0.975}$$

$$4 - 1.225 \sqrt{\frac{1}{4} + \frac{1}{6}}\,(2.776) < \bar{Y}_0 < 4 + 1.225 \sqrt{\frac{1}{6} + \frac{1}{16}}\,(2.776)$$

$$1.80 < \bar{Y}_0 < 6.20$$

Now suppose an estimate of the number Y_0 of requests is required for a new document (age 0). The point estimate would again be 4. The 95 percent interval would be

$$4 + \sqrt{1 + \frac{1}{n} + \frac{(X - \bar{X})^2}{\Sigma(X - \bar{X})^2}}\; t_{0.025} < Y_0 < 4 + s_{Y \cdot X} \sqrt{1 + \frac{1}{n} + \frac{(X - \bar{X})^2}{\Sigma(X - \bar{X})^2}}\; t_{0.975}$$

$$4 - 1.225 \sqrt{1 + \frac{1}{6} + \frac{4}{16}}\,(2.776) < Y_0 < 4 + 1.225 \sqrt{1 + \frac{1}{6} + \frac{4}{16}}\,(2.776)$$

$$-0.05 < Y_0 < 8.05$$

Note that, even though the same point estimate Y_0 is used in the last two situations, the confidence interval is much wider in the last one. A mean can be specified with greater precision than can a single value.

References

1. Cochran, W. G., *Sampling Techniques.* 2nd Edition. New York, Wiley & Sons, 1963.
2. King, D. W., *Evaluation During File Development of the Glass Technology Coordinate Index File.* Bethesda, Md., Westat Research, Inc., November 1967.
3. Lancaster, F. W., *Evaluation of the MEDLARS Demand Search Service.* Bethesda, Md., National Library of Medicine, January 1968.

Chapter Twelve
Sampling Methods

12.1 Introduction

Sampling is inherent in almost all evaluation activities, since it is seldom possible to observe *all* users at *all* times or to check the indexing of *all* documents, and so on. The sample selected for evaluation must be identified in accordance with fairly rigid rules, so that generalizations ultimately made about the sample population will be valid. Methods of selection, sample sizes, and some fundamental statistical concepts are discussed in this chapter.

12.2 Constructing the sampling frame

The first step in sampling is the definition of the population to be sampled. If one is sampling to determine indexing errors, the population might be all indexed documents in the file, all documents indexed after 1967, those indexed during a week, or those indexed by a particular indexer or group of indexers. Similarly, a user population might be defined to be those submitting requests during a given period, the scientists in a given discipline in the United States, and so on.

Once the population is defined, it is necessary to provide a means of identifying the units in the population so that, with respect to a sampling procedure, one can know with certainty whether or not the unit is in the sample. This is the *sample frame*. Some examples follow.

The complete list of document acquisition numbers provides a sampling frame for all documents in the system. A sampling rule such as, "Start with the seventh number and take every nineteenth number thereafter," will uniquely define a sample.

A listing of office space on a university campus by building, floor, and wing may identify all of the offices on the campus. A rule such as "Take all offices in the Xth wing on the Yth floor of the Zth building," will identify a "cluster" of offices to be included in the sample, and hence a cluster of potential users. Note that the total number of potential users in the population need not be known in order to construct such a frame.

Implied in the use of a sample frame is the ability to assign a probability to the selection of each sample unit in the population. The assignment of the probability is a function of the selection rule used, but the sample frame must organize the population in such a way that this assignment is possible.

Two kinds of populations must be distinguished – *finite* and *infinite*. Their connotations are obvious. Formulas used for estimating standard errors of statistical measures in finite populations are different from those used in infinite populations. The formulas for infinite populations are simpler.

In the field of documentation, nearly all populations are finite, but many of them are large with respect to the size of the sample drawn and, for these, it is appropriate to use the infinite population formulas.

As a rule of thumb, if the sample is less than 10 percent of the population, one may as well consider the population to be infinite. (See Sections 12.4 and 12.6 for details.)

12.3 Selection of sample units

A *sample unit* is some identifiable piece of sampling frame on which observations are to be taken, or which is to serve as the basis for identifying elements of the population to be observed. For example, in drawing a sample of items from an issue of *Index Medicus*, we might consider the pages to be sample units. Having drawn, say, 10 pages at random, we might draw five items from each page by some predetermined rule. This is a two-stage sample in which the page is known as the "primary" sample unit and the item as the "ultimate" sample unit. There may be primary, secondary, and further stage units.

A *selection procedure* specifies the rules for inclusion or exclusion of sample units with regard to a specific sample. Ordinarily, one is inclined to choose *random* sampling over other selection rules, and to depend on the unstructured nature of the random sample to protect against bias. Since statistical methodology is based mostly upon randomness, methods are available for estimating sampling errors and thus for forming judgments about the precision of estimates.

A random sample is one drawn in accordance with a *randomization procedure.* There are many such procedures, some of which are identifiable with "drawing numbers out of a hat." It is much more common, however, to use a "table of random numbers." One can consider these numbers to be predrawn by a randomization procedure, although they are usually prepared by computer by a "pseudo-randomization" procedure.

Although statistical methodology is based upon randomization, most samples are actually drawn systematically as a matter of convenience. Suppose, for example, that we want a sample of 25 out of 800 documents which are arranged alphabetically by title. To draw a random sample, we could number the documents from 1 to 800 and use a table of random numbers to draw three-digit random numbers which would identify the documents uniquely. We would have to decide ahead of time whether to permit a document to be drawn more than once (with replacement) or only once (without replacement).

A much more common procedure is to draw a systematic sample. We divide 800 by 25, obtaining a *sampling interval* of 32, draw a random number from 1 to 32 to identify the first document, and then take every thirty-second document thereafter. This is not a random sample, but is much easier to draw and should have the characteristics of a random sample if there is no alphabet-related trend or periodicity in the characteristic being measured.

12.4 Elementary statistical measures

Clearly, it is impractical to present a course in elementary statistics in a book on evaluation. However, some of the most important statistical concepts are so simple that the uninitiated can grasp them readily with a minimum of exposition. This section presents some of these concepts, with the knowledge that standard textbooks are readily available for the reader who wishes to have further exposition.

Most sampling activities are undertaken to answer one or more of the following questions:

(1) What is the *population total* (e.g., number in the population having a given characteristic or total quantity such as total indexing errors, total hours spent searching, and total references used)?

(2) What is the *average per sample unit* (e.g., average errors per document, average number of searches per user, average time spent searching per user or per search)?

Although we want to know the above things for the *population,* we have available to us only sample estimates which are subject to *sampling error,* so a third question is:

(3) How much sampling error is associated with the above estimates? This, too, can only be estimated.

Initially, we assume that all samples are randomly drawn from finite populations. We consider four cases after introducing the following notation:

N = number of sample units in the population
n = number of sample units in the sample
x_i = numerical value of interest which is associated with the ith sample unit
$\bar{X}$ = average over all sample units
X = total over all sample units

Case 1. We wish to estimate the population *average* from a sample.

We estimate it by the sample average

$$\tilde{\bar{X}} = \bar{x} = \sum_{i=1}^{n} x_i/n \qquad (1)$$

The tilde (~) indicates an estimate of the population parameter. Its standard error[1] is estimated as

[1] Meaning can be attached to the standard error of the mean as follows. Suppose n is large and N even larger, so that n/N is small, say, less than 0.05. Then, suppose one were repeatedly to draw independent samples of size n and compute their means (averages), $\bar{x}_1, \bar{x}_2, \ldots,$ etc. For most kinds of data encountered in evaluation of document transfer systems, about 68 percent of such means would lie within 1 standard error of the true (or population) mean, about 95 percent within 2 standard errors, and essentially all within 3 standard errors.

$$\tilde{S}_{\bar{x}} = \sqrt{\frac{\Sigma(x_i - \bar{x})^2}{n(n-1)} \frac{N-n}{N-1}} \tag{2}$$

Note that if N is large with respect to n (see Section 12.2), $(N - n)/(N - 1)$ is approximately 1.0 and this factor can be ignored in the computation.

Case 2. We wish to estimate the population *total* from a sample.

The estimator is

$$\tilde{X} = N\bar{x} \tag{3}$$

and its standard error is

$$\tilde{S}_x = N\tilde{S}_{\bar{x}} \tag{4}$$

Case 3. We wish to estimate the proportion of the population having a given characteristic.

The estimator is

$$\tilde{P}_a = n_a/n \tag{5}$$

where n_a is the number in the sample having the given attribute.

Its estimated standard error is

$$\tilde{S}_p = \sqrt{\tilde{p}_a(1 - \tilde{p}_a)/n} \tag{6}$$

Case 4. We wish to estimate the number in the population having a given characteristic.

The estimator is

$$\tilde{N}_a = N\tilde{p}_a \tag{7}$$

and its standard error is

$$\tilde{S}_{N_a} = N\tilde{S}_p \tag{8}$$

12.5 Sampling design objectives and sample sizes

Generally, it is desirable to have highly precise estimates of population parameters and at low cost. These are conflicting objectives, and part of the function of sample design is to resolve this conflict. Two valid specifications for sample design are:

(1) Design a sample which will yield the maximum precision (minimum standard error) for a given cost, or

(2) Design a sample to provide specified precision at a minimum cost.

Two factors – *sampling procedure* and *sample size* – affect costs and precision. Sampling procedures involve decisions about stratification, clustering, randomization, and similar matters. Some discussion of these techniques appears in the next section.

Here, however, we are concerned with the effect of sample size on precision[2] of *random samples* from infinite or large populations. Some preliminary concepts are useful. One is the *coefficient of variation* of the population being sampled. The coefficient of variation is the ratio between the standard deviation and the average. The standard deviation has the same meaning with respect to individual quantitative observations that the standard error has with respect to sample means. Thus, a coefficient of variation near zero indicates a tight clustering (in a relative sense) of the values around their average. A coefficient of variation of 1.0 indicates relatively wide variability – about the kind of variability one would expect in sampling for indexing errors per document where the minimum must be zero, but where there is a large upper limit to the number which can be found. Since the average number of errors is usually small, the variation below the average is much smaller than the variation above the average. Such populations are "skewed to the right."

Coefficients of variations of 2 or 3 or more are generally associated with highly skewed populations.

We refer again to the four cases discussed above.

[2]Note that precision is related to sampling error and excludes bias due to nonresponse, interviewers, questions, or any other source. Total error is the sum of sampling error and bias. It is a useful concept in sample design, but in practice it is difficult and often impossible to measure bias. Roughly, then, sampling error is *measurable error*.

Cases 1 and 2

$$CV_X = \sqrt{\frac{\Sigma(x_i - \bar{x})^2}{n - 1}} \Big/ \bar{x} \tag{9}$$

Cases 3 and 4

$$CV_p = \sqrt{\tilde{p}(1 - \tilde{p})} \Big/ \tilde{p} \tag{10}$$

Note that as $\tilde{p}$ approaches zero the coefficient of variation becomes large.

A second concept necessary in the determination of sample size is the concept of *allowable variation* of the estimate from its true value. That is, we may specify that we wish "to know the mean within 5 percent of its true value." Such a specification is incomplete because it does not account for the risk we are willing to run that the estimate may be in error. A more usable specification is "to be 90 percent certain of being within 5 percent of the true value."

The 5 percent in the above specification is referred to as the "permissible range" (*PR*) and the 90 percent as the "certainty factor" (*CF*). Table 12.1[3] presents sample sizes for well-behaved data, that is, for populations in which the estimators are approximately "normally" distributed (see any text on elementary statistics).

The table is used as follows:

(1) Estimate the coefficient of variation in the population (*CV*).
(2) Specify the permissible range (*PR*).
(3) Specify the desired certainty factor (*CF*).
(4) Read the desired sample size from the table.

The coefficient of variation is almost never known before the sample is undertaken. (If it were known, there would be no need to sample.) However, it is usually possible to guess at an average and the range of values expected. Since the range in well-behaved data may be expected to be no greater than six standard deviations, an estimate of the coefficient of variation is provided by one-sixth of the guessed range divided by the guessed average. In sampling for proportions, one

[3]This table was not prepared for the statistical purist, but for the nonstatistically oriented evaluator who needs a general guide to sample size determination.

Table 12.1 Sample Sizes for Random Samples from Infinite Populations

Coefficient of variation	Permissible range	Certainty Factor 0.68	0.80	0.90	0.95	0.997
0.05	0.01	25	42	68	97	225
	0.02	7	11	17	25	57
	0.03	3	5	8	11	25
	0.05	1	2	3	4	9
	0.10	1	1	1	1	3
	0.15	1	1	1	1	1
	0.20	1	1	1	1	1
	0.25	1	1	1	1	1
0.10	0.01	100	165	271	385	900
	0.02	25	42	68	97	225
	0.03	12	19	31	43	100
	0.05	4	7	11	16	36
	0.10	1	2	3	4	9
	0.15	1	1	2	2	4
	0.20	1	1	1	1	3
	0.25	1	1	1	1	2
0.20	0.01	400	658	1,083	1,537	3,600
	0.02	100	165	271	385	900
	0.03	45	74	121	171	400
	0.05	16	27	44	62	144
	0.10	4	7	11	16	36
	0.15	2	3	5	7	16
	0.20	1	2	3	4	9
	0.25	1	2	2	3	6
0.30	0.01	900	1,480	2,436	3,458	8,100
	0.02	225	370	609	865	2,025
	0.03	100	165	271	385	900
	0.05	36	60	98	139	324
	0.10	9	15	25	35	81
	0.15	4	7	11	16	36
	0.20	3	4	7	9	21
	0.25	2	3	4	6	13
0.40	0.01	1,600	2,630	4,330	6,147	14,400
	0.02	400	658	1,083	1,537	3,600
	0.03	178	293	482	683	1,600
	0.05	64	106	174	246	576
	0.10	16	27	44	62	144
	0.15	8	12	20	28	64

Table 12.1 Sample Sizes for Random Samples from Infinite Population (Continued)

Coefficient of variation	Permissible range	Certainty Factor 0.68	0.80	0.90	0.95	0.997
	0.20	4	7	11	16	36
	0.25	3	5	7	10	24
0.50	0.01	2,500	4,109	6,766	9,604	22,500
	0.02	625	1,028	1,692	2,401	5,625
	0.03	278	457	752	1,068	2,500
	0.05	100	165	271	385	900
	0.10	25	42	68	97	225
	0.15	12	19	31	43	100
	0.20	7	11	17	25	57
	0.25	4	7	11	16	36
0.75	0.01	5,625	9,245	15,222	21,609	50,626
	0.02	1,407	2,312	3,806	5,403	12,657
	0.03	625	1,028	1,692	2,401	5,625
	0.05	225	370	609	865	2,025
	0.10	57	93	153	217	507
	0.15	25	42	68	97	225
	0.20	15	24	39	55	127
	0.25	9	15	25	35	81
1.00	0.01	10,001	16,436	27,061	38,416	90,000
	0.02	2,500	4,109	6,766	9,604	22,500
	0.03	1,112	1,827	3,007	4,269	10,000
	0.05	400	658	1,083	1,537	3,600
	0.10	100	165	271	385	900
	0.15	45	74	121	171	400
	0.20	25	42	68	97	225
	0.25	16	27	44	62	144
1.50	0.01	22,500	36,980	60,886	86,436	202,501
	0.02	5,625	9,245	15,222	21,609	50,626
	0.03	2,500	4,109	6,766	9,604	22,500
	0.05	900	1,480	2,436	3,458	8,100
	0.10	225	370	609	865	2,025
	0.15	100	165	271	385	900
	0.20	57	93	153	217	507
	0.25	36	60	98	139	324

Table 12.1 Sample Sizes for Random Samples from Infinite Population (Continued)

Coefficient of variation	Permissible range	Certainty Factor 0.68	0.80	0.90	0.95	0.997
2.00	0.01	40,001	65,741	108,241	153,664	360,000
	0.02	10,001	16,436	27,061	38,416	90,000
	0.03	4,445	7,305	12,027	17,074	40,000
	0.05	1,600	2,630	4,330	6,147	14,401
	0.10	400	658	1,083	1,537	3,600
	0.15	178	293	482	683	1,600
	0.20	100	165	271	385	900
	0.25	64	106	174	246	576
3.00	0.01	90,000	147,918	243,543	345,744	524,287
	0.02	22,500	36,980	60,886	86,436	202,501
	0.03	10,000	16,436	27,061	38,416	90,000
	0.05	3,600	5,917	9,742	13,830	32,400
	0.10	900	1,480	2,436	3,458	8,100
	0.15	400	658	1,083	1,537	3,600
	0.20	225	370	609	865	2,025
	0.25	144	237	390	554	1,296

can perhaps do better, since a single guess as to the proportion provides the information necessary to compute equation (10).

The table should cover most sample sizes encountered in practice, but other sample sizes can be approximated by the equation:

$$n = \left(\frac{Z\,(CV)}{(PR)} \right)^2 \qquad (11)$$

where Z is identified with the certainty factor as follows:

Certainty factor	Z
0.68	1.0
0.80	1.28
0.90	1.64
0.95	1.96
0.997	3.00

A common misconception in sampling is that a 5 percent sample or a 10 percent sample will guarantee a certain degree of precision. Except for small populations, the percent coverage has little to do with precision. The important thing is the absolute size of the sample, and one of the most wasteful sampling practices is to take a fixed proportion of a large population.[4]

12.6 Specialized sample designs

One must occasionally depart from simple random samples because:

(1) The cost of obtaining the required precision by simple random sampling may be too great, or

(2) The construction of a random sampling frame may be too costly or impossible. In such cases, one may employ restricted randomization (e.g., stratified random sampling), systematic sampling (discussed previously), or cluster sampling. Some comments on stratified sampling and cluster sampling follow.

Stratified sampling separates the population into parts (strata) which are homogeneous with respect to the variable of interest, and then samples are taken within each of these. The practical effect is to make several homogeneous populations out of one heterogeneous population. The gain in precision can be remarkable, depending upon the effectiveness of the stratifying criterion.

In the field of documentation, users may be stratified by discipline or by education and experience levels, and documents may be stratified by age, by subject matter, or by mode of indexing. It is necessary to know the number of sample units in each stratum to achieve any gains.

Let N_h be the number of sample units in the hth stratum, n_h the sample size, $\bar{x}_h$ the sample mean, and so on. Then, for Case 1 we have

$$\tilde{\bar{X}}_s = (1/\Sigma N_h)\, \Sigma \bar{x}_h N_h \qquad (12)$$

[4]An obvious exception is the case in which one is interested in estimates for small subdivisions of the population as well as for the population as a whole. This is what justifies the 5 percent and 20 percent samples taken as a part of the Census of Population and Housing.

That is, the estimated population average is a weighted average of the separate strata averages.

$$\tilde{S}_{\bar{x}_s} = \sqrt{(1/\Sigma N_h)^2 \; \Sigma N_h{}^2 \tilde{S}_{\bar{x}}{}^2} \tag{13}$$

(See equation 11.)
The extension to Cases 2, 3, and 4 is straightforward.

Cluster sampling is employed when it is difficult or costly to identify a sample unit ahead of time but a cluster of sample units can be readily identified. It is also used when it is relatively less expensive to observe clusters than individual sample units.

For example, if we want a sample of entries from *Index Medicus,* we might well consider a page to be a cluster. Drawing a random (or systematic) sample of pages identifies a set of sample clusters. All of the entries on the sample page can be included in the sample or they can be subsampled. Clearly, one can draw a sample of pages more easily than a sample of entries.

If there is a high degree of homogeneity among the sample units within a cluster, we will lose precision for fixed sample size compared to random sampling. This loss must be more than offset by savings in cost if clustering is to be effective. It is also intuitively clear that with homogeneity within clusters we should subsample only a few sample units within each cluster, thus increasing the number of clusters which must be drawn into the sample.

As another example, consider the task of drawing a sample of articles from scientific journals. The journals are widely scattered and thus are costly to locate. Once they are located, it is relatively inexpensive to include additional articles from the same journal. Thus, the trade-off, depending on homogeneity, is between drawing many journals with few articles per journal or few journals with many articles per journal. The professional statistician can approach the decision problem analytically, but to present the methodology here would take us far afield.

The clustering and subsampling process can extend through several stages. At the grossest level, the clusters are called "primary clusters," at the next stage "secondary clusters," and so on, until the sample units of interest are identified. These units are called "ultimate sample units." The methodology for estimation is complex and will not be given here.

Chapter Thirteen
Experimental Design

13.1 Introduction

There are two kinds of research data. One is *observational* data, where no attempt is made to modify or control any part of the system which generates the observations. An example is the recording of the number of references cited by physicists in a given journal.

The second is *experimental* data in which one has purposely controlled or modified some of the facets of the system in order to measure the effect of the changes or to compare the responses of the system under different conditions or restraints. An example is the accumulation of data under controlled conditions to show the effect of experience on indexing accuracy.

Both observation and experimentation are important in document transfer system evaluation. One of the primary roles of observation is to indicate the kind of experimentation which might prove fruitful. As a general rule, we cannot determine cause-and-effect relationships from uncontrolled observations. We may, however, get ideas from observational data which lead to experiments whose principal role is the assignment of cause and effect.

The layman tends to think of experimentation as a laboratory technique in which one factor is varied, with all other factors held constant. Much of modern science was developed by precisely these methods. However, it is never possible to control all factors exactly, except the one whose effect is being examined. Technology is simply not that precise. In particular, the typical document transfer system is far too complex an operation for the useful employment of this simple "controlled" approach. It is frequently necessary to permit several things to vary in the same experiment, arranging the experiment in such a way that the effects can be unscrambled. This necessity has led to development of the field of experimental design. It is a large field of study, requiring several years' work at the graduate level for its mastery. However, there are a few basic principles which, if known to the experimenter, will permit him to construct many experiments intelligently and which will alert him to the necessity of seeking professional help for more complex cases.

13.2 Preliminary concepts

The variation which is not controlled in an otherwise controlled experiment is termed *experimental error.* It is a measure of the "repeatability" of an experiment. By convention, it is usually measured by the *variance*, which is the square of the standard deviation (see Chapter 11). The smaller the experimental error, the more sensitive the experiment, that is, the smaller the difference required to be statistically significant.

Generally, the more things one controls, the smaller will be the experimental error. This might lead one to believe that the best policy would be to control everything possible. This is what is done in the laboratory when it is important to determine a particular effect within narrow limits of error. However, in the field of document retrieval evaluation, it is important to be able to extrapolate the results to the real world, and too many controls on the experimental factors make this extrapolation difficult, if not impossible.

When we loosen experimental controls to permit generalization over a wider population, we must take more readings (i.e., do more experimentation) in order to achieve the same sensitivity. There is, then, a trade-off between the sensitivity and generality of the results. The proper balance in a given situation is a matter of judgment.

Generalizations about the real world of document transfer are presumed to be important, so that experimental conditions should, as nearly as possible, simulate the conditions of the real world. This means, generally, that experimentation is an expensive proposition. However, no one has yet come up with a substitute for it. The best we can do is to design the experiments in such a way that we get the most information for the money invested.

When an effect can be attributed to two or more factors and the portion due to each cannot be determined, we say that the effects of the factors have been *confounded.* For example, in an indexing experiment, if A indexes document D_1 by process P_1, and document D_2 by process P_2, we say that process differences are confounded with document differences. We cannot tell whether the observed difference between the indexings is due to the processes or to the documents, or both.

The statistical techniques for handling confounding are *replication, partitioning,* and *randomization.* Replication is the repetition of the same test using different experimental units, such as indexers, documents, and so forth. Thus, effects due to the choice of particular persons or documents are averaged out.

Partitioning is the process of separating the experiment into cells such that each cell is different from some other cell by a change in only one experimental factor. Thus, it is possible to identify differences in observed results with differences in factors. The most common illustration of partitioning is the "factorial arrangement" in which observations are taken with each possible combination of the experimental factors. For example:

	Factor A			
Factor B	A_1	A_2	A_3	A_4
B_1				
B_2				
B_3				

Randomization is the use of random process (such as drawing numbered tags out of a jar) to select, for example, the documents to be used in the experiment and to assign them to particular individuals. Such a process does not *guarantee* that the documents selected will be representative of the population, but it does insure that no conscious or unconscious bias can influence their choice. It also assures us that valid statistical inferences can be drawn from the experiment and that the estimate of experimental error is unbiased. It is possible, of course, to obtain a "bad" sample by random selection, but if the number of items selected at random is reasonably large, the probability of obtaining a really bad sample is extremely small. This is not true if the total number of selections is small, say, one or two. In such cases, it can be demonstrated that the conscious selection of a case which is "representative" will yield better results on the average than the selection of a single case at random. It has also been shown that the reverse is true as soon as the sample size gets to be as large as four or five. So, in all but highly special cases, one can rely upon the randomization process to yield a "representative" selection.

Experimentation with human beings is always difficult. One of the reasons is that they behave differently when they are being observed. Another reason is that the human being is an intelligent and highly adaptive creature; in spite of detailed instructions, he can find numerous ways of modifying or interpreting those instructions so as to take advantage of his own peculiar skills, prejudices, and experience. He may perform poorly on a given search system simply because he has no confidence in it, or he may perform well because he exerts extra effort to "prove" the worth of a system in which he believes.

Some of the problems associated with human behavior can be controlled by careful experimental design – others cannot. Where they cannot be controlled, at least they should be recognized, and the conclusions drawn from the experimentation modified (or limited) accordingly.

13.3 Some specific designs

One problem which must always be faced is that a user learns from searching for documents by any method, so if he searches a file by method A there is not much point in having him search by method B if one is interested in comparing the two methods. There is a carry-over effect which may destroy the validity of the comparison.

Let us consider two alternatives for handling the problem. Suppose method A is hand searching the file and method B is searching by use of a coordinate index. We might give every user involved in the experiment an even number of search requests, assigning half of them, at random, to the group in which method A is to be used first. The experimental arrangement is called a "crossover" design, and might be portrayed as follows:

	User 1				User 2			
Order of search	S_1	S_2	S_3	S_4	S_5	S_6	S_7	S_8
First search	A	B	A	B	A	B	A	B
Second search	B	A	B	A	B	A	B	A

There could be as many users as desired. Whether they should do the same searches, or a different set, is a point we will discuss subsequently. Note that, for each user, method A is used first half of the time and method B is first half of the time. Unfortunately, there can still be bias in the results if the carry-over effects are not equal.

Suppose that the variable of interest is search time, and that the "true value" for method A is 10 units of time and for method B is 20 units of time. Assume that, if a person searches by method B (coordinate index) first, his search time under method A (hand search) will be cut in half. On the other hand, use of method A first may not help much in the use of method B. Let's assume it doesn't. Then, if there were no error, the search times would be as follows for User 1:

	S_1	S_2	S_3	S_4
First search	(A) 10	(B) 20	(A) 10	(B) 20
Second search	(B) 20	(A) 5	(B) 20	(A) 5

The average time observed for method A is 7.5, while for method B it is 20. Thus, the unequal carry-over effect will cause us to estimate that the difference is 12.5 units rather than 10 units.

We could, of course, consider only the first searches, in which case we would get unbiased results, but the second searches would be wasted unless we could figure out a way of correcting for the bias.

An alternative design can be constructed by having each user do only one search on each set of requests. The design could appear as follows:

User 1		User 2	
A	B	A	B
S_1	S_5	S_9	S_{13}
S_2	S_6	S_{10}	S_{14}
S_3	S_7	S_{11}	S_{15}
S_4	S_8	S_{12}	S_{16}

Each user does four searches by each method, thus producing a total of 16 separate searches.

The design might also appear as follows:

	Specifications							
User	S_1	S_2	S_3	S_4	S_5	S_6	S_7	S_8
User 1	A	B	A	B	A	B	A	B
User 2	B	A	B	A	B	A	B	A

This design utilizes half as many search requests (specifications), but each set of requests is searched by both users. Either design should result in unbiased estimates. If the effect of the search specifications is highly variable (which is likely to be the case), the second design is considerably better than the first because we have a comparison of both methods within each of the search specifications. Thus, we have eliminated specification differences in comparing methods, leaving only user differences and random differences. The user differences can be averaged out over all of the searches. In the first design, A can be compared with B only in the presence of user effects and specification effects. It is true that they will average out over all observations, but the experiment is likely to be considerably less sensitive than the last one given.

Another concept which is important to the designer of experiments is the concept of *interaction.* Consider the effect of experience on method A (hand searching) and method B (coordinate index searching) which was discussed above. Assume that enough users are available so that estimates can be derived for both experienced and inexperienced users. Suppose, again, that we are interested in search time and that the following results are obtained:

Users	Method A	Method B	Average
Experienced	10	20	15
Inexperienced	20	10	15
Average	15	15	15

If we look only at the averages of the two methods, we will observe no difference between them. Similarly, if we look only at the averages for each experience level, we will again observe no difference. But the two methods are, in fact, quite different, method A being much better for experienced users and method B much better for inexperienced users. The hypothetical illustration is exaggerated, of course, but shows that one must always be aware of the possibility of differential effects. These effects are called *interaction.*

Note that method B shows an increase of 10 units over method A for experienced users but a decrease of 10 units for inexperienced users. The difference between the 10-unit increase and the 10-unit decrease (i.e., 20 units) is a measure of the amount of interaction. Where interaction is present, one must report the averages for each of the cells in the table.

Here is a case in which there is no interaction, although at first glance there may appear to be:

	A	B
Experienced	10	30
Inexperienced	20	40

B is 20 units greater than A at each level of experience; hence, the interaction is zero. Furthermore, the 10-unit difference in means of the experience groups truly reflects their relative value. Also, it is perfectly proper to interpret the mean of B as being 20 units greater than the mean of A.

13.4 Use of standard designs

Generally, professional statistical advice should be sought in the design of document transfer experiments. The problems of sequence, interactions, learning curves, and system changes over time often make it difficult, if not impossible, to design experiments by reference to standard published designs. However, some knowledge of the standard designs and their assumptions and limitations will help in communicating the experimental conditions to the statistician. Also, "cookbook designs" do occasionally fit the experimental situation satisfactorily. With this in mind, some of the common experimental arrangements are discussed below. Methods of estimating differences due to experimental treatments are given, but only selective reference will be made to the analysis of variance through which the reliability of such estimates can be judged.

Completely randomized designs are the simplest. Suppose there are k "treatments," i.e., things to be compared. For example, there might be four indexing procedures, or two search methods, or three kinds of document surrogates. One proceeds to "design" an experiment as follows:

(1) Determine a measure by which a single trial of the experiment is to be characterized (e.g., search time, cost, judge's score of usefulness, number of documents retrieved).

(2) Form an aggregation of possible trials (experimental units) and separate them by random selection into t groups of approximately equal size. These are the "treatment groups."

Example (a). Hand indexing is to be compared with machine indexing. A collection of documents selected at random from the population of documents to be indexed is an aggregate of experimental units and is divided at random into two groups – one to be hand indexed and the other to be indexed by machine.

Example (b). Same as Example (a), except that there are three indexers. Each document in the "hand-indexed" group is given a probability of one-third of being assigned to each indexer. Thus, the effect of indexers is averaged out.

Example (c). Same as Example (b) except that documents come from two subject-matter fields. Drawing is the same as above, except that the aggregation is formed by selecting documents from the two subject-matter fields with probability proportionate to the number of such documents in the population.

The experimental layout takes the following form:

	Treatment groups			
	1	2	---	t
	X_{11}	X_{21}	---	X_{t1}
	X_{12}	X_{22}	---	X_{t2}
	---	---	---	---
	X_{1n_1}	X_{2n_2}	---	X_{tn_t}
Means	$\bar{X}_{1.}$	$\bar{X}_{2.}$	---	$\bar{X}_{t.}$

Note that the number of trials need not be the same in all treatment groups, but, if one wishes to compare group means, efficiency will be lost by not having them essentially the same size.

The group means (averages) are unbiased estimates of the means of the subpopulations which they represent. A measure of experimental error is the pooled within-treatment variance:

$$s^2 = \sum_i \frac{(n_i - 1) \sum_i (X_{ij} - \bar{X}_i)^2}{\sum_i (n_i - 1)} \qquad (1)$$

where n_i is the number of trials in the ith experimental group. It is assumed that the variances within groups are reasonably homogeneous.

The standard error of the ith treatment mean is

$$s_{\bar{x}_i} = \sqrt{s^2 / n_i} \qquad (2)$$

The usefulness of this simple random design is frequently overlooked. Its principal advantage, other than its simplicity, is that results obtained in this manner are immediately generalizable to the population from which the experimental units were drawn. It is assumed, of course, that randomization was accomplished as outlined above, so that the experimental *units* are a randomized representation of the population about which generalizations are desired. Thus, it is a highly desirable design to use in "real world" experimentation.

Randomized complete blocks designs control one source of experimental variation in addition to the treatment factor. They are so named because of their development in agricultural experimentation. All agronomic treatments are compared within one "block" of land so that major differences in soil are eliminated in comparing treatments. A collection of such blocks constitutes the replications of the experiment.

The same principles may apply in document transfer experiments. "Blocks," for example, may refer to document classes, or to abstractors, or to document representations, and so on. The basic experimental layout is as follows:

	Treatments				
Blocks	1	2	---	t	Means
1	X_{11}	X_{21}	---	X_{t1}	$\bar{X}_{.1}$
2	X_{12}	X_{22}	---	X_{t2}	$\bar{X}_{.2}$
---	---	---	---		
b	X_{1b}	X_{2b}	---	X_{tb}	$\bar{X}_{.b}$
Means	$\bar{X}_{1.}$	$\bar{X}_{2.}$	---	$\bar{X}_{t.}$	$\bar{X}_{.}$

Example (d). Treatments are kinds of surrogates for document screening and blocks are users. Each of b users submits t questions, each one of which is screened by using exactly one of the document representations. The variable of interest (X_{ij}) is the number of false drops.

Treatment means are the simple averages over all blocks. A measure of experimental error is obtained as follows:

$$s^2 = \sum_{ij} \frac{(X_{ij} - \bar{X}_{i.} - \bar{X}_{.j} + \bar{X}_{..})^2}{(b-1)(t-1)} \qquad (3)$$

The standard error of the ith treatment mean is:

$$s_{\bar{X}_i} = \sqrt{s^2/b} \qquad (4)$$

Validity of the estimate of the standard error requires an absence of interaction (see Section 13.2) between blocks and treatments.

Note that, while the design controls an extraneous source of error, it has some disadvantages as well over the simple random design. First, the design specifies "balance," that is, each treatment is compared with every other treatment in each block. Frequently, observations are lost for a variety of reasons, and this requires one to modify the procedure for computation of means and standard errors. The required adjustments will not be discussed here.

More important, the conclusions about treatment averages are not so easily generalizable to the real world as they are in the completely randomized design because of the restraint that each block receive equal weight in the computation of the means. If, as in Example (d), each block represents a user (or group of users), they will almost certainly not be making equal use of the system in practice. The conclusion, "The difference between Treatments 1 and 2 is 2.4 documents if all users are equally represented" may not have much meaning if, in fact, users are *not* equally represented in the real world.

In spite of this limitation, the design has proven quite useful in document retrieval experiments.

Latin square designs control another source of variation but stereotype one's conclusions even more than randomized blocks designs. The design can be explained through an example. Consider example (d) and assume that personnel with varying levels of skill and experience are available to do the document screening. We will call these "skill levels." Suppose there are four treatments (i.e., document representation forms). Then one must select four user groups and four skill levels and form r replications of the following basic pattern:

	Skill levels				
User groups	1	2	3	4	Means
1	X_{A11}	X_{B12}	X_{C13}	X_{D14}	$\bar{X}_{.1.}$
2	X_{B21}	X_{D22}	X_{A23}	X_{C24}	$\bar{X}_{.2.}$
3	X_{C31}	X_{A32}	X_{D33}	X_{B34}	$\bar{X}_{.3.}$
4	X_{D41}	X_{C42}	X_{B43}	X_{A44}	$\bar{X}_{.4.}$
Means	$\bar{X}_{..1}$	$\bar{X}_{..2}$	$\bar{X}_{..3}$	$\bar{X}_{..4}$	$\bar{X}_{...}$

The first subscript indicates the treatment (A through D), the second subscript the user group, and the third subscript the skill level. Note that each treatment appears once in each row and once in each column, so that effects of skill levels and user groups are balanced in the comparison of the treatment means, $\bar{A}$, $\bar{B}$, $\bar{C}$, and $\bar{D}$ (not shown in the diagram).

The design, as shown, is unrandomized, since a pattern having the desired properties of each treatment exactly once in each row and column was just written down.[1] In practice, randomization can be accomplished by random permutation of columns, followed by random permutation of rows of a basic latin square pattern.

Treatment means are found as simple averages of each treatment over all replications of the experiment. Note that it is assumed that the experiment is replicated r times in that many independently randomized latin squares, so that the number of observations on each treatment is rt (i.e., $4r$ in the given illustration).

An estimate of experimental error is provided by

$$s^2 = \sum_{k\alpha} \sum_{i,j} \frac{(X_{\alpha ij}{}^{(k)} - \overline{X}_{\alpha ..}{}^{(k)} - \overline{X}_{.i.}{}^{(k)} - \overline{X}_{..j}{}^{(k)} + 2\overline{X}_{...}{}^{(k)})^2}{r(t^2 - 3t + 2)} \tag{5}$$

where the superscript (k) denotes the kth replication of the latin square design and the subscript α indicates the particular treatment (A, B, C, D, etc.). The standard error of a mean is then

$$s_{\bar{x}_\alpha} = \sqrt{s^2/rt} \tag{6}$$

Validity of this estimate requires that there be no interaction (see Section 13.2) among treatments, columns, and rows.

Missing values can be handled by methods reported in many textbooks. Interpretation is even more difficult than in the randomized blocks design because of the equal weighting which is assumed with respect to *two* controlled factors. In the given example, the differences between the means are representative of differences between treatments in a population in which all skill levels and all user groups are equally represented.

Factorial arrangements provide a means for subdividing treatments into meaningful groupings in order to display direct effects of experimental "factors" and their interactions with other factors. Factorial arrangements are not to be confused with "factor analysis," which relates to the identification of relationships among variables in multivariate analysis.

Consider four document surrogates and three methods of announcement. It is clear that there are 12 possible treatment combinations, represented as follows:

[1] Rules for selection and randomization of latin square designs can be found in R. A. Fisher and F. Yates, *Statistical Tables for Biological, Agricultural and Medical Research*, Oliver and Boyd, Edinburgh, 3rd ed., 1948, or in most textbooks on experimental designs.

	Surrogates				
Methods of announcement	1	2	3	4	Means
1	X_{11}	X_{12}	X_{13}	X_{14}	$\overline{X}_{1.}$
2	X_{21}	X_{22}	X_{23}	X_{24}	$\overline{X}_{2.}$
3	X_{31}	X_{32}	X_{33}	X_{34}	$\overline{X}_{3.}$
Means	$\overline{X}_{.1}$	$\overline{X}_{.2}$	$\overline{X}_{.3}$	$\overline{X}_{.4}$	$\overline{X}_{..}$

The column means show surrogate effects averaged over methods of announcement and the row means show announcement effects averaged over all surrogates. A difference $\overline{X}_{ij} - \overline{X}_{.j} - \overline{X}_{i.} + \overline{X}_{..}$, except for that portion identifiable with experimental error, is representative of interaction between surrogate forms and methods of announcement.

Means of the cells, averaged over all replications of the experiment, represent estimates of what one can expect from the given combination of treatments, with the limitations on interpretation created by the design itself.

The factorial arrangement of treatments can be utilized in any of the designs given above, since it represents a way of identifying treatment combinations and therefore is not influenced by external influences which are controlled by "blocks" in the randomized blocks design or by "rows and columns" in the latin square design.

The statistical methods appropriate to analysis of factorial arrangements will not be discussed here, but can be obtained from most standard textbooks on the analysis of variance or experimental designs.

Other designs are available in a perplexing array of possibilities, but they should be undertaken only under the guidance of a professionally trained statistician. Simplicity in design is a highly desirable characteristic, and in the real world of documentation one is likely to gain by putting extra resources into additional trials of a simple experiment rather than into complex design and analysis of fewer observations in a sophisticated design. The ability to generalize the results to the real world in a simple design has no counterpart in complex designs.

Index